PAUL BAKER AND JO STANLEY

Hello Sailor!

THE HIDDEN HISTORY OF GAY LIFE AT SEA

Longman

An imprint of **Pearson Education**

London · New York · Toronto · Sydney · Tokyo · Singapore · Hong Kong · Cape Town ·
Madrid · Paris · Amsterdam · Munich · Milan

PEARSON EDUCATION LIMITED

Head Office:
Edinburgh Gate
Harlow CM20 2JE
Tel: +44 (0)1279 623623
Fax: +44 (0)1279 431059

London Office:
128 Long Acre
London WC2E 9AN
Tel: +44 (0)20 7447 2000
Fax: +44 (0)20 7447 2170
Website: www.history-minds.com

First edition published in Great Britain in 2003

© Pearson Education Limited 2003

The right of Paul Baker and Jo Stanley to be identified as Authors of this Work has been
asserted by them in accordance with the Copyright, Designs and Patents Act 1988.

ISBN 0 582 77214 1

British Library Cataloguing in Publication Data
A CIP catalogue record for this book can be obtained from the British Library

Library of Congress Cataloging in Publication Data
A CIP catalog record for this book can be obtained from the Library of Congress

10 9 8 7 6 5 4 3 2 1

Set by Fakenham Photosetting Limited Fakenham Norfolk
Printed and bound in China

The Publishers' policy is to use paper manufactured from sustainable forests.

In tribute to the thousands of brave gay
seafaring men who persisted – and
sometimes had fun.

Contents

THE FORTNIGHTLY CLUB

cordially invite you to a

MASKED BALL

at the Quality Street, Methodist Hall

Tuesday, 24th October, 1961 at 11.30 p.m.

The Fortnightly Club masked ball invitation.
'Method Hall' refers to the nickname of someone's cabin.
Picture courtesy of private anonymous donor.

Preface

All the nice girls love a sailor
All the nice girls love a tar
For there's something about a sailor
Well you know what sailors are
Bright and breezy, free and easy
He's the ladies' pride and joy
Falls in love with Kate and Jane
Then he's off to sea again
Ship ahoy! Ship ahoy![1]

(Music Hall Song, circa 1909)

Ships may be floating hotels that take us to exotic places, but for gay sea-farers in the mid-twentieth century such vessels were one of the only places where they could be open about their sexuality. When the UK's punitive laws and pathologising attitudes meant that gay men had to be closeted, on some liners they had a ball. Mainly in their teens and twenties, they sashayed their way across the world's oceans. Thousands of excited young men dressed like Hollywood stars by night, but efficiently manned great vessels by day.

These men were not generally butch icons such as the cutely bell-bottomed sailors who could be hired as a bit of uniformed rough from the armed services. Rather, they were men of the Merchant Navy (transporting people and freight, not fighting wars as in the Royal Navy) who might wear Hawaiian shirts or the occasional evening gown. They were hotel workers – stewards, waiters, pursers, but also some officers – not horny-handed Able Seamen or the sweating stokers of legend. And if someone said 'Hello, sailor' they might look around expecting that a fanciable Royal Naval sailor was being addressed, not themselves. However, for all that, they too were seafaring men.

This was a new breed: men who did hospitality work on ships almost *because* it was a place to be gay, rather than because they had an affinity with brine. Male company, exotic destinations and avoidance of problems at home were also a lure. But these were not people who *particularly* sought a life on the ocean wave; it was often just a place to be freely themselves at a time when homophobia was rife ashore.

Partying in male company below decks. Picture courtesy of
private donor.

And until now their story has only been known by other people who
have been to sea: their straight and gay colleagues, and passengers. So this
book reveals an overlooked aspect of gay history and of maritime history.
It puts maritime occupations into gay heritage. And it gives those newly-
developing subjects – gender at sea, and Sailor Jack's masculinity[2] – a
whole new dimension, raising such questions as: How could gay men at
sea be tolerated when women aboard were superstitiously seen as wreck-
ers? Was Jack's 'girl' in every port actually a young man? Do novels such
as *Treasure Island* have to be read quite differently in respect to relationships? What was behind sexism at sea – a desire for an all-male world far
from shore? And was this quite what British Prime Minister Winston
Churchill meant when he said that the navy succeeded because of rum,
bum and baccy?

The story of these gay men is often one of fun and irreverence. Unlike
the sailors of old who embarked with their ditty boxes and souwesters,
these seafarers minced up gangways with record-players, sewing machines
and eyeshadow to match their flip-flops, though they may have had
concertinas and rope in common. Instead of disembarking with their
painstakingly scrimshawed whale molar for mum, they flounced off with
the latest frocks from Manhattan and porn from Paris. Their affairettes
give a new angle to the usual fantasies concerning liner romances. When

Photographed on board
R.M.S. "QUEEN MARY."

Miss Everton too was a seafaring man – seen here with a crowd mourning
Everton Football Club's disastrous performance. Picture courtesy of the Oral
History Unit, Southampton City Council.

there were wedding bells at sea, both the bride and the groom could be
crew. And these seafarers' special language was not one about ship's parts
but about men's parts. Their undercover language – Polari – made gay
men on ships a special community with its own covert ways of communi-
cating.

In *Hello Sailor!* we show what it was like to be gay at sea during a time
when land meant straightness. With oral testimony from a number of men

who were seafarers from the 1950s to the 1980s, this is a story about a secret fraternity, which sheds new light on that masculine institution, the Merchant Navy.

Notes

1. Perhaps the phallic essence of the seafaring man figure is underlined by the entirely penetrative emphasis in the bowdlerised version of the song: 'All the nice girls love a candle / All the nice girls love a wick / Cos there's something about a candle / that reminds them of a prick. / Nice and greasy, slips in easy', etc.

2. See Ayers, P. (1999) 'The Making of Men: Masculinities in Inter-war Liverpool', in Walsh, M. (ed.), *Working Out Gender*, Ashgate, Aldershot, pp. 66–83; Burton, V. (1999) ' "Whoring, Drinking Sailors": Reflections on Masculinity from the Labour History of Nineteenth-Century British Shipping', in Walsh, *Gender*, pp. 84–101; Burton, V. (1991) 'The Myth of Bachelor Jack: Masculinity, Patriarchy and Seafaring Labour', in Howell, C. and Twomey, R. (eds), *Jack Tar in History: Essays in the History of Maritime Life and Labor*, Acadiensis, New Brunswick, NJ, pp. 187–8.

Acknowledgements

We'd both like to thank our interviewees, particularly those who read the draft chapters. The book could not have been done without them and they were generous as well as helpful. Their bravery and co-operation made all the difference.

We also thank those people who know about seafaring life and offered contextual information: James Cowden, Sheila Jemima, Rick Norwood, Stephen Rabson, Don Trueman and Derek Warmington. For appropriate historical information we appreciate Tony Tibbles and John Walton. Many people were generous in letting us use their pictures. These include James Cowden, Wayne Stanley for the images in *Physique Pictorial*, *On Our Backs*, Sailors Sauna, Southampton City Council/Jane Hunter Cox of Ocean Pictures, Toto Tours, The Tom of Finland Foundation, Ian Wallace and Warwick Modern Record Centre.

Additionally, thanks to Colin Richardson, editor of *Gay Times* for publicising our project and enabling us to find informants, and Heather McCallum and Bree Ellis at Pearson for being such supportive colleagues.

Paul would like to thank: Jo, for bearing the load so well; Tony, for cups of tea and encouragement; John, for advice and insight; Helen for being a sounding board and providing an alternative point of view; Bryon for his artwork, and his parents John and Marianne for being supportive when he told them about this 'racy' book.

Jo would like to thank: Paul, for being so equable and diligent; Dave, who put me on to the subject in the first place; members of the maritime historiography community worldwide for their (sometimes gloriously bawdy) assistance. Behind every book there is not only a talented cat or two but also a good health care practitioner: I appreciate Ruth Joynes and Dawn Mills for help with RSI when it struck; Ruth Ejankowski-Leeson for dazzling domestic support; Marie Osborne for fast and thorough work on the NUS archive; and Jo Wardman for her energetic work as amanuensis.

Books are composed in recreational time, as well as work time. I'm lucky that John came into my life and offered not just succulent reasons for taking time off, but stunningly insightful support for the book itself.

Several organisations were profoundly useful: the Oral History Unit, Southampton City Council, who were outstandingly co-operative about the use of their material; Warwick Modern Record Centre, which helped Jo as their 2000–2001 Research Fellow using the National Union of Seamen archives; the Caird Library at the National Maritime Museum; and the Hotel and Catering International Management Association Library. The British Library, Bradford and Lancaster University libraries and Bradford Central Library played essential parts. We thank them.

We have tried to obtain permission to include pictures and photographs wherever possible. In some cases we have had no replies or no luck in finding copyright holders. We would be delighted to hear from them if they write to us care of the publishers.

Some of the historical detail in this book has been changed slightly or made opaque in order to protect the identities of our informants, for example some ship's names and dates of voyages have been excised. Many of the men are concerned about a homophobic backlash and so our first responsibility was to make sure they and the people they mention could not be recognised.

The inclusion of people who appear in the photographs and pictures in this book does not imply anything about their sexual orientation either then or now.

Sailor Jack: the Other Side

Popular ideas of seafaring men

Historically, seafaring men (particularly the lower ranks) were seen as a rabble outside society. Maritime historian of seafarers, Charles Napier Robinson, describes them as a separate breed: lewd and disorderly knaves, they were people over-punished with keel hauling, flogging, tongue scraping or hung with weights round the neck.[1] 'Sailors have seen and done strange things, like to nothing that happens on shore. They pass their time on a wild and wonderful element, remarkable for its strength, its capriciousness and its cruelty'[2] he suggests, rather romantically. 'Seamen were ... of a different character from landsmen, and their rude and boisterous humour, ill-disguised contempt for the softer habits of those who lived ashore, the quaint expressions of their profession, with their wider knowledge of the globe, all appealed to people, or enforced and emphasised the distinctive attributes of the sailor, with manners, customs and language of his own.'[3] Sailors were seen both in contradistinction to people on land, and to femininity.

They were exceptionalised in popular thinking, and may not have been able to win the public relations battle, should they have ever chosen to try. Characterised as too indulgent in alcohol and promiscuous heterosexual sex, a much more muted story is that of their homosexuality. In literature and song, if not in reality, it has traditionally had two forms: first, a romantic and not necessarily sexual brotherhood; secondly, objectifying, inter-generational sexual use or abuse. Recently, Queer Studies (an academic discipline which we explain later in this chapter) has turned its literary lens to American maritime fiction such as that by Herman Melville. The classic example of this kind of gay sexuality in the merchant fleet comes from the most famous maritime novel of all, Moby Dick, where Queepueg and Ishmael are 'wedded'; and Ishmael sees the former as his 'dear comrade and twin brother'.[4]

By comparison to this heartfelt and noble affinity of masculine equals who love the sea, there were unequal relations, where degrees of

A kind of brotherhood of the sea. 'The Tritons' by Kenneth Kendal, from *Physique Pictorial*, Fall 1954. Picture courtesy of Wayne Stanley, Athletic Model Guild.

masculinity (expressed in age and seagoing experience) determine who has respect and who plays a superior role. As historian of gay pirates, B.R. Burg argues, 'fo'c's'le humor abounds with stories of below deck encounters in which salty bosuns initiate tender cabin boys into the arcana of the sea'.[5] The lack of love and the forceful inequality in this kind of relationship is connected to the great status divides on ships, to which Chapters 2 and 7 refer, but which is more true of periods before the mid-twentieth century on which we focus. As ex-bellboy John Taylor Caldwell writes of sailing on the Anchor line's the *TSS Caledonia* from Glasgow to New York in 1928: 'The various departments of crew had little love for each other, and all were at one in contempt for the stewards, unjustly considered "pansy-waists" who fawned on passengers expressing willingness

Seafaring life was sometimes a masculine brotherhood. Picture courtesy of Bill.

to empty their chamber-pots. Bellboys were the small fry of this despised brood.'[6]

The abuse of minors comes out in a well-known fictional description of life at sea. James Hanley's novel, *Boy* (1931), shows how desperate 12-year-old Liverpool stowaway, Arthur Fearon, is sexually approached by the second steward, the cook and the bosun's mate.[7] The book refers several times to the climate aboard: men who think that boys are both there to be used and 'much better than a woman anytime' as the carpenter argues.[8] Such a work could be taken to a make a firm and negative *de facto* connection between homosexuality and abuse at sea. But other factors need to be looked at. There is a pecking order on every ship, based on age, calls, seniority, status and masculinity. Young uneducated feminine boys are lowest in this order and as such they suffered all sorts of hostility. Sex in this context was more about men exercising power over other men than about gay identity. As an old salt tells Fearon, many boys were used as 'brownies' and the practice was passed on from generation to generation. 'My first trip, we rounded the Horn in a bloody hurricane. I had to go aloft with two of the seamen. I was like a girl in those days, with silky skin and slender hands. Those two buggers tried to do me one all right when we perched Aloft ... ever since... I hate boys.'[9]

By the mid-twentieth century, not only had steam long ago displaced sail but also motorised ships had replaced steam. Passenger ships were seen – often derisively by those who held a romantic preference for the 'masculine', sooty-funnelled days – as floating chocolate boxes. Increasingly regular schedules meant the danger, uncertainty and

The Man at the Wheel.

Changing images of seafarers. The logos that appeared with editorials in NUS journal, before and then after March 1939. Picture courtesy of RMT.

adventure was gone. The picaresque man of the waves described by Robinson had largely vanished – if he ever actually existed. The editorial logo on the seafarers' union journal, *The Seaman*, is a clear sign of this. After the Second World War, the rugged, bearded Cap'n Birdseye figure at the stormy wheel in his sou'wester was replaced by a virile young man.

Kenneth Williams. Picture courtesy of V.E. Stanley.

He was still at the wheel rather than carrying a tray of cocktails or duster, and he didn't, of course, have his hand on his hip or wear a satin fishtail frock.

Seafarers in popular culture

The focus in literature and entertainment, such as Gilbert and Sullivan's *HMS Pinafore*, the musical *South Pacific*, and the opera *A Night on the Town* tends to be on non-merchant navies. There is little camp activity but a lot of interest in uniform, including trousers. Jerome K. Jerome writes about the stage sailor's pulling up of his trousers, along with dancing the hornpipe and points out that 'the thing the stage sailor most craves in his life is that someone should shiver his timbers. ... But nobody ever does it.'[10] Pirates are popular figures in light entertainment, and there have been several novels about transgression in the form of women taking up buccaneering.

Since cruises took off in the 1930s, novels with titles such as *Sea Air, Luxury Liner* and *Mystery on the Queen Mary* have offered crime and heterosexual romance among passengers, but no gay escapades by the people who sailed the ship. Seafarers' biographies also omit the subject, sometimes surprisingly. For example, Cunard masseur John Dempsey writes of gay actor Noel Coward's camp *bon mots*, but not of any gay shenanigans in the massage suites of the *Berengaria, Queen Mary and Queen Elizabeth*.[11] Most movies and television series about passenger ship life show romance and adultery (particularly *The Love Boat*)[12], and also refer to homosexuality. A remarkably early exception is Kenneth Williams in *Carry on Cruising* (1962), the camp First Officer on the *SS Happy Wanderer*.[13]

Gay seafarers in popular culture

James Hanley's *Boy*[14] is the best-known novel about male–male sex in the Merchant Navy, as described above. Mary Renault's *The Charioteer*[15] sensitively evokes a naval officer's relationship with a young medical orderly in a hospital after Dunkirk was evacuated – a far cry from camp flouncing on passenger ships. But the most recent works of gay seafarer fiction are pure erotica. Ken Smith packs in sexual stories in his *Virgin Sailors*.[16] The cover blurb of *The Captain's Boy*, by Sam Stevens, asks 'Just how far will men go to satiate their carnal desire?' And the hero, Robert Marchant, finds out when 'he and his crewmates are captured by

'Boiler Room', by Tristano, an English artist. It appeared in *Physique Pictorial Summer* 1958. Picture courtsesy of Wayne Stanley, Athletic Model Guild.

pirates intent on regular man-on-man orgies'.[17] Gay pirates were also the focus in Clay Wilson's underground comic strip *Captain Piss-Gums and His Pervert Pirates*.[18]

Seafarers in compromising positions are also found in gay high culture. Examples include the photographs of sailors by Robert Mapplethorpe,[19] and Rainer Werner Fassbinder's film *Querelle* (1982), based on Jean Genet's 1947 novel. Fassbinder's interpretation was artfully homoerotic, starring Brad Davis as the sexually experimental lead. In addition, Stuart Edelson's novel *Black Glass: A Sea Myth*[20] describes young sailor Michael Silver's time in Vietnam, 1965. He falls in love with a straight sailor and makes sexual discoveries in Far Eastern ports.

Within the gay world's popular culture, the sea and homosexuality have been linked for five decades, although the focus has been on sailors as part of national, not merchant, navies, and on butch rather than feminine sailors. In the 1950s and 1960s the photographer Bob Mizer took hundreds of photographs of nude and semi-nude sailors (or good-looking men partially dressed in sailors' uniforms) for his Athletic Model Guild. Many of these photographs found their way into early gay magazines, with names like *Tomorrow's Man, Vim and Physique Pictorial*. These magazines also featured drawings of sailors by artists like Tom of Finland and Etienne.

From the 1950s to the 1970s there were also many underground erotic novels based around sailors, although they were almost entirely about the US Navy, not the merchant fleet. They largely feature butch men, not queens, although many have a fragile young newcomer receiving sadistic treatment. They mainly fall into two categories: those about sex between sailors, on ships, and those between naval men and landlubbers, in port. These novels about sex between sailors in the US Navy show that rank, and degree of masculinity, are crucial factors. They include *Navy Meat*,[21] *Hank's Navy Buddies*,[22] *Navy Discipline Below Deck*,[23] *Porthole Buddies*,[24] and *The Brig Boys*.[25] A common theme in these novels is of butch Marines who desire to be passive partners because they long for a break from endlessly putting on a macho show. The second category of novels shows US Navy personnel having sex, sometimes paid, with men ashore who are fascinated by their uniform and sometimes by their roughness. Often the men ashore are older and wealthier. Books such as *San Diego Sailor*,[26] *Seafood Platter*,[27] and *Navy Blues*[28] read as if they are written for and by such men.

The theme of sexy sailors continues with popular music. In 1979 the pop group The Village People released the song *In The Navy*, which, like their debut hit, *YMCA*, was quickly established as a gay anthem. A team from *HMS Dog* danced to it in Manchester's 2000 Gay Pride march. Both songs contain the theme of an all-male institution being an enjoyable haven for lonely young men. And most tellingly of all, a glance at the X-rated gay video porn of today continues the theme of (usually the US) Navy as a prime site of erotic fantasy: *Naval Escort*, *A Sailor in Sydney*, *The Anchor Hotel*, *Seamen First Class*, *Sailor in the Wild* and *Good Sailors Gone Bad*.

Maritime history

So much for views of the seafarer in fiction and popular culture. But what of the non-fiction world? No serious maritime histories have included the history of these thousands of camp gay men on liners,[29] although some scholarly articles have studied the maritime homosexuality in the Royal Navy,[30] and two books have investigated gay activity on pirate vessels.[31] However, this was a different period, a different type of seafaring, and a much less open, joyous and camp culture.

By contrast, gay men (and women) in the US Navy and military have had some attention in non-fiction,[32] though those in the US Merchant Navy have not. The most relevant of these books to our history is Steven Zeeland's *Sailors and Sexual Identity*, which tells the stories of gay naval servicemen through his own – often sexual – encounters with them.

Armchair travellers have for years had access to celebratory books such as John Maxtone Graham's *The Only Way to Cross* and John Malcolm Brinnin's *The Sway of the Grand Saloon*.[33] Although such works cover the style and grandeur of life on passenger ships, few deal in any detail with the staff and none refer to homosexuality. Perhaps one of the most interesting books to re-read, with cross-dressers in mind, is a compilation of ship's photographers' work in the 1950s. Such concessionaires on ships were paid to portray glamour at sea, and *The Golden Age of Transatlantic Travel: 1936–59* refers to the frocks and stars but certainly not to the gay guys who emulated these women's styles.[34]

Gay history

Non-fiction books on gay history have barely included seafarers. For example, Kevin Porter and Jeffrey Weeks's anthology of the lives of gay men 1885–1967, *Between the Acts*, includes only a brief reference to an interlude with a married sailor lover ashore in 'A Dancer's Life'.[35] Lisa Power's history of the UK Gay Liberation Front refers to an activist who was formerly a seaman.[36] Two autobiographies deal substantially with gay life, George Melly's story of his time in the Royal Navy just after the

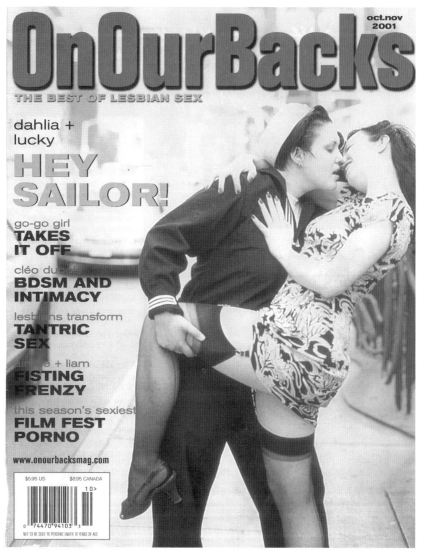

Lesbian women find the idea of sailors erotic too. Cover *On Our Backs*,
Oct./Nov. 2001. Picture courtesy of *On Our Backs* magazine.

Second World War[37] and Jack Robinson's accounts of wartime in the
Merchant Navy.[38]

More generally, the entertainment world (particularly in the USA) has
shown substantial interest in flamboyant cross-dressing and transcen-
dence of gender using naval clothing and iconography. For example, the
November 2001 editions of the two main international lesbian erotic
magazines (*Flirt* and *On Our Backs*) published pictures of lesbian women

Sailors are such popular gay icons that even a London sauna uses the image. Picture courtesy of Sailors Sauna.

dressed as sailors; the Orange mobile phone network in 2002 used two women in sailor gear to illustrate its holiday promotion; and in the UK, designer Jean-Paul Gaultier used a cross-dressed woman in a sailor bar for one of his television adverts in 2000. His marketing manager said the message was 'Things are not always what they seem'.[39] There's also a London sauna called Sailors.

The erotic appeal of seafarers

So why are seafarers endowed with an almost mythical aura of intense sexuality and masculinity? There are several reasons for the appeal of 'the sailor' as an iconic figure. Travellers can be seen as sexually exotic. Seafarers are the new boys in town, bringing with them the glamour of faraway places and providing new sexual opportunities for people who may have exhausted their regular stock of trade. The phenomenon of women who meet ships in order to have sex with the men on them – wharf angels, seagulls or shipgirls[40] – testifies to this appeal.

Also, seafarers are fleeting presences. The sense of casualness offered by sex with a seafarer is also attractive. For those who don't want to be tied down to marriage or a long-term relationship, a seafaring man functions as an ideal one-night stand or occasional boyfriend. His ship may only be in dock for a few days, and then he'll be gone for months. As the song

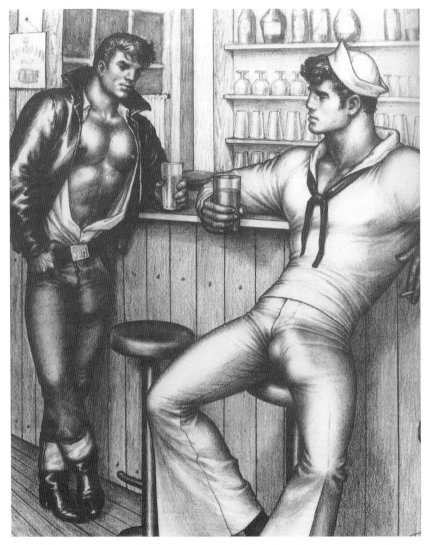

The stereotype: an iconic, hyper-masculine sailor. Picture courtesy of
The Tom of Finland Foundation (1962).

goes: 'Falls in love with Kate and Jane, then he's off to sea again.' While
a seafaring man may have a girl (or boy) in every port, some of their
shore-side partners had a sailor on every ship too.

A sense of living high and wild is also appealing. The association of
sailors and heavy drinking suggests that their sexual inhibitions are likely
to be relaxed in certain situations, particularly on long voyages or during
shore leave. 'The automatic union of . . . sailors ("rum, sodomy and the
lash") and the gay world is clichéd, politically no doubt far from correct,

but unavoidable'[41] argues lexicographer Jonathan Green. And part of the erotic appeal lies in the fetishisation of the uniform. Most importantly, uniforms function as anonymisers. Put someone in a uniform and they are defined first by their occupation: differences between particular people are excised. Someone's uniform becomes the foremost signifier of his or her identity.

There is also the homoeroticism of nominally all-male organisations, including the military. For centuries the army and the navy have been places that largely exclude, deny or minimise women's presence. Military cultures are 'masculine' by default – the majority of men who inhabit them are young, healthy and at their physical peaks. Masculinity is performed through the profession: the handling of machinery, weapons and large vehicles, the austere living conditions and the physical exercise. Also, the (only recent) decriminalisation of homosexual acts in the armed forces or merchant ships has simply served to make the idea of gay sex with a seafarer even more compelling than ever.[42] The excitement of sanctioned sex pales in comparison to 'forbidden', dangerous sex.

And single-sex institutions are almost always endowed with a high level of sexual mystique or tension. Men at sea may be expected to endure long periods of time away from their homes and families. This physical distance from zones of familial responsibility may mean that a seafarer's indiscretion could be excused as an occupational hazard.

What does this stereotype leave out?

It must be said that this stereotypical and objectifying view of the sailor as a desirable, bronzed hunk is focused on the uniformed, usually US, sailor – in a country's fighting force, such as the Royal Navy. He's often in the lower ranks, and he's in fighting – not hospitality – work. It is not something that was true of most of the merchant seamen whose stories helped make this book. They were mainly stewards.

The iconic 'sailor', that ultra-butch symbol of a particular kind of sexuality – horny, macho and stiff-pricked – was not a part of their lived daily life though he could be something *they* fantasised over. They didn't wear bellbottoms, though some queens might go for a man who did. Chris, a gay steward who gave us his story, illuminates this distinction. He was attracted to sailors in the Royal Naval uniform with its plunging neckline and tight bellbottoms. He enjoyed dressing his lovers afterwards, putting their lanyard straight, but he did so as any lover might, not particularly as a fellow seafarer. And merchant seafarers traditionally did not wear a uniform more than they had to. Some gay seafarers of the time would have

Seafarers camping it up in the British Merchant Navy. Picture courtesy of
private, anonymous donor.

preferred Palm Beach loafers, if not stiletto-heeled sling-backs, to uniform
boots, and cool cocktail frocks to brass-buttoned jackets.

Although generally young and necessarily energetic, many of these men
were not at their physical peak like the iconic 'Sailor'. Catering workers
traditionally suffer from bad feet and poor digestion. Irregular, snatched
meals and alcohol abuse take their toll. Heavy lifting for some involved
wielding trays of champagne through packed dining rooms, not manhan-
dling ships' tackle.

So they might be able to spot a Norman Hartnell gown at 50 paces
better than they could detect the class of a frigate on the port bow. In the
cases of stewards, their skills were in cuisine, couture and emotional lore.
Masculinity in the institution, on passenger ships, was diluted by women's
presence as passengers and, increasingly, as staff. It was only below decks
in their quarters that there was a male-only environment.

And, unlike the myth of the horny sailor-for-rent, none of the sailors
who were interviewed for this book sold sexual favours for money, and
none saw himself as an exotic bit of rough. Some may have seen themselves as beautiful, but to be liked or at least accepted was more important. The point, with our informants, was not that they fancied shipboard
colleagues because they were seafarers (although some of the butch,
below-deck characters had appeal). It was simply that they could enjoy

the company and proximity of lots of men, some of whom might be available. And while officers were generally expected to 'butch it up', camp or effeminacy was tolerated, or at least sanctioned, within the ranks of stewards and kitchen staff.

And this is perhaps the most interesting aspect of this history of gay seafarers. Not that so much gay sex went on – passenger ships were places where a lot of sex occurs anyway – but that a large camp subculture was allowed to flourish in such a traditionally masculine territory. It was a situation in which something illegal and reprehensible ashore became an exceptionalised and accepted 'bit of fun' to thousands of passengers and seafarers. Butch-femme roles were played out long after such behaviour was seen as oppressive by gay activists ashore. But gay sexuality was flaunted on ships at least 20 years before the Gay Liberation movement started. And what is also fascinating is the difference between navies. For example, Royal Naval prohibitions, even as late as 1990s, led to the disciplining of a Royal Navy senior officer Duncan Lustig-Prean. His famous 1999 European Court victory against homophobia[43] highlighted just how much the Merchant Navy situation in the mid-twentieth century was unusual.

About this book

Why write it?

We wrote *Hello Sailor!* in order to highlight two important and often over-looked facts: that gay life happened in this ostensibly unlikely place; and that gay seafarers were not (necessarily) the stereotypically butch icons found in sailor porn.

Stories of maritime life have too often omitted accounts that are related to gender and sexual orientation. As other historians of masculinity have argued, 'making men visible as gendered subjects has major implications for all the historian's established themes'.[44] It exposes some of the hitherto hidden subjective experiences and patterns of power relations on ships. And one benefit that studies of history from a gay perspective can offer is not only to refute the myth of the sea as a masculine and heterosexual place, but to question why it has so long been portrayed as such. Even today, few seafarers will talk of the secret: the extent of camp gay performance and how it worked in the interest of shipping lines who liked 'feminine' service, passengers who relished camp wit, and gay men who could at last express and explore hidden aspects of themselves. Equally, no one has yet explored in print the oppressive shipboard relations, heterosexual hegemony and patriarchal patterns that are both masked and exposed when queerness is handled as comic masquerade, not serious option.

Our book has two roots: Paul's interest in Polari (a secret form of language used by gay men) and gay social history and Jo's in gendered maritime history. Paul was interviewing gay seamen, among other gay men, about how they used this language variety in order to construct identities during the repressive 1950s and 1960s. And Jo had for years wanted to find out more about the subjective reality of the legendary queens who starred in stories told her by ex-seafarers. Their Hollywood nicknames, sumptuous gowns, fighting fists and scintillating tongues suggested that there was a lost history of the sea that illuminated gender relations in the Merchant Navy.

Gay people were simply not present in maritime history books and maritime museum displays. As someone studying women, and therefore gender polarities, in shipboard culture Jo thought that to understand gay male behaviour might be to understand masculinities on ship, and hence femininities, and that seems a very deserving and overdue study. Paul did most of the initial interviewing of the nine gay men whose testimonies form the basis of this book. Together we wrote a paper for a maritime conference in Fremantle, then saw that the subject could be a book and exhibition too. We were delighted to find a publisher who liked the idea.

Sources

In dividing the job between us Paul has focused on the gay life-stories and gay context, while Jo has written the parts that put gay sea life into a maritime context. As our basis we used contemporary oral testimony with gay male seafarers (see Appendix 1 for their brief biographies), plus substantial general anecdotal evidence from other straight and gay seafarers. The men's names have been changed for their protection, except in the case of two men who felt it a matter of principle to be out about themselves. We worked out pseudonyms for all of the gay people referred to. These are in keeping with their identities, for example the name of 'Carol Baker' (the blond bombshell) was given to a sea queen who normally used the name of another movie star of the same period. Ship's names have been omitted where we have thought it would compromise the story-giver.

Paul's additional sources include material gathered for his PhD thesis on Polari, information from the Hall-Carpenter Archives and other gay social historians, and additional interviews with a number of non-seafaring gay men who gave details about gay life and language use in the 1950s and 1960s in the UK.

Jo's sources include much informal oral testimony from seafarers of both sexes, shipping line personnel workers, and other maritime historians; shipping company archives at Liverpool and Greenwich; material gathered for her PhD thesis on women domestic workers on ships; seafaring union archives at Warwick Modern Record Centre; and popular literature on sea travel.

Using information

We encountered a number of problems with the sources that we used in order to understand what seafaring life was like for gay men. First, we were unable to interview every gay seafarer who existed. But our sample is representative, consisting of stewards, waiters, engineers and officers, from the early 1950s up until the 1980s. We interviewed men who were camp and others who were butch – some who were openly gay while at sea and others who had not revealed their sexuality to anyone.

Another possible problem when using oral testimonies is that there is sometimes reticence, over-politeness and a tendency to see the past through rosy spectacles. Oral historians[45] today now focus on *how* things are remembered and said as much as *what* is said. 'Mistaken' memories are welcomed because of what they reveal about unconscious fantasy. They also show how popular memory affects individual memory: others' ideas of what happened affect what individuals think happened and can get mixed with, or even override, the subjective feelings. For example, being young, experiencing the ethos of sexual liberation of the 1970s, meeting famous people and being on cruise ships tended to be remembered in a positive way partly because people expect it to have been happy. Evidence for this book was often presented in a frivolous and jocular way. This suggests that some may strategically deny the seriousness of homosexual oppression when talking about painful history. Making light of troubles – then and now – is a way of coping with the threats to your identity. However, it means that the full story of homophobic trouble on ships has yet to be told. Our difficulties with some people's stories – contradiction, exaggeration, generalisation and evasion – actually reveal just how problematic gay sexuality still is in our heteronormative society, as well as raising such questions as 'Was it *really* OK to be out on that ship? Did people actually have so much sex? Just how gay was *that* kind of ship in *that* period?'

But these rich, subjective stories, in feminist historians Gluck and Patai's words, turn up 'the muted channel'. Gay seafarers' amplification of the somewhat secret world of ships enables us to view maritime history in full stereo, not heterosexist mono.[46]

Language

It is useful here to explain how we have used language in this book. We have usually used the current term 'gay' to describe men who had romantic and sexual relationships with other men. However, some gay, lesbian, bisexual and transgendered people today have now recuperated the term 'queer' in the same way that people of colour have reclaimed the label 'black' and some feminists have recuperated terms like 'stroppy cow' and 'crone'. But for many men who suffered stigma in the last century 'queer' and 'homosexual' have pejorative meanings, so we have avoided using these terms where they might offend people. Indeed, prior to the early 1970s, many men who had sex with other men did not consider themselves to be 'gay'. The word only came into popular usage in the UK with the advent of Gay Liberation. In the 1950s and 1960s some of these men simply had no words to describe their sexual orientation, or would have used a euphemism such as 'artistic' or 'so'. Others may have used the Polari word 'omee-palone'. So, while the word 'gay' is used in this book to describe men who self-identified as mainly being sexually and romantically attracted to other men, we acknowledge that some men would not have used this word to describe themselves, until long after they had left the Merchant Navy, if ever.

Also we have used the term 'seafarer' rather than 'seaman' for two reasons. First, to make the point that seafarers are not solely male. Women were officially called 'British Seamen' too. Secondly, to avoid confusion about status on ship: 'seaman', 'sailor', and 'crew member' are often taken to describe the lowliest manual deck workers on ship and not the full range of seafaring people in general, from navigating officers to galley scullions. 'Seafarer' covers all ranks. Our glossary in Appendix 2 explains some of these terms.

Queer Theory

And what do we mean by 'gay sexuality' or 'homosexuality'? And are gay people born or made? There have been many lively disputes between these two different viewpoints. Social constructionists see sexuality as something that is heavily influenced by society, while essentialists regard sexuality as something that people are born with.[47] More

recently, it has been argued that both 'sides' of the debate have important contributions to make, and that sexuality is most likely a combination of both 'nature' and 'nurture'. This book explores gay seafarers
by using new perspectives and theories from the academic world of
Queer Studies, which has been influenced by such thinkers as Judith
Butler, Eve Kosofsky Sedgwick, Diana Fuss and Michel Foucault.[48]
Queer Studies examines areas, such as ship's companies, which would
not normally be seen as the terrain of sexuality. It uses a queered (gay
aware) lens to look at subjects and situations that seem superficially to
be heterosexual or non-sexualised. For example, the seventeenth- and
eighteenth-century plays about seafarers which feature girls dressed as
cabin boys[49] could be seen not as testimony of women's presence, but
actually a sanitised way of acknowledging that cabin boys were the
feminised lovers in gay partnerships.

Queer Theory is different from conventional gay and lesbian studies,
argue Queer Studies writers Stein and Plummer.[50] This is because Queer
Studies sees sexual power as embodied in different levels of social life. It's
expressed through *how* we talk about it. And it's imposed through arbi-
trary and reductive divisions, the most obvious of which is gay versus
straight. Unlike gay and lesbian studies, Queer Studies does not uphold a
civil rights point of view, such as 'gays should be accepted as equal members of society'. Instead it favours 'a politics of carnival, transgression,
and parody'. That coincides with the very idea of themselves that sea
queens expressed and acted out on the ships. They celebrated difference
and refused to seek assimilation.

Queer Theory also acknowledges that sexuality is fluid and constantly
subject to reinterpretation. And as many seafarers found out, categories
like gay and straight are not inscribed in stone. Men could be straight on
one voyage and gay on the next. By concentrating on Queer Studies,
rather than gay and lesbian studies, we can write about the experiences of
seafarers who may have had sex with other men but who did not consider
themselves to be gay. 'Queer' in this case is set up in opposition to whatever is established as 'normal', a much wider category than self-identified
gay men and lesbians. However, there are potential problems with Queer
Theory. For example, it has been accused of creating a form of academic
discourse that excludes non-academics,[51] and its disruptive nature may
mean that it can lack coherence. But for the purposes of this book, we
believe that a broadly queer perspective is one that can be usefully implemented in the study of the sexualities of seafarers.

Sexuality

We are writing about sex for both light reasons (because it's interesting and fun) and for more serious ones. Today, sexuality is regarded as 'that bodily domain of pleasure, power and personal identity', argues Scott Bravmann, a writer on gay sociology.[52] The controversy about sexual intercourse on Royal Naval ships, which developed after WRENS were allowed to go to sea in 1991, indicates just how it is an area of public concern. Sexual orientation is tied up with how we see ourselves, how we are treated by others – straight and gay – and how we handle daily life, including work and recreation.

So there is an important social aspect to sexual orientation. Gay sexuality, therefore, can become based around what Lave and Wenger call a 'community of practice', 'a set of relations among persons, activity and world, over time and in relation with other tangential and overlapping communities of practice. A community of practice is an intrinsic condition for the existence of knowledge.'[53] However, gay sexuality is not a simple unified and coherent thing. It has many class, race and gender tensions and conflicts that divide gay men as well as unite them. For example, some of the men in our study led a life that excluded members of the opposite sex, while others were married. Ships are highly stratified spaces. Class, occupational status and age mattered. Passenger vessels were often – like hotels – full of snobbery as well as status rivalry, so a gay but closeted navigating officer was far removed from an out steward, camp purser or experimenting bellboy.

Masculinity and femininity

And why does this book refer to women as well as men on ships? 'Removing women from the field of study also obscures the connections between masculinity and social power', argue masculinity theorists Graham Roper and John Tosh.[54] And the power to have sex with very specific members of shipboard society, and to act in camp ways, was a product of social status and visible masculinity. To understand what 'masculinity' is we have to understand the differences between men by seeing them in the context of sexual politics. Such a context includes older men's power over younger men, heterosexual men's power over homosexual men in the last 100 years, and men's power over women. Masculinity is therefore a product of the differing social powers of men, and is at the centre of how male–female relations are organised in societies.

Additionally, this book is part of the growing sociological trend towards focusing on those who populate ships, rather than the vessels themselves. That trend also recognises that gender is important. This has been evidenced by academic interest in sailor Jack's masculinity,[55] gendered transport conferences and the forming of women's maritime networks.

The organisation of this book

The following chapter summarises what attitudes to homosexuality were like ashore, particularly during the 1950s and 1960s. This helps to explain why, in contrast, some men could experience ships as the gay heaven and place of freedom we describe in Chapter 2. The community that gay seafarers built up was enabled and enriched by their secret language, Polari, which is explored in Chapter 3. While being part of gang was crucial, so were relationships. These, in all their diversity, are revealed in Chapter 4. For some gay men, dressing up in order to perform camp or 'female' identities was an essential part of stating that they were gay, so Chapter 5 records the sequins and style that were put on when the uniform was taken off. While frocks were part of off-duty pleasure on ship, getting off in foreign countries was also a form of recreation. Chapter 6 describes some of the ways that being a seafarer could enable men to mix with gay or gay-friendly people in distant ports. Overseas, gay seafarers could visit gay clubs, brothels and bath-houses, and discover that attitudes towards sexuality where often less repressive than in the UK. Chapter 7 outlines the complex set of social and sexual relations that gay seafarers had with their straight colleagues and the passengers. A ship could be a space for gay men where feminised behaviour such as domesticated neatness and outrageously camp performance was accepted, even welcomed, as it was in no other occupation. But it was a party that had to be left at some point, as Chapter 8 details. Seafarers who 'swallowed the anchor' were both pushed and pulled by personal and social conditions, and they returned to a much less permissive shore with very different ideas about gay life from when they first walked up the gangway.

So voyage with us all, if you will, in these extraordinary and often happy waters and learn exactly why queer things happened at sea.

Notes

1. Robinson, C.N. (1911) *The British Tar in Fact and Fiction*, Harper and Brothers, London.

2. Ibid., p. 153.

3. Ibid., p. 157.

4. See Bender, B. (1987) *Sea-Brothers: The Tradition of American Sea Fiction from Moby-Dick to the Present*, University of Pennsylvania Press, Philadelphia, PA, p. 160. Also for a fictionalised but entirely plausible and beautiful version of Ishmael's gay life after leaving the sea, see Naslund, S.J. (2000) *Ahab's Wife or The Star-Gazer*, Women's Press, London.

5. Burg, B.R. (1983) *Sodomy and the Perception of Evil: English Sea Rovers in the Seventeenth Century Caribbean*, New York University Press, New York, p. xvii.

6. Caldwell, J.T. (1999) *With Fate Conspire: Memoirs of a Glasgow Seafarer and Anarchist*, Northern Herald Books, Rastrick, Yorkshire, p. 29. Caldwell has a rather interestingly sex-free idea of why young men were not in older men's cabins. As a steward in a 12-berth cabin on the *Caledonia* in 1938, he noted that the bellboys had been taken from their collective cabin and each allocated to an adult's cabin. 'The men did not allow bellboy visitors in, on the grounds that they would be a talking, laughing, horse-playing disturbance (besides, some of them might be light-fingered)' (p. 133).

7. Hanley, J. *Boy*. First published in a limited edition of 145 copies in 1931, in a cheap edition by Borriswood in 1934, and this edition by Andre Deutsch in 1990, p. x. The book describes such bleakness (aboard the *Hernian* to Alexandria) that the police took action against it. It became a *cause célèbre* in the challenge to Britain's Sedition Act, according to Anthony Burgess in the introduction. E.M. Forster, himself gay, endorsed the book and fiercely denounced official squeamishness at the International Congress of Writers in 1935, p. 76.

8. Hanley, J. *Boy*, p. 100.

9. Ibid., p. 97.

10. Jerome, J.K. (no date) 'The sailor' from *Stageland* at http://gaslight.mtroyal.ab.ca/stg-sail.htm.

11. Dempsey, J. (1992) *I've Seen Them All Naked*, Waterfront Publications, Poole.

12. See, for example, the autobiography of Cruise Director Jeraldine Saunders (1998), *Love Boats: Above and Below Decks with Jeraldine Saunders*, Llewellyn Publications, St Pauls, MIN.

13. *Carry on Cruising* was directed by Gerald Thomas and made by Anglo Amalgamated Film Distributors. The 1993 video version is distributed by Warner Home Video.

14. Hanley, J. *Boy*.

15. Renault, M. (1965) *The Charioteer*, Mary Renault, Longmans, Green and Co, London.

16. Smith, K. (2000) *Virgin Sailors*, Prowler Books, London.

17. Stevens, Sam (1999) *The Captain's Boy*, Prowler Books, London.

18. For a brief summary of this and other material on gay piracy, see Newlin, J. (2002) *Madam John Dodt's Legacy*, #3 at http://www.ambushmag.com/lega3.htm.

19. See discussion 'I love a Man in Uniform (I need an Order)' at http://www.stonewallinn.com/Features/DirtyEx4.html.

20. Edelson, S. (1993) *Black Glass: A Sea Myth*, Dimi Press, Salem, OR.

21. *Navy Meat*, no author, Male Photo Illustrated – 114, Star Distributors, New York, 1979.

22. *Hank's Navy Buddies*, Parker Schaeffer, Spade Classics, Star Distributors, New York, 1979.

23. *Navy Discipline Below Decks*, Black Knight Classics, Guild Press, Washington DC, 1970.

24. *Porthole Buddies*, Black Knight Classics, Guild Press, Washington DC, 1969.

25. *The Brig Boys*, Barton Lewis, Greenleaf Classics, CA, 1981.

26. *San Diego Sailor*, no author, Black Knight Classics, Guild Press, Washington DC, 1969.

27. *Seafood Platter*, Andrew Martin, His 69 Surrey Books, Star Distributors, New York, 1987.

28. *Navy Blues*, J.J. Proferes, Guild Press, Washington DC, 1966.

29. Two exceptions are Michael Gavin's 1982 article 'Gays at Sea', *Mister*, 35, Millivres Press, London, pp.26–8. There is also a section on sea queens in Kirk, Kris and Heath, Ed (1984) *Men in Frocks*, Gay Men's Press, London.

30. The lack of information has been particularly discussed by gender historians working in the maritime field, such as Margaret S. Creighton. The main references to gay seafarers are Gilbert, A. (1976) 'Buggery and the British Navy, 1700–1861', *Journal of Social History*, 10, pp. 72–98; Gilbert, A. (1977) 'Sexual Deviance and Disaster during the Napoleonic Wars', *Albion*, 9, pp. 98–113; Chauncey, G. Junior (1985) 'Christian Brotherhood or Sexual Perversion? Homosexual Identities and the Construction of Sexual Boundaries in the World War I Era', *Journal of Social History*, 19, pp. 189–212; Chauncey, G. Junior (1994) *Gay New York: Gender, Urban Culture, and the Making of the Gay Male World, 1890–1940*, Basic Books, New York, especially Chapter 3. In relation to piracy there is B.R. Burg's *Sodomy and the Perception of Evil*, and Hans Turley's scholarly (1999) *Rum, Sodomy and the Lash: Piracy, Sexuality and Masculine Identity*, New York University Press, New York and London. See also Burg, B.R. (1994) *An American Sailor in the Age of Sail: The Erotic Diaries of Philip Van Buskirk*, Yale University Press, New Haven CT. Further feminist writings about masculinity include Creighton, Margaret S. (1996) 'Davy Jones' Locker Room: Gender and the American Whaleman 1830–1870,' especially p. 28 and Laura

Tabili (1996) ' "A Maritime Race": Masculinity and the Racial Division of Labor in British Merchant Ships 1900–1939' p. 184, both in Creighton, M.S. and Norling, L. (eds), *Iron Men, Wooden Women: Gender and Seafaring in the Atlantic World 1700–1920*, Johns Hopkins University Press, Baltimore, MD, and London. Literary Queer Studies scholars have also examined homosexuality in Herman Melville's *Billy Budd* and *Moby Dick*. See also Naslund, *Ahab's Wife*.

31. Burg, *Sodomy or The Perception of Evil*, and Turley, *Rum, Sodomy and The Lash*.

32. Zeeland, S. (1995) *Sailors and Sexual Identity*, Harrington Park Press, New York; Shilts, R. (1995) *Conduct Unbecoming: Gays and Lesbians in the US Military*, St Martins Press, New York; Bérubé, A. (1991) *Coming Out under Fire: The History of Gay Men and Women in World War Two*, Penguin, London; Dyer, K. (ed.) (1990) *Gays in Uniform: The Pentagon's Secret Reports*, Alyson, Boston, MA.

33. Graham, J.M. (1983) *The Only Way to Cross*, Patrick Stephens, Cambridge; and Brinnin, J.M. (1971) *The Sway of the Grand Saloon: A Social History of the North Atlantic*, Macmillan, London.

34. Hunter-Cox, J. (1989) *Ocean Pictures: The Golden Age of Transatlantic Travel 1936–59*, Webb & Bowyer, with Michael Joseph, London.

35. Porter, K. and Weeks, J. (eds) (1991) *Between the Acts: Lives of Homosexual Men 1885–1967*, Routledge, London, pp. 104–5.

36. Power, L. (1995) *No Bath but Plenty of Bubbles: An Oral History of the Gay Liberation Front 1970–73*, Cassell, London.

37. Melly, G. (1977) *Rum, Bum and Concertina*, Futura, London.

38. Robinson, J. (1988) *Jack and Jamie Go to War*, Gay Men's Press, London.

39. See http://www.commercialcloset.org/cgi-bin/iowa/portrayals.html?record=520.

40. Ship girls are researched by Jan Jordan. See *Ship Girls: The Invisible Women of the Sea*, unpublished paper given to the Women and The Sea conference, Wellington Maritime Museum, New Zealand, December 1993. Jeraldine Saunders, *Love Boats*, refers to them as 'seagulls' on p. 179.

41. Green, J. (1987) 'Polari', *Critical Quarterly*, 39 (1), pp. 127–31.

42. Part XI of the Criminal Justice Act and Public Order Act 1994 made homosexual acts in the armed forces and on merchant ships no longer a criminal offence in the UK. However, homosexual acts were still grounds for administratively discharging a member of the armed forces or a crew member on a merchant ship until 1999, when a ruling by the European Court of Human Rights finally removed the ban.

43. See *Last Night I dreamt of the Sea Again*, http://www.davidclemens.com/gaymilitary/duncan.htm. Interestingly he writes of working for the captain on the *HMS Ambuscade* who said ' "If you ever think one of your stewards is gay, please allocate him to me as my steward." "Why, Sir?" I asked, genuinely shocked.

"Because, Duncan, gay men make the best stewards, they know how to look after a man."'

44. Roper, M. and Tosh, J. (1991) 'Historians and the Politics of Masculinity', in Roper, M. and Tosh, J. (eds), *Manful Assertions: Masculinities in Britain since 1800*, Routledge, London, p. 1.

45. These new developments in oral history particularly use the ideas of Alessandro Portelli and Luisa Passerini. For a useful overview, see two volumes: Perks, R. and Thomson, P. (eds) (1998) *The Oral History Reader*, Routledge, London; and Samuel, R. and Thompson, P. (eds) (1990) *The Myths We Live By*, Routledge, London.

46. Gluck, S.B. and Patai, D. (eds) (1991) *Women's Words: The Feminist Practice of Oral History*, Routledge, London, p. 11.

47. For reviews of social constructionist theory, see Stein, E. (ed.) (1990) *Forms of Desire*, Garland, New York, and Mass, L. (ed.) (1990) *Homosexuality as Behavior and Identity, Vol. 2: Dialogues of the Sexual Revolution*, Harrington Press, New York. For examples of essentialist arguments, see LeVay, S. (1991) 'A Difference in Hypothalamic Structure between Heterosexual and Homosexual men', *Science*, 253, pp. 1034–7 and Allen, L.S. and Gorski, R.A. (1992) 'Sexual Orientation and the Size of the Anterior Commissure in the Human Brain', *Proceedings of the National Academy of Sciences of the USA*, 89, pp. 7199–202.

48. For further reading on this see, for example, Butler, J. (1990) *Gender Trouble: Feminism and the Subversion of Identity*, Routledge, New York; Sedgwick, E.K. (1991) *Epistemology of the Closet*, Harvester Wheatsheaf, Hemel Hempstead; Fuss, D. (ed.) (1991) *Inside/Out: Lesbian Theories, Gay Theories*. Routledge, New York; Foucault, M. (1976) *The History of Sexuality, Vol. 1: An Introduction.*, trans., Robert Hurley, New York; for an overview, see Seidman, S. (ed.) (1996) *Queer Theory/Sociology*, Blackwell, Oxford, whose bibliography refers to the key books by Butler, Foucault, Fuss and Sedgwick.

49. See Robinson, *British Tar*, for example p. 190, but also Dugaw, D. (1992) '"Rambling Female Sailors": The Rise and Fall of the Seafaring Heroine', *International Journal of Maritime History*, IV (1) June, pp. 179–94. She has also written about them in Dugaw. D. (1989) *Warrior Women and Popular Balladry, 1650–1850*, Cambridge University Press, Cambridge.

50. Stein, A. and Plummer, K. (1994) ' "I Can't Even Think Straight": "Queer" Theory and the Missing Sexual Revolution in Sociology', *Sociological Theory*, 12 (2), July, pp. 178–87.

51. Watney, S. (1993) 'The Spectacle of AIDS', in Abelove, H., Barale, M.A. and Halperin, D.M. (eds), *The Lesbian and Gay Studies Reader*, Routledge, New York, pp. 202–11.

52. Bravmann, S. 'Post-modernism and queer identities', in Seidmann, *Queer Theory/Sociology*, p. 334.

53. Lave, J. and Wenger, E. (1991) *Situated Learning: Legitimate Peripheral Participation*, Cambridge University Press, Cambridge, p. 29.

54. Roper and Tosh, 'Historians and the Politics of Masculinity', p. 4.

55. See Ayers, P. (1999) 'The Making of Men: Masculinities in Inter-war Liverpool', in Walsh, M. (ed.), *Working Out Gender*, Ashgate, Aldershot, pp. 66–83; Burton, V. (1991) 'The Myth of Bachelor Jack: Masculinity, Patriarchy and Seafaring Labour', in Howell, C. and Twomey, R. (eds), *Jack Tar in History: Essays in the History of Maritime Life and Labor*, Acadiensis, New Brunswick, NJ, pp. 187–98; and Burton, V. (1999) ' "Whoring, Drinking Sailors": Reflections on Masculinity from the Labour History of Nineteenth-Century British Shipping', in Walsh, *Gender*, pp. 84–101.

Chapter 1

When Queer was Covert

'On the maiden voyage of the *Canberra* ... there must have been 500 gay men on that ship. It was like heaven working there.' Frank.

'These abnormal practices have no place in a sea-going community.' Mr Marshall, Tower Hill branch of the National Union of Seamen.

To understand just how and why some ships could be alleged (at least retrospectively) to be gay paradises in the 1950s, 1960s and 1970s, we need to know something about that counterpart of heaven: hell. Gay men describe ostracism, stigma, loneliness and misery in the homophobic world ashore.[1] These make clear how much a gay-friendly ship – a community where they could be out – could be so balmy in the years when Connie Francis, Barbra Streisand, Kathy Kirby and Dusty Springfield were top of the hit parade and stars like Judy Garland and Jayne Mansfield were camp icons.

This chapter begins with a description of the gay context over the twentieth century, focusing first on land, then at sea.

The gay context of the period

A gay man, like any human being, is not simply an individual acting alone but someone who interacts with his society. We are all products of our mentors, lovers, critics, family members, employers, enemies and friends. Queer theorists such as Ken Plummer have stressed the importance of interaction, of how people's sexuality is affected by the ways that societies perceive and handle them.[2] So in considering gay people as subjects, we need to view them in their social contexts.

Non-heterosexual encounters have occurred throughout history in many contexts. In different countries and periods of time, two men having sex together could be quite unremarkable. Some of those encounters

Robert on deck. Boarding school had
prepared him. Photo courtesy of Robert.

happened in all-male spaces, including in armies and on ships, in cultures
where there were varying degrees of homophilia (love or affiliative connections between people of the same sex). A number of studies have found
societies which had positive studies of gay men in cultures in the eleventh,
twelfth, seventeenth, eighteenth and nineteenth centuries.[3] Most post-
1980s histories of how sexuality is viewed in societies show that it is only
since the nineteenth century that homosexuality has been set up as a condition and a sickness. Gay people were characterised as particular *types*,
not simply human beings who engage in certain sexual acts. The French
philosopher, Michel Foucault, famously argued that the meaning of
homosexuality moved from being about *behaviour* (the sexual act) to
character type (the pathologised and excluded queer).

In Britain's history the key foundational law was an Act in 1533 which
condemned all acts of buggery – whether it was with women, animals or
men. The penalty was death. This law continued, at least nominally, until
1885. That is, significantly, it was a prohibition against an act not a type
of person. Jeffrey Weeks believes that most men prosecuted under these
laws were probably penalised for gay behaviour (sodomy).[4] Behind that
law lay two interesting ideas: that all people were potentially capable of
such acts, and that reproductive sex in marriage must be protected. The
áct was particularly seen in religious terms as a sin against nature, an
abomination against 'right-thinking' folk.

One of the most serious prosecutions – on land or at sea – was that of
the four sailors on *HMS Africaine* who were executed for buggery in

February 1816.[5] Buggery was seen to be as serious as desertion, mutiny and murder in the navy. It was not until 1861 that the death penalty was removed. The Offences Against the Person Act reduced the sentence to ten years-to-life. However, in 1885, the decade in which steamships began to rule the waves, section 11 of the Criminal Law Amendment Act (known as the Labouchère Amendment) made *all* male homosexual acts (vaguely described as 'gross indecency'), whether committed in public or private, illegal. Unsurprisingly, the Labouchère Amendment was also known as the 'Blackmailer's Charter'. A few years later the Vagrancy Act of 1898 punished people who 'solicited or importuned for immoral purposes', which included homosexual men.[6] And for almost a century afterwards one of the main stated objections to having gay men in the armed forces was that they were open to blackmail and could thereby weaken a nation's strength.

Until just before the First World War the Labouchère Amendment continued to be used in order to regulate and punish homosexual men. The 1912 Criminal Law Amendment Act invented the term 'importuning for immoral purposes', which might today be phrased as cruising or chatting someone up and agreeing to go and have sex.

The twentieth century saw major changes in how homosexuality was perceived and handled.[7] It moved from being a criminal state to a pathologised and clandestine state to an increasingly normal state and finally to a proud and resistant state. This shift was particularly notable in the 1940s during the Second World War. The war meant that service personnel, as never before, were together and out. Alan Bérubé, an historian who has examined homosexuality during this period, demonstrates the extent to which clubs and bars and meeting spots emerged.[8]

It was a troubled time for military officers who sought to manage or eliminate gay sexuality. But it was the start of an unstoppable tide. The Second World War caused attitudes towards homosexuality to be temporarily relaxed in some situations – for example, many homosexual men served in the army and described how same-sex relationships were often tolerated, if not made explicit,[9] especially while serving in India. In London, the atmosphere of heightened emotion, coupled with the blackout and the presence of American and Canadian servicemen,[10] meant that every kind of sex was available, including homosexual sex. Jack Robinson, who became a merchant seaman, described it as a time when 'Under the trees of Leicester Square painted young men hung around the lavatories. Smart young men [wearing Cherry Blossom uniforms] in leather kneepads polished the shoes of the wealthy ... diamond earrings flashed beneath the nightclub lights' and the clerk at the YMCA immediately asked if Jack and his mate wanted to share a room.[11]

Chris, a former steward, remembers being told by an older seafaring colleague about the great gay sex you could have even at a bus-stop, with a sailor or soldier standing there, because the black-out obscured all activity. However, as Bérubé points out, many found that they were fighting two wars: on the one hand for country, democracy and freedom and, on the other hand, for their survival as gay people,[12] sometimes facing ethical dilemmas about fighting for a country that was fighting against them.

In 1948 American zoologist Alfred Kinsey (1894–1956) created the first path-breaking report on human sexuality. In it he challenged the ideas of gay men and lesbians as 'queer' because his surveys found that most humans had both heterosexual and homosexual feelings. However, this news and the legacy of wartime development, did not bring any easy progress towards accepting homosexuality as a legitimate choice in the opening years of this study. Instead there was a swing back to sexual regulation. Servicewomen and men returned home and were expected to get married and have children. In the UK, the Archbishop of Canterbury gave a sermon which called for Britons to reject 'wartime morality' and start living Christian lives.[13] Marriage increased by 50 per cent in 1946, and family values were back in fashion. As the cross-dressing legend Quentin Crisp, who appreciated sailor's uniforms,[14] wrote, 'the horrors of peace were many'.[15]

One of the worst aspects of this was the ignorance, as Alan, a future wireless officer, found. Class and location made all the difference to his ability to acquire knowledge. As a young man in the Midlands, far from London life, he knew that he was different, and had mutually masturbated other boys at school. But he didn't know what the difference was. When he looked up the word 'homosexual', thinking that this word might be something useful to his understanding, the dictionary only offered the definition 'same sex'. So he ended up without the explanation that would have helped him feel less isolated and puzzled. By contrast, Robert, a Junior Assistant Purser in the same period, had witnessed and taken part in a lot of gay sex at his boarding school. 'At least half the beds were empty every night.' He also had access to the nearest thing there was to gay pornography: 'body-building' magazines that he bought discretely from a small shop in St Martin's Court, in the heart of London's Theatreland. These magazines included *Physique Pictorial*, which showed photographs and drawings of muscular, semi-naked men in close proximity, with just posing pouches or airbrushed underpants disguising their genitals. A random survey of its 1951–60 issues shows that nautical or seaside scenes were among the most popular, along with stud farms, ranches, logging camps, garages and scenes from classical antiquity. That is, already a gay man with access to this material could see visual confirmation that the

Alan crossing the Indian Ocean on the *British Kestrel*, August 1962. Picture
courtesy of Alan.

sea and sailors had a clear connection with gay sex, albeit American, as
we have discussed in more detail in the Introduction.

While homosexuality was perceived as a social problem, theatrical concert parties starring be-frocked men (initially ex-servicemen, often gay)
were pulling in crowds from Warrington to London's West End. 'Visiting
American megastar Lena Horne couldn't fill the Theatre Royal in Leeds
but ... *Men in Frocks* played to capacity houses.'[16] As Chapter 5 details,
cross-dressing – whether 'cod' (not pretending to be female, wearing mops
for wigs, etc.) or very successfully deceptive – was both a gay activity and
a key way that straight people encountered gay men in the 1940s and
1950s.

But some politicians, legislators and church leaders in the 1950s saw
homosexuality at worst as a form of moral degradation which could cor-
rupt youth and at best 'a fit subject for music hall humour'. As Cunard

steward Chris remembered: 'In those days . . . the culture then, was, in the outside world . . . so suppressed. Homosexuality was regarded as dirty old men in raincoats. And you really didn't have anyone to turn to. You were literally in isolation in those days. It wasn't until you [had what] . . . you commonly call cottages [public toilets], and you started finding other people like yourself. . . . Cottaging was almost like a self-support group, and that's why I picked it up.'

During the years from 1921 to 1963, according to Hugh David, there was an almost exponential year-on-year increase in the number of reported indictable (male) homosexual offences. It peaked in 1963 at a level 24 times higher than it had been in the earlier years of that century.[17] Blackmail was also becoming a lucrative business in the 1950s. One team of blackmailers were reported as making at least £100 a night and netted £15,000 within seven months, acquiring £26,000 from one of their victims.[18]

From 1950s scandals involving such prominent men as novelist Rupert Croft-Cooke and two sailors and *Daily Mail* diplomatic correspondent Peter Wildeblood, we can see that gay seafarers were operating in a climate of risk but also of possibility: gay partners *were* available. And some had a taste for men in uniform, if cross-class sex was acceptable to them. These well-publicised trials and scandals brought homosexuality into the open, making it the subject of discussion in private homes and workplaces – including ships – as well as in the law courts. Such trials also brought gay men on to ships as a refuge, argue Kris Kirk and Ed Heath, writing about men in frocks:

The Merchant Navy had been known as a good bolt-hole for gay men who were the victims of clean-ups on land which always followed the breaking of a gay 'scandal'. Some of the Sea Queens recall an influx of gay men in 1954, the year that the Montagu and Wildeblood affair made banner headlines.[19]

Parliament began considering the penal laws for homosexual offences in 1954. In 1957 the Wolfenden Committee recommended that 'homosexual behaviour between consenting adults in private is no longer a criminal offence'. Parliament refused to pass the Report six times, and the Sexual Offences Act was only passed in July 1967. Nicknamed, even by some gay men, as 'The Buggar's Charter', it legalised homosexual acts in private between consenting adult males over the age of 21 (it was 16 for heterosexuals). However, it did not apply to members of the armed forces, merchant seamen on ships, or residents of the Channel Isles or the Isle of Man where homosexuality still remained illegal.

Indeed, both shipping line employers and the National Union of Seamen (NUS) put on such pressure that the Merchant Navy was specifically excluded.[20] The union climate was highly disapproving. At the NUS's 1966 Annual General Meeting Mr Marshall of Tower Hill branch tried to move a motion against proposed legal change: 'These abnormal practices have no place in a sea-going community.' His colleague, S. Leek, even argued that 'in fact various discrepancies on ship penalise the heterosexual rather than the homosexual'. And although the conference chairman tried to silence him, because the press was there, he went on to say: 'Various figures have been given in relation to exact amount of homosexuals in this country, between one and five per cent, but what we do know for certain is that the percentage on board ships is much larger than that ... Whilst I would hesitate to say that the British Merchant Navy has become a haven for homosexuals we have them aboard in ever increasing numbers, and whilst some people may treat them as a laugh, there is no doubt of the damage they do in regard to the corruption of younger ratings. ... The ultimate irony, if this Private Member's [Mr Humphrey Barclay, Conservative, Lancaster] Bill had become law would have been the freedom of the homosexual to commit their own grossly indecent acts of perversion without redress, yet the heterosexual who took a female aboard with ideas of performing a natural function, would no doubt be the recipient of prompt disciplinary action.' The chairman got the resolution laid on the table (effectively withdrawn) on the grounds that the Bill had already been defeated.[21] However, the hostile climate was clear and the Executive used Resolution 67 to bring pressure against the Bill that later became the Sexual Offences Act.[22]

NUS members' unease continued despite the Bill being passed, although they seemed to become aware they were being offensive. At the May 1968 AGM, Sid Carthew of Liverpool said: 'This is a rather difficult thing to speak about. Possibly as difficult as the racial question that was brought up this morning – something that we wish to put under the carpet and keep out of the way. But these things have got to be faced, because they are problems. ... I wouldn't wish a son of mine to go away to sea and find himself placed in a cabin with this type of person that commits these acts. ... I would like to see anybody who commits any act of this type, be expelled from this union.' Mr E. Brown, perhaps concerned at the loss of membership dues that might result, responded that 'it is still an offence on board a ship. I feel if we find any of those who are involved in this kind of thing we should just put them out of the industry, kindly.'[23] No dissent was recorded.

The Act was part of a general tendency towards liberalism, as evidenced by changes in abortion law. Lisa Power, a writer on gay history, believes that 'many of the politicians supporting it saw it primarily as a humanitarian attempt to minimise blackmail against homosexuals, and were horrified by the growth of gay visibility that followed'.[24]

Despite the flurry around the Act, many people ashore in the UK lived similarly to before – it took time, she found, '[b]ut the changed law was a prelude to being able to meet more openly'.[25] They met in the rare gay pubs such as the Salisbury, which was featured in *Victim*, the movie that, by showing gay blackmail, gave support to the 1967 Act and starred the iconic actor Dirk Bogarde. A few member-only drinking clubs in Soho offered sanctuary. Mainly they met in other people's homes, to which temporarily visiting seafarers did not have the same access as did people who were around long enough to develop networks.

Popular culture only offered particular gay figures who were cast as effeminate, comedy stereotypes such as Julian and Sandy in *Round the Horne* (1964–69; see Chapter 3), the camp (but not explicitly gay) Mr Humphries in *Are You Being Served* (1972–84) and Honky-Tonk in the *Dick Emery Show* (1963–81). However, these were acceptable, 'funny' representations that were more likely to be contested by groups such as The Campaign for Homosexual Equality rather than by the mainstream British public.

In the 1970s homosexuality's existing stigma was not eradicated overnight. Sexual *acts* between men had been decriminalised, but *attitudes* towards homosexuals continued to be ambivalent throughout much of the 1970s and 1980s. Gay men and lesbians continued to suffer discrimination in workplaces ashore, although by that time gay men were well recognised by shipping lines as good stewards. Gay men could still be convicted for 'importuning', although at sea such behaviour may have been difficult to detect and enforce. Ashore, many religious leaders continued to deny that gay lifestyles were acceptable. Although the social climate changed substantially, hysteria emerged in a changed form in the 1980s as gay men were blamed for the spread of HIV, and consequently AIDS, by a number of tabloid newspapers. These included *The Sun*, which consistently stated that AIDS was a 'gay disease', *The Daily Mail* and *The Daily Express*, which followed the line that homosexuals were to blame for the appearance and spread of HIV.[26] The introduction of Clause 28 in 1988, which stated that a local authority should not 'promote homosexuality or publish material for the promotion of homosexuality ... promote the teaching in any maintained school of the acceptability of homosexuality as a pretended family relationship by the publication of such material or otherwise' placed a further legal stigma upon gay lifestyles. Unsurprisingly, according to a number of British Social Attitudes surveys, negative attitudes towards homosexuality rose during the 1980s, peaking in 1987, the year before the introduction of Clause 28.[27]

The history of homosexuality in the UK has therefore been one of moral regulation, erasure, ridicule and ignorance. It is a history of difficulty for gay men, including destructive pathologisation and consequent defensive responses such as self-parody and secrecy. The period just before and at the start of our study was one in which the critical mass was growing – there were many more 'out' and active gay people than ever before. And despite the many problems, it was a history of (slow-) growing tolerance. A possible reason for this was that the British Empire was declining – there was not the same precious idea that the British population (ashore and at large) had to be seen to be the epitome of moral rectitude. Additionally, because of demographic and economic trends, there was not the need to procreate quite so much.

That, then, is an outline of the gay context by which the men in this study were shaped. The following section examines how the social climate ashore relates to what was happening on ships in that period.

The shipping context

Homosexuality at sea was a known but stigmatised phenomenon, as was homosexuality ashore, up until at least the end of the Second World War and in some cases long afterwards. But of course, on all-male ships where men were away from land for months, sexual release has always been sought in a variety of ways. It is through the Royal Navy (a branch of the armed services), rather than the Merchant Navy (commercial transportation of human and other freight), that homosexuality on ships throughout history comes mainly to public notice. However, it is under-reported and unsatisfactorily interpreted. The most famous incident involved the Royal Naval trials and executions of the four men on the *HMS Africaine* in 1816.[28] But given thousands of men involved over 300 years in an organisation with the tradition of 'rum, bum and the lash' there were oddly few prosecutions.[29]

There are two possible reasons for this absence: either homosexuality was ignored, or it didn't exist. Naval historian Suzanne Stark notes that during her reading of detailed reports of courts martial proceedings it was clear that justice was flawed – people would be let off if they were liked, pilloried if unpopular. This suggests that much may have been tolerated, in the interests of keeping crews intact and happy, and retaining trained personnel. Ships are notoriously places where officers turn blind eyes in the interests of keeping a community stable while far from the safety of shore (mutinies are costly trouble). Additionally, travel acclimatises people to many unusual customs and behaviours: it can create a workforce that is exceptionally tolerant of personal difference. The point, as many seafarers in this study report, is teamwork. If you pull your weight, then you can be forgiven almost anything in that family, the ship's company. That gay guy was seen as all right if he was '*our* gay guy'. He was defended against hostile outsiders just as black workers can be protected by colleagues who say 'leave him alone, he's *our* black'.

The second reason for the lack of evidence of homosexuality – that gay relations actually *did not occur*, or not occur *much* – is argued by a leading historian of the Georgian Royal Navy. N.A.M. Rodger found evidence of only a handful of cases over a period where hundreds of thousand of people were employed. In the Seven Years War (1756–63) there were 11 court martials for sodomy and seven charges of indecency or uncleanness at a time when the seagoing population was 70–80,000, and where 75 per cent of the crew were unmarried.[30] Rodgers asserts, 'it is difficult to believe that there can have been any serious problem with a crime so much detested, but so seldom mentioned. If senior officers were concerned about it, they gave no hint of it in their correspondence. Everything suggests that it was an insignificant issue.'[31] And he contends that if it had existed, people would have known. It would have been hard to conceal almost the only crime in the navy for which death was the penalty.[32] But it appears that concealment is a complex business; class loyalty is just one of the factors involved. Officers' cases never came to trial. 'The purser of the *Newcastle*, for instance, "detected in some things not so decent to name" deserted before he could be arrested.' The surgeon of the *Mercury* and captain of the *Canterbury* who 'confronted with a complaint from one of his men, denied and shot himself', Rodger reports.[33] Brother officers did not want to report each other. It says much about the court's attitudes to race that a black seaman was the principal prosecution witness in a sodomy court martial at the Nore in 1761. Two men were hanged as a result.[34]

The lack of existing formal evidence today should be read not as evidence of homosexuality's rarity. Rather it could be seen as evidence that it was too minor an offence to be punished from on high, just as the presence of women on board was ignored by officials unless it was seen to result in trouble. Similarly, it could indicate that this behaviour was so prevalent that the large number of prosecutions would have wasted too much time.[35] Many commercial shipping lines today feel that the point is the men's ability to serve well, not their personal behaviour. This suggests that we could equally re-read Rodger's findings as demonstrating that homosexuality was something that was normal and ignored in the interest of keeping a ship fully staffed and relatively happy.

Rodger also cites young men's active pursuit of women when ashore (evidenced by incidences of sexually transmitted diseases) as proof of vigorous heterosexuality. It could also be read as simply a human desire for intercourse, male interest in penetration, and the social acceptability of those interests and desires taking the form of prostitution and casual romance (both heterosexual). Homosexuality was preferable to having to lose crew through disease and desertion because of lack of sexual contact. A realistic officer could surely accept that young men, isolated at sea, become sexually voracious. Homosexuality was a way of controlling that and therefore a method of damage limitation. That is, if men must have sex, then let them do so in ways that are convenient to the organisation for which they work.[36]

The negative labelling of homosexuality was intermittent rather than continuous. So one possible explanation for the extraordinary absence of buggery and sodomy from works on seafaring men[37] is that the writers of that period did not write about gay sexuality because of the discourse of the time, not because they were actually absent practices.

The problem of lack of evidence became particularly thorny in the Newport, Rhode Island, naval scandal of 1919. Effeminate sailors from the training school there were caught by a US Navy undercover operation. Brawny sailors were set up to solicit gay sex off these 'Ladies of Newport' – and happened to trap an Episcopal minister too. A Senate investigation was set up and the Navy spies' activities were deemed 'reprehensible'.

Certainly Royal Naval sailors were very interested in 1950s drag shows in Britain, as Kirk and Heath attest. Lots of sailors were Stage Door Johnnies, so keen that 'often they'd follow us home' remembers Loren Lorenz.[38] Another queen, Poppy Cooper, says: 'When we went to Portsmouth the theatre was packed with ... hundreds of matelots. Looking out from the stage you could see all these white hats in the gallery. And when we came out of the stage door, they filled the streets; you would have thought royalty was arriving.'[39]

Whatever sexual acts were or were not known to have been committed, in both the Royal and the Merchant Navy, there is still evidence that ships were sites where people played with gender identity, even if they were not consciously doing so. That evidence is in early photographs of seemingly innocent shipboard revelry. There was a long-established tradition of carnivalesque cross-dressing for entertainment during long voyages. Shipboard fancy dress parties were arranged – by passengers and by crew in different situations – in order to pass the time. Several crew members in *foo-foo bands* in the early twentieth century wore frocks. And at the Neptune ceremony, a key rite of passage, a range of characters, including Neptune/Triton and mermaids, were arrayed in home-made costumes. As Chapter 5 explains, and photos attest: a ship was a place where no one was bothered if men dressed as Cleopatra or Mrs Mop for the night, and women as highwaymen or kings. The meanings of identity, roles and

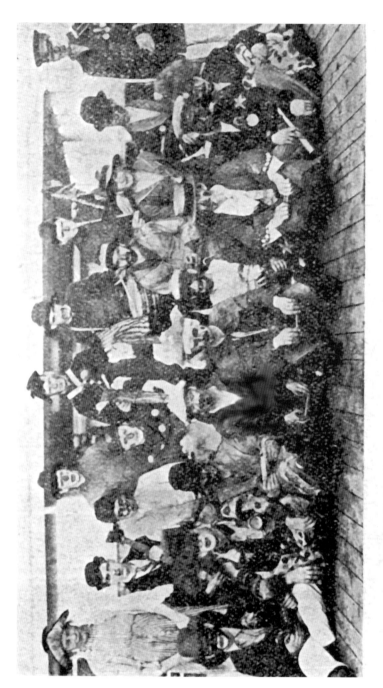

FOO-FOO BAND.—Engine Department of s.s "Celtic."

Picture courtesy of RMT

sexual relations were explored through clothing if not through sexual action. Gender subversion was explored temporarily but repeatedly: a man might quite unremarkably parade in women's wear at least once a month while at sea.

Evidence about gay activity on ships in the interwar years is harder to find. Inevitably, it is the minority – abuses – and not the majority – consensual relationships – that have been reported. Journalist Michael Gavin reports that 'One elderly gay was sent to prison after being found entwined round a laundry boy in a cruise ship linen locker. Another, a cook and not so elderly, got off with a caution when a tanker captain happened upon him examining the galleyboy on the table in the ship's hospital.'[40]

The main explanation for this lack of prosecution is that a merchant vessel was not a situation where the honour of the realm, as embodied in a particular stiff-upper lip kind of masculine performance was required. Gay sexuality on merchant vessels was not the same threat to culture or national security. Blackmailers could gain little political advantage in threatening to expose a lowly cook.

Additionally, there is testosterone. Male workers on ships seek sexual release and this takes several forms, including masturbation, mutual masturbation and use of non-human orifices, the classical one being a skate nailed to the mast. Skate have a mouth shaped like a woman's genitals and this was penetrated by men aboard.[41] With the advent of mass passenger shipping from the 1880s, ships were places where (hetero)sexual activity was regulated. Migration literature shows us chaperones and firm segregation of the unmarried women from single men aboard. If voyages turned men's thoughts to sex, then a shipping line saw its job as to protect 'the innocent' from men's animal lusts.

By the mid-twentieth century, new technologies and increasingly regular schedules meant the danger, uncertainty and adventure was gone. The mass invasion of hotel workers domesticated the ships. Many more men were married, with children. The census shows that in 1931 48.2 per cent of enumerated British stewarding workers were married (11,567 out of 23,956).[42] Some left settled homes for the quick trips to New York almost as routinely as city commuters leave the Kent suburbs for London's Waterloo.

Oral evidence from ex-seafarers confirms that in the interwar years there were gay men, both married and single. The majority appear to have been stewarding staff on passenger ships. They particularly worked as cabin stewards, but did not openly flaunt their sexuality. Some of their colleagues thought they were oddly effeminate, or wondered why they 'didn't bother with women', but there was little knowledge of who they had sex with. They were simply 'fairies' but what 'fairy' meant was not understood in those sexually naive times. Gay men on the freighters and passenger ships of the mid-twentieth century appear to have been quite covert, until the postwar years, though tolerated. Older seafarers such as Alan, a wireless operator, now believe this is partly because of general ignorance about sexual matters. Gay men didn't necessarily know what was possible, so did not do it. And straight people simply were not in an informed enough position to recognise gay men. As stewardesses of that period have reiterated: 'You people today just can't imagine how *innocent* we were then.'

The meeting of gay men and ships

The gay men we talked to report that older colleagues told them that gay men had worked at sea for decades before the Second World War and in the war too. However, 'out gay men' and 'passenger ships' became very evident partners after World War Two. Even – or perhaps especially – monumental vessels that were the epitome of nationhood, such as the *Queen Mary*, had substantial proportions of gay men flouncing down their august corridors. Of the P&O *Canberra*'s maiden voyage in the

So many men ... – a masked party below decks. Picture courtesy of private donor.

1960s, Martin recalled: 'I could honestly say ... there was a thousand crew, and out of the thousand crew there was 500 gays on that ship ... It was like heaven.'

But how is it that such a gay-friendly employment situation arose? It was not thanks to the National Union of Seaman.[43] Members and officials had a history of despising stewarding staff as men 'who weren't proper seamen', as its records show. The very fact that the job appealed to so many gay men further lowered 'feminine' stewarding work in the union's eyes. The explanation for gay-friendliness lies much more in company policy and inability to stop a tide once it had started.

There appears to be two main explanations for gay entrée into this sparkling world of white palaces speeding to the Caribbean, New York, the Antipodes and Africa. One was the pull of shipping firm employment demands. The other was the push of men who wanted to be in a situation that was less difficult than on land.

First, those luxurious passenger ships needed service personnel who would offer a high quality of care to passengers – stewards, cooks, waiters and so on – to compete with air travel. Shipping lines were attracted to men whose supposed 'femininity' made them likely to be efficient, neat, clean and discreet. Gay men also had the advantage that they would not proposition female passengers and cause the company trouble. Given the commonly talked about sexual friskiness of women during the war, it was better that female passengers were tended by servants who were sexually out of bounds. Gay men fitted the bill. 'It was almost *de rigueur* for stewards to be gay, and not at all the difficulty it was on land', says Robert. 'I wouldn't say there was homophobia as such, not really. In fact that company I was with almost had a tendency with their cabin stewards then because there was never any trouble with the female passengers. They [the company] figured the other passengers could look after themselves, but there wouldn't be any sort of impropriety with the female passengers.'

Several interviewees believe that on many P&O passenger ships 30–40 per cent of the crew were gay. On some voyages as many as 50 per cent were gay and they think that among bedroom stewards it was as high as 90 per cent. Some Cunard, Canadian Pacific, Glen Line, Blue Funnel, Shaw Savill, Royal Mail and Union Castle passenger vessels were similarly a haven for gay men. At around the turn of the 1950s in a large ship's catering department 'you could roughly reckon, generally speaking, 25 per cent. I'm trying to be realistic. ... If it was a popular ship like the *Queen Mary*, or if it was a big ship like the *Arcadia* or the *Iberia*, there might be a higher percentage as opposed to the little ones I was on,' says Chris.

How could such an extraordinary figure be true? Cruise ship writer Garry Bannerman explains: 'Once a ship reaches a point where a large portion of the men are homosexuals, it can be assured that the percentage will rise dramatically as time goes on. Friends lobby on behalf of friends, stories circulate throughout the world, and the personnel companies become unknowing agents.'[44] That is, shipping lines were not necessarily gay-friendly, but their spaces were utilised by gay men to create that heaven. And shipping lines that focused on recreational as opposed to business travel were more likely to be relaxed about 'out' and camp gay activity. Finally, the freedom common in any liminal (marginal) zone, such as Brighton or Blackpool, enabled it, particularly on cruises.

And why did some companies have higher proportions of gay staff than others? The answer was unlikely to be actively gay-positive company policy but was partly to do with the length of a particular trip and the type of customer. Stephen Rabson, the P&O archivist, suggests that reasons for this could include the fact that P&O made longer voyages (to Australia) than most lines, and therefore a ship developed its own culture for the voyage.[45] Being away from land for so long necessitated more group tolerance, created a climate where any entertainment was welcome in the absence of ships' cinemas and casinos, and led to the development of contingent sexual relationships. 'The heat and the gin' also played a part, argue some informants. Ships doing short hops across the cold Atlantic to New York were places where gay activity was less likely, Chris points out. Also the fact that P&O had a 50 per cent white crew meant that, unlike the other lines with their mainly Goan stewards, this company offered employment to British stewards. And stewarding departments were where gay men congregated.

The 'push' factor was that the sea could offer a more positive experience than ashore. Gay men needed a space in which to be more comfortably out. In particular, queens needed a place to perform after the advent of television depleted audiences for the great drag show spectaculars ashore.

A gay man told historian of homosexuality Jeffrey Weeks that he could never relax in clubs for fear of raids and arrests: 'I wish I was dead.'[46] The idea of being transformed from an outcast individual to a member of a social group, and transmuting a 'spoiled identity' to one of respect of value was barely dreamable. And so, the sea beckoned. Geoff, who worked for P&O in various stewarding capacities, explains that 'a lot of people went to sea for that reason. There was not so much control [over homosexuality] in a lot of cases [on ships]. They went to sea because they knew that. He found ships 'teeming with gay people, about 75 per cent of stewards and 50 per cent of others'.

Others went to sea as an alternative to conscription. Frank said 'of course, the young gay ones went there, because they had [to do National

Service], it was two years in the army ... but if you went into the Merchant Navy you could do six years, without doing the National Service, so basically that was an attraction for a great number of people, and of course everything happened [sexually]'.

Many knew what they were doing. Chris, who did stewarding work for Cunard from 1959 to 1965 remembers, 'It was generally known, underground, that ... it was quite gay in the Merchant or in – come to that – the Royal Navy but that's another story. But nobody [else] really quite knew. Once again we go back to the culture. Everything was really rather kept low-key or kept taboo. One didn't speak to these sorts of people.' He too joined as a way to avoid the extreme restrictions facing conscripted men. 'I had the option of going in the forces as a National Service and I thought, "Oh blow it, I'll go in the Merchant instead."'

Dave joined the Merchant Navy because he needed a job and had already understood that the Merchant Navy offered gay men a much more enjoyable life than ashore. '[I was] out of work. Previously I was in the Royal Navy and as part of my seven year stint, I volunteered to join the Australian Navy, rather nice to get away from the wartime rationing that was in operation then, and see a bit of the world. And of all the hundreds that volunteered, I was selected. ... So we set out and did our nice four-week voyage to Australia, living the life of luxury on this passenger liner, and then came back the same way. During that time I got to know various members of the crew and I thought this is all very camp – camp as arseholes, this lot. I had a great time. And of course the Sexual Offences Act hadn't been cast and things were still dodgy here at home. And I thought, "this is rather nice". I never thought any more about it. When I came out of the Royal Navy, and got working at the local airport ... I got fed up for that. And I went to work as a cinema manager and I got disenchanted with that. I found myself unemployed ... I thought to myself, "I dunno, what about that old P&O?" So I wrote to them and got taken on. They first said, "no vacancies", so I got the train and got up there, borrowed the seven and six [37.5p] fare from my mum and yes, I got taken on. Within seven days I was sailing from Tilbury. Absolutely exciting ... and it was excellent.'

Many of the fears that gay men expressed about life on land did not have to be the case at sea. Such fears included: being recognised; being shamed; the unknown; becoming involved in the criminal underworld; being bashed up; being alone; and getting in trouble with the police.[47] On gay-friendly ships recognition was not an issue, you were already known. Shaming had less stigma when so many – even the majority – were gay. For hotel-side workers it already was a 'criminal underworld', but one that was fairly petty and internally controlled by catering crew. Casual

Homophile friendships between masculine men developed on cargo ships.
Picture courtesy of Bill.

beatings from homophobic strangers were less likely as everyone was a colleague (though not a friend). And it was mainly officers who needed to fear losing their job.

Cargo ships were different. The main reason is that without passengers there were not such large populations of stewards, who were the mainstays of the gay community on ships. Nor was there the same holiday atmosphere. However, gay men did exist on cargo ships. And they were there in stereotypically gay roles, such as on the purser's staff or in catering. Some were there for homophile reasons: they liked being in other men's company and they disliked the 'bother' of having passengers, particularly women, around. Some had relationships while at sea, and some had relationships with crew members after they left the ship. It seems that gay men who were not into high camp were happier with this discreet and un-camp world, even though it was usually at the cost of their silence. Martin likened them to guest-houses as opposed to Hiltons: informal, teamwork, being your own boss, casual dress except in the evening and a sense of friendliness: 'If you wanted a quiet honeymoon you'd go on a cargo ship.'

In summary, the meeting of gay men and ships was enabled by four factors. First, the opportunity for expression of sexual desires of all kinds, as well as the opportunity to appropriate the clothing of other sexes, those key indicative envelopes of the body. Secondly, it was a situation where casual sexual relationships were usual and therefore expected. Thirdly, there was the physical need for sex. Fourthly, the shipping line needed

Working on their tans – seafarers sunbathing on deck. Picture courtesy of Dave.

particular kinds of people to carry out 'feminised' work and it was prepared to overlook off-duty revelry provided it didn't interfere with the
passengers. The companies' needs created a particular kind of workforce,
and that workforce developed its own culture, in which gayness became
normal. 'I don't know about it being illegal. It was obligatory, dear',
Martin joked.

NOTES

1. See, for example, Porter, K. and Weeks, J. (eds) (1991) *Between the Acts: Lives
of Homosexual Men 1885–1967*, Routledge, London and New York.
2. Plummer, K. (1996) 'Symbolic Interactionism and the Forms of
Heterosexuality', in Seidman, S. (ed.), *Queer Theory/Sociology*, Blackwell,
Oxford.

3. See, for example, Boswell, J. (1980) *Christianity, Social Tolerance, and Homosexuality*, Chicago University Press, Chicago, IL; Bray, A. (1982) *Homosexuality in Renaissance England*, Gay Men's Press, London; Weeks, J. (1977) *Coming Out: Homosexual Politics in Britain from the Nineteenth Century to the Present*, Quartet, London.

4. Weeks, *Coming Out*, p. 45.

5. Burg, B.R. (1983) *Sodomy and the Perception of Evil: English Sea Rovers in the Seventeenth Century Caribbean*, New York University Press, New York, p. xv.

6. Weeks, *Coming Out*, pp. 11–22.

7. The term 'homosexual' had been coined by Karl Maria Kertbeny in the 1860s as a preference to the existing word that was used at the time to describe men who had sex with other men: 'pederast'. Kertbeny claimed that many homosexuals were more masculine than other men, being superior to 'heterosexuals'. He hoped that the word would help to eliminate the oppressive Paragraph 175 in Germany. However, the term was instead adopted by doctors. These included Richard von Krafft-Ebing (1840–1902), a neurologist and psychiatrist interested in sado-masochism, who in 1882 concluded that homosexuality was a form of inherited mental illness, resulting in effeminacy. This 'sickness' model was to dominate western thinking about men who had sex with other men for much of the first two-thirds of the twentieth century.

8. Bérubé, A. (1991) *Coming Out under Fire: The History of Gay Men and Women in World War Two*, Penguin, London.

9. David, H. (1997) *On Queer Street*, Harper Collins, London, pp. 143–6.

10. Calder, A. (1969) *The People's War: Britain 1939–45*, Jonathan Cape, London, p. 308.

11. Robinson, J. (1988) *Jack and Jamie Go to War*, Gay Men's Press, London, pp. 58–9.

12. Bérubé, *Coming Out*, p. 7.

13. Jivani, A. (1997) *It's Not Unusual*, Michael O'Mara Books, London, p. 89.

14. Royal Naval Seaman George Melly noted this when he met Quentin Crisp: 'I'm not denying that the sailor suit may not have been something of a turn-on', Melly, G. (1977) *Rum, Bum and Concertina*, Futura, London, p. 76. He wore his bellbottoms ashore. However merchant seamen were told to dress in civvies off ship.

15. Crisp, Q. (1968) *The Naked Civil Servant*, Penguin, London, p. 68.

16. Kirk, Kris and Heath, Ed (1984) *Men in Frocks*, Gay Men's Press, London, p. 16

17. David, *On Queer Street*, p. 153.

18. Jivani, *It's Not Unusual*, pp. 114–15.

19. Kirk and Heath, *Men in Frocks*, p. 31.

20. Weeks, *Coming Out*, p. 177.

21. *Report of the Proceedings at the* 74th *AGM*, May 1966, pp. 168–70, MSS. 175A/box 3, Warwick Modern Record Centre.

22. *Report of the Proceedings at the 1968 AGM*, 1968, p. 20, MSS. 175A/box 3, Warwick Modern Record Centre.

23. Ibid., pp. 115–16. The minutes of the AGM procedures do not adequately convey the lobbying that took place in the union, according to Don Trueman.

24. Power, L. (1995) *No Bath but Plenty of Bubbles: An Oral History of the Gay Liberation Front 1970–73*, Cassell, London, p. 9.

25. Ibid., p. 10.

26. Sanderson, T. (1995) *Mediawatch*, Gay Men's Press, London, p. 46.

27. See Jowell, R., Brook, L., Prior, G. and Taylor, B. (1992) *British Social Attitudes, the 9th Report*, Ashgate, Aldershot, p. 124; Jowell, R. (1996) *British Social Attitudes, the 13th Report*, Ashgate, Aldershot, p. 39; Jowell, R., Curtice, J., Park, A. and Thomson, S. (1999) *British Social Attitudes, the 16th Report: Who Shares New Labour Values?*, Ashgate, Aldershot, p. 348; and Jowell, R., Park, A., Thomson, K., Jarvis, L., Bromley, C. and Stratford, N. (2000) *British Social Attitudes, the 17th Report: Focusing on Diversity*, Sage, London, p. 112.

28. Burg, *Sodomy and the Perception of Evil*, p. xv. Two other crew members, John Parsons and Jack Hubbard, were lashed 200 and 170 times respectively for 'uncleaness', the then term for deviant sexual behaviour.

29. Harvey, A.D. (1978) 'Prosecutions for Sodomy in England at the Beginning of the Nineteenth Century', *Historical Journal*, XXI, p. 939. See also Gilbert, A. N. (1976–77) 'Buggery and the British Navy 1700–1861', *Journal of Social History*, X, p. 72.

30. Rodger, N.A.M. (1986) *The Wooden World: An anatomy of the Georgian Navy*, Fontana, Glasgow, p. 79. The proportion of men in the Royal Navy at that time who were permanently married (as opposed to formally claiming wives when convenient) was between one fifth and a quarter. They were mainly young men without ties.

31. Ibid., p. 81.

32. Ibid., p. 80.

33. Ibid., p. 80.

34. Ibid., p. 159.

35. Ibid., p. 80.

36. Ibid., p. 80.

37. As well as Rodger, see Lloyd, C. (1970) *The British Seaman 1200–1860: A Social Survey*, Paladin, London; the contributors to Howell, C. and Twomey, R. (eds) (1991) *Jack Tar in History: Essays in the History of Maritime Life and Labor*, Acadiensis, New Brunswick, NJ; Stark, S. (1996) *Female Tars: Women Aboard Ship in the Age of Sail*, Naval Institute Press, Annapolis, MD; Robinson, C.N. (1911) *The British Tar in Fact and Fiction*, Harper and Brothers, London;

and Ommer, R. and Panting, G. (eds). (1970) *Working Men Who Got Wet*, Maritime History Group, Memorial University of Newfoundland.

38. Kirk and Heath, *Men in Frocks*, p. 24.

39. Ibid., p. 24.

40. Gavin, M. (1982) 'Gays at Sea', *Mister*, 35, Millivres Press, London, p. 25.

41. This practice was so common that in the eighteenth and nineteenth centuries skate were routinely examined for traces of hereditary syphilis. The Ministry of Agriculture and Fisheries currently have no record of such a practice but seafarers repeatedly report that this was the case, and as late as the twentieth century.

42. By contrast 16.4 per cent of women doing stewarding work in 1931 were married.

43. The body that represented the men, the National Union of Seamen, was far from being the creator of a such a tolerant space, unlike the US's West Coast Marine Cooks and Stewards Union. Allan Bérubé, who writes about gay men and lesbians in the military, found that 'from the early 1930s to the 1950s, the communist, multiracial and queer-positive MCSU ... created a multiracial work culture and union-based movement which "developed their own collective strategies to achieve the broad political goal of surviving with dignity as working-class queers" '. However, the union fell victim to the FBI, coast guards and anti-communist, white, male union members. It was part of the anti-labour suppression of radical and cross-social boundary organising in that McCarthyist period. Its banned members were unable to get work. See Bravmann, S. (1996) 'Postmodernism and Queer Identities', in Seidman, *Queer Theory/Sociology*, pp. 350–1. Bravmann was drawing on several works by Allan Bérubé, but particularly, ' "Dignity For All": The Role of Homosexuality in the Marine Cooks and Stewards Union, 1930s–1950s', a paper presented at the Annual Meeting of the American Historical Association, San Francisco, 6–9 January, 1994. Its abstract was printed in the *Committee on Lesbian and Gay History Newsletter*, January 1994, p. 6.

44. Garry Bannerman, G. (1982) *Cruise Ships: The Inside Story*, Collins, Toronto, p. 110.

45. Stephen Rabson, private conversation with JS, 21 September 2001.

46. Porter and Weeks. *Between the Acts*, p. 81, quoting his own research notes, 27 September 1970.

47. Ibid., p. 81.

Chapter 2

A Place of Freedom

On passenger ships gay men found a playful atmosphere, a culture and community to which they could belong, a tradition of entertainment that took cross-dressing for granted and the space and opportunity to have sex without fear of police intervention. This chapter opens by taking a broad look at what it was like to be on a ship in the mid-twentieth century. What were the ship's general meanings for anyone on board? It explores the sense that being on a ship was time off and space away. As part of that, a voyage could seem like a metaphor for transition: you were on the way to being somewhere and someone else, the old was left behind, maybe forever. It was often holiday fun. The heady feeling was echoed by the physical giddiness of being on the sea, particularly in ships with inadequate stabilisers. And in this novel place to meet lovers, there was a social climate of fleeting love, romance and sexuality. Of course this varied for passengers, heterosexual crew and gay men, so separate sections of this chapter deal with how differently the ship was experienced for each category of person. But our fundamental argument is that gay seafarers could experience a ship as a place of (limited) freedom because it was like that for most people aboard anyway. Gay men benefited from the *general* climate.

Life at sea in the mid-twentieth century

A ship is both a vessel and an hotel, both a means of getting somewhere and a temporary end in itself. With its network of decks and departments it's a cluster of new space on the way to new spaces on the other side of the sea. A ship can be a holiday camp afloat[1] or a nest, a refuge from the ocean's vastness,[2] and, of course, a workplace. It was particularly passenger, more than cargo, ships that provided havens for *camp* gay men. Rudyard Kipling made a distinction that still largely stands: the

One of the ships on which some of our respondents worked in the late 1950s.
Picture courtesy of Dave.

liner is 'a lady, an' she never looks nor 'eeds. The Man o' War's 'er
'usband and 'e gives all she needs, But oh the little cargo-boats ...
They're just the same as you and me a-plyin' up an' down.' While cargo
ships were functional and more masculine spaces, passenger ships,
especially cruise vessels, could be both sexy and sexualised: far more
than simple vehicles.

It can be difficult to imagine what passenger ships were like in the
1950s and early 1960s, so it may help by thinking about old movies of
seaside guesthouses and luxury hotels. The Hollywood movie, *Titanic*[3]
was set in 1912, decades before the seamen in these pages travelled, or
were even born. But it shows how much ships could be seen as a social
situation with a means of transport and some changing scenery attached.
Forty or fifty years on, luxuriousness and style were not as great but they
were still present. That recreational frisson was there. And the absolute
extremes of snobbery and poverty were not so apparent – partly because
many of the flagrantly rich already travelled by that new phenomenon,
commercial aeroplanes.[4] No longer were hordes of poor migrants dancing
down in steerage's squalor. Mass migration to the USA had largely ended,
although many thousands were still making assisted passages to
Australia.[5] Also, the gender segregation so important in Victorian[6] times
had waned. Sexual morality was starting to become not quite such a con-

cern. In the 1970s and 1980s, as the holiday industry developed, cruising became affordable. A sunny version of the cruising life was presented by television series such as *The Love Boat* in the USA[7] and *Traumschiff* in Germany. Cruise operators' brochures in today's travel agencies perhaps give another clue to what ships were like for the people who give their stories here. Or try imagining a slightly up-market, latter-day British holiday camp like Butlins[8] or the early Costa Brava, but at sea and with a subtle difference: gay people and gay acts could be tolerated there. The picture that should emerge is one of fun, licence, packaged adventure and organised, but tasteful, hospitality for an increasing mass of tourists, more extravagant but less wild than it can be today.

Time off and space away

Such ships offered voyages of five days (for example, from Southampton to New York) or cruises of several months, when land might not be seen for days and home belonged to that category of 'so far away it doesn't quite count'. People on ships experienced themselves as belonging to their own world, away from the usual. Passengers – and those crew who worked with a recreational attitude, as some of the gay stewarding workers did – were in spaces that existed outside usual society: spaces where behaviour that was not usually permitted, could happen. Ships were exceptional places where people took time *out* from their usual lifestyles, and time *away* from usual situations.

Time on the ship was, for passengers, time off from routine work dominated by employers' clocks.[9] Sundays ashore were still seen as precious, even sacrosanct, days of rest. So every holiday moment had to be enjoyed in full because as late as 1951 the majority of working people on land only received one week's holiday a year and by 1969 two-thirds were still not entitled to annual holidays of two to three weeks.[10] In a society where the privations of war remained in people's minds, this 'annual liberation from labour discipline' that John Walton identifies[11] was truly recreational, even though it could cause some difficulties, such as getting on well with others who wanted to use their time differently. But generally a ship's inhabitants – staff as well as guests – could mark off this time as being there to assist long-term well-being, although they would not phrase it so. For working-class people it was a space of exception and unprecedented mass festivity, where, unlike a street party, almost everything was provided and done for them. Wild behaviour could feel justified because it was only temporary. Normality would be restored when they returned to land – and that applied to casual workers as much as passengers.

Above all, ships were liminal spaces, a concept that is much discussed by cultural geographers today. Rob Shields and Victor Turner take liminality to mean 'moments of discontinuity in the social fabric, in social space and in history. These moments of "in between-ness", of loss of social co-ordinates ... classically ... occur ... when people are in transition from one station of life to another, or from one culturally-defined space in the life-cycle to another.'[12] It's an intermediate ritual phase where people entering an unfamiliar society learn new social rules and develop complex bonds with other initiates. During the voyage (which could be conceptualised as a process of initiation) people's anomalous social position is changed as they leave their old state. A passenger ship was a place where people could learn about a hedonistic, less work-oriented, less conformist way of living, as the leisure industry developed at an unprecedented pace throughout the twentieth century.

When people's bodies are literally 1,000 miles away from home, it enables them to imagine themselves 1,000 miles from all the rules of

A culture of excess: waiter service and pre-paid food, where waiters could secretly ogle passengers. Picture courtesy of Dave.

home. Although the ship is still a highly regulated system, it somehow *feels* different. Un-moored, the normal order of things may be felt to be suspended, questionable, irrelevant or even wrong. Unlike Southend, Blackpool or Torreomolinos, where there might be the possibility of running into neighbours from home, on a ship there would be less possibility of being exposed by critical gazes from your land life. People who are usually marginalised were unusually free in this context.[13] This meant that people on ships – passengers and workers – could try on different kinds of behaviour. They could enact fantasies via fancy dress parties, helped by duty-free booze. And they could act in accordance with the social mores of the ship, which increasingly in the 1970s, 1980s and 1990s meant partying. It was a culture of excess, not least because all food was already paid for and people enjoyed filling their plates, and because romance – or at least sex – was in the air.

The voyage as metaphor for transition

Characteristically, a voyage is a space where personal change and emotional development occurs because of the changed perspective. Voyages can enable people to become 'better' versions of outmoded selves, just as economic migrants go to new worlds for 'improvement'. Such rites can be a moment when life-changing decisions are made after profound reflection and an old restricted sense of self is left behind. The sea passage on many types of ship is used in novels as a metaphor for mental and spiritual exploration and social passage.[14] Within that passage new identities are constructed partly through social relationships, the most intense of which are usually romances. Perhaps the most classic celluloid example of this is the character of Charlotte Vale played by Bette Davis in *Now Voyager* (1942).[15] Charlotte boards the ship as an ugly duckling and disembarks as a beautiful and successful socialite, after an oceanic romance with Jerry Durrance (Paul Henreid), which affects her ability to befriend others. The movie illuminates the denotation of romance as social success, and proof of improved social skills, as well as escape.

In the quest for a changed self and/or future, romance and sex get mixed up. Sociologist Anthony Giddens argues that

Romance gears sexuality into an anticipated future in which sexual encounters are seen as detours on the way to an eventual love relationship. Sex is, as it were, a sparking device with romance as the quest for destiny ... [but] having sex with a new partner may be the start of the fateful encounter which is sought after.[16]

The holiday, particularly the voyage-quest, appears to offer the conditions for sexual encounters that people hope may result in a fulfilling soulmate for life. But flings feel justified too.

Holidaying

As spaces where people were taking time off and time out, and where identities could change, postwar passenger ships were not only vessels taking people to a holiday destination, they were part of the holiday experience *in itself*. As a result, there was a climate of play and excess, with swimming pools, nightclubs and shopping malls being common features on many ships. The difficult economic conditions in shipping in the 1960s[17] meant that this new money-making enterprise had to woo customers by ensuring that ships felt like palaces of pleasures, not floating utilitarian buses. For many working-class people in a pre-television era, ships were their first contact with luxury. 'Never before had my eyes observed such splendour', said 14-year-old bellboy John Dempsey of his first sight of the *Mauretania*'s restaurant. 'All that panelling, large ornate doors, tables set with silver cutlery, flowers, and waiters in wing collars with black bows ... I had seen it at the movies, of course, but there was nothing like the real thing.'[18]

Ships were no longer just public transport to a destination but holiday destinations in themselves. What was a seaborne ship, after all, if not a mobile beach, a floating pier, a shop-lined promenade and a bathing beach near cafés – all rolled into one? And the seaside had long been synonymous with a particular type of open-air consumable amusement, as writers on Blackpool and Brighton argue.[19] With fantasy names that included words such as *queen, princess, halcyon, carnival, discovery, ecstasy* and *inspiration*, ships were holiday zones or even sites of the carnivalesque.[20] Anarchy, misrule, rudeness and excess are characteristics of the carnivalesque: people engage in behaviour that is transgressive or unexpected. There could be an almost Rabelesian sense of 'naughtiness' in this unusual situation where the social order could be overturned – low people could be high (and vice versa). Carnivalesque moments are a bit like the classic mid-summer madness: revelry, temporary fever, the servants might shaft the gentry, drink and food would be consumed in excess, but at the end of the trip all would be restored to normal.

Whoops-a-daisy

Added to these traits was the constant movement of the sea and the physical unsteadiness it created. Fairgrounds 'celebrated strangeness and excess, and undermined dignity and control by offering unexpected movement and physical excitement:'[21] the Roller Coaster's wild dips, the tilting floors of the Crazy House and the vertigo of the Big Wheel. A similar sense of unpredictability was experienced while at sea. A ship could lurch and roll you off your feet – or even into someone's arms. The sea – and the invigorating maritime air – could be blamed if someone became 'out of control', or simply different from their usual selves at home.

One of the ways that people mentally deal with physical unsteadiness and the fear it can evoke is to tell themselves that the feeling has another, less unsettling cause. Attribution theory in social psychology proposes that people experiencing a heightened feeling, such as fear, decide to attribute some reason or another to it, even if that link is not warranted.[22] So people on a ship could label a feeling as 'love' when it actually was caused by something else, such as fear of the unknown or a sense of agape (love for humankind) that was induced by the oceanic nature around them.

Romance and sex

Why would feelings be attributed to love or sex? There are several psycho-biological explanations that are not satisfactorily proven. The most important of these is that the ship's rhythms are said to increase libidinal arousal, something which is common 'knowledge' among seafarers.[23] Secondly, there is the possibility that the bright light (reflected off vast seas) may cause increased serotonin levels, the biochemical that triggers sensations of happiness, making people more suspectible to romance. Thirdly, being on gay-friendly ships meant that gay men were sexually successful rather than social outcasts. It's possible that the more sexual successes that were achieved, the more the biochemicals that create a sense of happiness were generated.

All of the inhabitants on a ship, including the workers, can be seen as a kind of tourist, and so some ideas from tourism sociology can be useful in helping us to see the general atmosphere in which seafarers operated and sometimes took part. Tourists are often in search of excitement and myth. Such myths include the idea that 'This is It!' or 'I am the exciting person that this other person sees me as being'. Part of the excitement is physical: sensory stimulation and interaction with the elements (wind in your hair, strange tastes on your lips, spray on your skin, not to mention a foreign head on your pillow and strange words shaped by your tongue). The fling can be the crucial marker of the success of this special time out and your success: you relate well; you can get your dream fulfilled. That the romantic adventure takes place at sea makes it even easier to enjoy without alarm because it's conducted within the spatial and social confinement of the ship. Your hair is ruffled while you are safe on deck, and near a hair salon; the foreign food is cooked by people who share your own standards of hygiene; brine can be showered off by your familiar soap from home. So a shipboard affair is not something that happens with the worryingly-unboundaried – a foreign person on their own soil. Instead people can have flings with someone on board who is *slightly* other, an inhabitant of a foreign place, but who, like you, is on the ship.

Tourism sociologist Richard Sharpley proposes psychological motivations for tourism,[24] from which it can be inferred that romance on a voyage offers people in transition two crucial opportunities. This can be applied to both workers and paying passengers, and both homosexual and heterosexual flings. First, such romances offer people a way to feel better about themselves during what may be a time of self-questioning. Secondly, they can provide an escape from the peculiar kind of loneliness that can accompany a voyage, or a sense of community during a period of disconnection from the places people feel they belong to, although homophobia means that gay people can feel lonely and disconnected ashore too.

Evidence from passengers and workers affirms that on ships there were more sexual and romantic liaisons than on land. Popular culture abounds with examples of the passenger's quest for salt-water smooches on balmy decks, a phenomenon on which today's cruise operators focus. For example, on St Valentine's Day in 1998 Princess Cruises enabled 5,000 couples to renew their marriage vows. The dearth of men on passenger ships – and women's interest in them – has been handled by the employing of 'gentleman dance hosts' like Walter Matthau and Jack Lemmon's characters in the 1997 US movie *Out at Sea*.[25] Romance had become part of people's expectations of a voyage, long before the Second World War. Writer H.V. Morton evokes the pattern of what he identifies as liner love or sea fever, postwar. 'The girl who could not, if she wished, become engaged during a sea voyage, is, imagine, with a few rare exceptions, non-existent.'[26] The climate is one of dangerous delusion, Morton believed. 'A man who falls in love at sea falls fathoms deeper than he would fall on land. ... Liner love can be compared only to those romances which afflict young people at masquerade balls where, isolated in a little space of unreality, they conceive a poetic fancy which dies, if not at dawn, possibly with the dawn after that!'[27]

So passenger ships offered temporary frivolity and lack of inhibition, an acceptance that fleeting flings occur in which both parties accept the temporary nature of the relationship. In many cases it would be this passing nature that adds to the appeal, a point which is often reiterated in gay pornography based around sailors. Robert, a purser, notes that gay seafarers referred to these sorts of encounters as *affairettes*. They were too restricted by circumstance to have much profound meaning but they had all the brief passion of an affair, made all the more poignant or wild because you knew you'd probably never see each other again. What you did together didn't have to matter.

Romances also occurred because ships were a heady new site for trysts.[28] Ashore, heterosexual people could meet in ice-rinks, dance halls, cabarets and picture houses, but gay people's options were more limited to private and often dingy places, as the last chapter shows. So a ship, this glamorous setting known only to most people through newspaper pictures of high society stars leaning against its railings, was a major addition to this repertoire.

Organising the idea of liner love

Romance and sex on ships were there partly because they were put there. Desires are not just spontaneously created, they are also socially constructed. Postwar shipping lines marketed good health to be gained and new sights to be seen as the main products of a voyage, but romance as a major by-product. Many adverts for cruise travel feature (opposite-sex) couples standing together in twilight embraces on moonlit decks, eyes on the calm seas and distant horizon that attest that all the usual problems are far away.

What ideas have to be consumed or ignored for people – workers or passengers – to construct a passenger ship as a site waiting for romance to happen? People have to be (put) in a mood to accept the idea that a fleeting encounter will occur, and they have to ignore their usual social standards. Alcohol enabled this, but so too did what seem to be deep and established psychic imaginings of what a ship means in our culture.

They were echoed by the products of popular culture, particularly cruise novels. Published from the 1930s onwards, some of these, as discussed in our introduction, set up expectations of affairs with all kinds of people on board and sometimes people (usually ex-patriots) in foreign ports. And it's no accident that *Now Voyager* was scored by Max Steiner, who also composed for the romantic classics *Gone with the Wind* and *Casablanca*. Cinema-literate people entered passenger ships with this model in their heads. What they did not find there already they could create.

Ships could be places of fun for the crew, on and off duty. Picture courtesy of Ian.

Seafaring workers

What were ships like for crew in this period? One of the recurring themes that we encountered during our interviews with seafarers was that their ships were fun, meaning that work was approached in a light-hearted way and didn't loom as depressingly large as it did on shore. Fun often meant many sexual relations. Jack Tar traditionally had a girl in every port, but seafarers on passenger ships might also have lovers on each and every deck, on each and every voyage.

Seafarers were part of the 'party' that they and the passengers were creating. The sexual climate that we described above meant that although passengers and crew were not supposed to fraternise, they sometimes did. The forbidden nature of such relationships often helped to make them all the more attractive, while the testosterone-soaked atmosphere served to spur on many men to sexual conquest.

Three of the main gains for gay men on ships were partners, 'play-acting' and parties. If neither female passengers nor female personnel were available, then some seafaring men with a more fluid sexual identity might readily turn to male sexual companions as a substitute, as Chapter 4 describes. For other seamen, with a stronger homosexual identity, a passenger ship offered a number of conditions that enabled gay sexual

Skull-duggery during a performance of 'Snow White and the Seven Dwarves' on an Elder Dempster vessel in the 1960s. Picture courtesy of The Cowden Collection.

activity to take place: places to have encounters, cheap alcoholic drinks, and the freedom to dress as glamorously as they fancied.

As many old voyage accounts and posed photographs attest, people on ships have always put on outrageous garb, for fancy dress parties. They do so to pass the time, and to indulge in the fantasy that just as you *were* somewhere else, so you could temporarily *be* someone else, as Chapter 5 shows. And not only was it normal to masquerade as someone else, role models were available too. The presence of so many movie stars and denizens of society gossip columns as passengers on ships brought ordinary people, including gay seafarers, into contact with the most extreme glamour – plus the knowledge that these figures were only human. They too could be seasick, sunburnt, drunk or made queasy by foreign food. Famous people were accessible for the duration of the voyage, and could therefore be emulated. It is no accident that many seagoing queens called themselves by the names of their favourite movie stars: Gina (Lollabrigida), Marilyn (Monroe), Rita (Hayworth), Lana (Turner) and Dolores (del Rio), some of whom they'd transported.

Ian, a waiter, sums up the atmosphere he found 'particularly on the *Sea Princess*, [where] gay definitely reigned. [It was] a very camp ship to work on. I think they [gay men] created an atmosphere for the passengers, that

Burlesque fun on the *Queen Mary* in the early 1950s – ship's bollard in the background. Picture courtesy of the Oral History Unit, Southampton City Council.

really made cruising so special, because it made an atmosphere, wherever you were on the ship, whether you were working or below decks, there was always a laugh. You could always hear people laughing or joking, or having camp jokes all the time, just laughing. It just sort of rubbed off, I think. I'm sure the passengers must have just felt this as soon as they came on. As soon as you get on, it's really relaxed and everyone was happy, genuinely happy. It wasn't a put-on thing, like when you go some places today when they're told what they've got to say and it's false. But it wasn't there, we weren't told anything, we were just being ourselves, being ourselves all the time. It was so natural, and I'm sure that's why they valued the gay community on the ships, because it helped the overall atmosphere.'

Four main points need to be understood if we are to see what life was like for gay seafarers at this times. First, ships were experienced differently by different seafarers. An individual's openness about his homosexuality, the job he did, his social class and the ship he was on were important factors. Secondly, ships offered a particular type of employment situation. Thirdly, they offered a special kind of culture, even a community. And fourthly, ships had spaces that gay men could use to their advantage.

Stars made a point of meeting staff, as did film actor Rock Hudson here on the *Queen Mary* with the catering officer. Picture courtesy of the Oral History Unit, Southampton City Council.

Different experiences

To make sense of the relationship between gay men and the ships, we need first to consider the level of openness that individual seafarers displayed, regarding their sexuality. Some were totally covert, while others were more or less 'out' to everybody. And then there were those who occupied the spaces in between, at different times and in different circumstances. A ship was also very different for officers than it was for ratings (people who were not officers, such as stewards). The former had more freedom but also far more to lose. Particularly in the years before 1980 an officer could lose his job, and all the benefits resulting from years of painstakingly accumulating knowledge and status, if he were found to be gay.

Sociologist Carol Warren defined the polarities between covert and out gay men in a way that corresponds clearly with the shipboard situation. First, she identified men who saw themselves as 'essentially normal, deviating *only* in the choice of sexual partner, a deviance that they could conceptually minimize'.[29] They curtailed their contact with the gay world and chose to be quite marginalised from the homosexual community. This was the pattern for several of the gay officers we talked to, particularly those who worked on cargo vessels. These covert gay men hid their sexuality from straight people. And they did what sociologist Erving Goffman described other stigmatised groups as doing: managing their 'discreditablity' in straight people's eyes.[30] They did so through controlling their personal front – how they behaved in public – and through limiting the amount of personal information they disclosed to others.

Many of these men were influenced by a desire to avoid guilt by association. But it was much more necessary to be covert on cargo ships where gay people did not *visibly* rule. Geoff, a writer and steward from 1950 **to** 1982 with P&O, sailed mainly on passenger ships to India, Japan and Australia. But his 'favourites were cargo ships, the smaller ships, because there were no passengers'. There was far less of a holiday feel. If there were any passengers at all, it would be a maximum of twelve and no special treatment was laid on for them. Unloading freight meant that the ship's complement had a week in port where they could mix with locals – sometimes forming sexual relationships – unlike time ashore allocated to cruise ships, which could be as little as half a day. And for Geoff, cargo ships had a much more irresponsible atmosphere than a 'cattle boat' full of starched, frenetically-socialising officers. On hot days he, the chippy (carpenter) and the storeman would just sit around quietly drinking beers with a towel wrapped round them. It was an opportunity for peaceful male sociability. No shows, and usually no sex.

But at the other end of the spectrum were men who, according to Warren, saw 'themselves as *completely* outside society ... [they] organize their entire lives, including their working lives, around the self-definition and the deviance'.[31] That is, they cope with being part of the usually-stigmatised group by flaunting their difference. This marking of 'otherness' was achieved by wearing flamboyant clothes, employing particular mannerisms and talking in a special language. And these traits tended to be more popular with the screaming queens, who were usually ratings (i.e. not officers) engaged in stewarding work on passenger ships. Often loud and declarative about their sexuality, they made sure that they were recognisably gay and 'in your face' with it. At a time when transvestism was still unusual and transsexuals even more rare, they were unusually theatrical and stereotypically feminised.

The second factor that divided gay men's experience of the ship was social status – based on class and the occupational rank they held. Ships were particularly status-conscious places to work in and many gay officers felt they could not mix with gay ratings, or at least be seen to be fraternising. Robert, a purser, knew it would be 'career suicide' if he were found chatting up a crewman he fancied. On his very first ship he noticed that 'the strange thing was in the Merchant Navy [that] ... while it was quite

Mixing it. Catering crew and deckhand (third left) play act Cinderella. Picture courtesy of private donor.

accepted for stewards and cooks and all those people to be gay, as an officer you really had to keep it covered up'.

In any case, stewarding staff did not necessarily mix with the ordinary seamen who were employed to carry out manual labour. This was partly because of the tradition of manual workers having a macho, homophobic culture which was very class-conscious and not appreciative of upper-working-class types who were considered to be snobbish and status-seeking. Workers entering ships encountered not just the formal division based on rank assigned by the shipping line, but also minute informal divisions based on how 'posh' someone acted. As happened on land, many of the more socially ambitious service personnel aped the manners of their 'social betters' and took pride in being indistinguishable from, or even better than, their upper-class passengers. One of the odd side-benefits of a gay man being on a gay-friendly ship was that, as Warren found with gay people ashore,[32] joining the gay subculture could enhance class status (for example, a knowledge of art and *haute couture* fashion might be gained). Similarly, some gay men at sea learned to look and behave like 'real ladies'. Photographs show how extremely aloof and elegant these cross-dressed, counterfeit social stars could appear.[33] Invitations to private soirées were printed in French. Lower class gay seamen might be morally

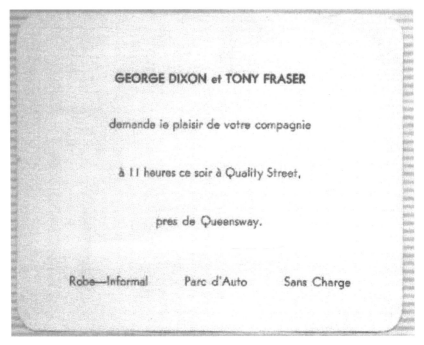

GEORGE DIXON et TONY FRASER

demande le plaisir de votre compagnie

à 11 heures ce soir à Quality Street,

près de Queensway.

Robe—Informal   Parc d'Auto   Sans Charge

The gay culture onboard offered class enhancement, as this invitation to a private soirée, printed in French, suggests. Picture courtesy of private donor (anonymous).

despised and socially avoided by those from the higher classes, but Esther Newton, who writes about gay and lesbian communities in the USA, found that ashore such 'lower' men might, 'by their flamboyant stylization and distinctive adaptations to extreme alienation, rival and even surpass the uppers. This applies especially to the low status queens, who represent a role-model of extraordinary coherence and power.'[34] On ships, one way that camp gay men could avoid shame at possessing an inferior social status was to become the kind of 'ladies' who wouldn't be seen dead with the kinds of men that some officers were. It could also be a way of parodying upper-class women: imitation as the insincerest form of flattery.

Employment

Gay-friendly ships offered a kind of employment to gay men that was similar to that encountered in the theatre on land. It was accepted and normal to be gay if you were a steward on ship, just as it was whether you were an on-stage star or front-of-house personnel in the red, plush palaces ashore. Jobs on ships were relatively easy to find for skilled, gay, white stewarding staff, before South East Asian crew were increasingly recruited from the 1960s onwards. And gay men working on the hotel side of the ship, particularly as stewards, found themselves to be in a devil-may-care situation because it was only casual employment. Catering work had long been a casual and seasonal trade in the UK.

The people attracted to hospitality work often saw it as a temporary way of earning money, not as a career. Some even saw it as a way to get a kind of holiday, with pay. Waiting at tables and making endless beds was just the price that was paid for being by the seaside, among people enjoying themselves. So it was at sea. People largely did the hotel-type jobs for the perks: extrinsic rather than intrinsic reasons. However, for ships' engineers and navigating officers it was a lifetime career. And it is noteworthy that most of the gay informants for this book were catering workers, not engineers, and their repeated refrain was: 'We had the time of our lives.' It was time out, for people who were not interested in taking a seafaring career seriously and for those who did not feel bound by Protestant work ethics. However, with that said, many were extremely keen on performing a good service and perfecting everything with the nicest of touches.

By contrast, covert gay men in non-hotel work on ships, particularly if they were of a higher rank, experienced a more disciplined situation in which respectability and status depended on not being out. Those who had been in the services and at boarding school adhered to the unspoken rule – thou shalt not be *found* to be queer – sometimes for their whole careers.

Community

Ships could offer gay men a community where they could be gay and sometimes very out (and outrageous). It was often gratifyingly different from the situation on land, as described in Chapter 1. They were able to express feelings, explore outlawed desires, gain new knowledge, and belong to a culture, if not a community. That culture had its own rules about how people should behave (for example, with tolerance, or with loyalty to other gay men, not to officers). And it had its own institutions and rituals: nightly visits to the ship's bar; weekly drag shows set up as entertainment for all; group visits to agreed pubs ashore. Newcomers were welcomed and initiated. Leading figures – such as the senior queen – expected all the respect given to a mayor or squire ashore.

Weekly drag shows were commonplace on many cruise ships, and 'Brownie', of course, had two meanings. Picture courtesy of the Oral History Unit, Southampton City Council.

To be 'out' on a ship was not only to express your personal feelings but also to join a collective that asserted the importance – indeed the normality – of being gay. Newly gay seafarers became part of the process of making publicly visible what had, ashore, been private offensiveness. It was an affirmation both of the individual and of the newly visible culture of which he was a part.

Communities, of course, are places of peer surveillance as well as of shared fraternity. As Chapter 4 shows, gossip and jealousy could make the gay communities on ships feel claustrophobic at times. Today many people believe that both social and genetic factors determine sexuality – some people believe they are born gay, while others adopt or construct a gay role that can change over time. So not all men who had gay sex automatically became members of a gay community. Some returned to wives or girlfriends when they went ashore, their membership status in the gay community only being temporary or non-existent.

Shipboard spaces

A ship offered a range of spaces that were utilised by gay men, from public to semi-public and private. Shipboard spaces such as the dining room and bars were shared with other crew and passengers, although with different levels of equality. Those shared only with crew included the crew messes (dining and recreation areas) and the working corridors. When Frank (a steward) went to work for a cruise ship, 'I must have been 26, basically, it was just unbelievable, because there was nowhere ashore in those days, there were no bars or anywhere to meet, [but on the ship] you'd go down the corridor: "Morning Doris, Elsie …" and they'd be in drag or heels, or maybe fighting over their boyfriends and things.' As Chapter 5 shows, there were places where sometimes there was deliberate performance, as in shows put on in the crew messes.

Gay men on ships found they had a floating network, the like of which was not available ashore except in cities like San Francisco. It focused much on drinking in the ship's bar, participating in cross-dressing shows and parties; and in having a pool of gay colleagues who could be both potential lovers, playmates and shoulders to cry on when affairs went wrong. Warren found that for gay men living ashore '[b]ars are the most important public community places',[35] and they were on ships too. Robert, a former purser who has travelled the world with many shipping lines, affirms the scale of gay socialising with alcohol as the focus. 'On the bigger ships there were actually gay bars … passengers could be invited down there [even though they were crew bars]. … Ships like *the Queen Mary* and the *Queen Elizabeth*, they had huge gay bars where all the gay crew went. And all the straight crew went to other bars. … They would occasionally mix, but basically they kept themselves to themselves. In fact one of the last ships I was on was … the *Ocean Monarch* coming back from Australia and there was a gay bar on there. … Quite a few of the passengers used to come down to that. Sometime the crew's mess room was used.' Dave, a waiter from 1956–1963, remembered that when he was with P&O, 'you had a crew room which, theoretically, when the ship was built you were supposed to eat there with everybody. The waiters used to take food from the dining room and ferry it forward, and eat the passenger food. There were lots of crew meals provided, but in the catering division, you ate from the first-class or second-class menu. So the crew room wasn't used all that much. But it was an area which we could use and people would have parties [there].'

But unlike gay-friendly cities like San Francisco, a ship's limited space could not allow access to other, more sexualised spaces that gay men ashore might use: bath-houses, beaches, gyms, cinemas and cruising spaces, for example. However, some men simply used the dark unused spaces of the ship. Dave remembered one of the main trysting sites was 'up on the forecastle, behind the winches. You'd be joking about how the grease off the cable came in handy. We used to call it the Forecastle Head

Follies. If we had passengers, then it was out of bounds during the day as they could look over and see. But at the dead of night, there'd be no cargo lights on, so it was all pretty dark up there. Any activity going on behind the great big winches might be spotted from the bridge, which was higher than where the passengers would be. If the activities got a bit heavy, with bums bouncing around, then officers might get a bit panicky, and think, "God, passengers might see that going on." They'd flick the cargo lights on a couple of times and that would put the fear of holy Moses into people and they'd scarper. It would calm everything down until the next time.'

Thinking in terms of who has power, we can see that places like the deck were 'contested spaces' to which different citizens of the shipboard community felt they had different rights. Ownership was implicitly negotiated: the crew's gay sex had to be carried out in a space where passengers who might feel affronted could not see.

Sociologist Erving Goffman has usefully made the distinction between back-stage and front-stage spaces: places in life where we put on different kinds of show: for example, the hotel receptionist desk or dining room versus the hotel kitchen or boot-room. For gay men on ships there were different spaces where they could be gay, or were expected to appear straight. Building on Goffman's theory, Carol Warren noted that in the gay community she studied there were two kinds of gay social behaviour in front-stage straight spaces: overt and dramaturgical.[36] What counts as overt? It included invasions into public, 'straight' spaces, by people who acted in such a way as to get themselves labelled as gay, for example, kissing, quarrelling, fiddling with each other's clothes or hair. Sometimes this was done deliberately in order to shock, challenge or make people laugh. In contrast, dramaturgical behaviour was used for playing the part of a woman. Here it is a great secret pleasure to appear as a woman and have no one suspect that you were actually a man.

Most of the gay men we interviewed enjoyed being present in straight spaces in transgressive ways, in taking over territory – playfully but with the deeply serious intention of claiming their right to be gay on ships. Warren explains that people can feel very proprietorial about space:

Invasion of space in both contexts [overt and dramaturgical] can increase the feeling of community in gay people. In the act of keeping others out of gay bars and homes, gay people reinforce the in-group, out-group division of the gay world, without challenging the stigma or the secrecy behind such actions. In the act of treating straight spaces either as real worlds or as stage settings for the invasion of outsiders, gay people continue to define themselves as outsiders and as strangers to the straight world. As Robert Frost once said, walling in and walling out are aspects of one act.[37]

By contrast to these public spaces on ships, gay seafaring males also made use of a space that was partially private: their cabins. Cabins were spaces where two important events occurred: sexual encounters, which could often be quite domesticated, and back-stage preparation for front-stage appearances in drag. Such spaces, though nominally private and back-stage, could often be quite public because cabins were shared and divided by very thin walls. The *trade curtain* which could be pulled across a bunk, was one way of maintaining a minimal form of privacy in multiple occupancy cabins, although you also had to rely on the discretion and tolerance of your cabin-mates. Dave, a steward, said the way cabin mates dealt with that exposure was to create a kind of private space in the mind. 'They had curtains across the bunk, and everyone else would have to close their minds. Or listen like hell!'

A cabin is someone's home while at sea: borrowed, flimsy, too crowded but at least a space where they are not visible to the passengers or officers; a site of un-duty, like a garden shed or hut.[38] Characteristically in the gay world ashore, especially in the 1950s, 1960s and 1970s, gay men made great efforts to establish a home where they could entertain lovers and other gay friends, where they could be secret and safe. A ship's cabin offered a similarly (largely) unsupervised space free of unwelcome cultural values, often for the first time in young working-class men's lives. Here they were free from the possibility of police or family raids. Pictures of beefcake could decorate walls and frocks could be stored without

Workers on ship made their cabins their own, including the trade curtain (swagged back, front right). Picture courtesy of Ian.

derision. It could be home and a place of new self-expression. Martin explains 'You'd do your cabin up with nice curtains with big bows on them, like they do now in *Changing Rooms*' [the British television programme about home make-overs]. And senior men with some job security could make their cabins a home from home. They could physically establish a congenial, delineated space that acts as a metaphor for the established nature of their homosexuality. Alan, a radio officer from the 1950s, remembers his chief steward: 'as camp as they come [he had] chintz curtains and all that . . . [he] brought his own curtains and cushion covers.'

Martin points out that cabins could be used as a private but common space. 'On the newer ships there were double-berthed cabins, we'd always say married quarters. One ship I was on, it was an eight-berth cabin. But some nights there were up to 16 people in it: eight queens and five omees [straight men] or whatever. If we were on a passenger ship with a six-berth cabin, which sounds mental, but it was paradise, you'd have six queens in there. And all the queens would be in there, fighting, trying to get ready for the saloon, because you used to put semi-makeup on for the saloon evening at night.' Indeed, there could be a whole cluster of cabins that were absolutely recognised as gay territory – often nicknamed Balmoral (because the queen took her holidays there) or Quality Street. These little colonies could be seen as a resort, like the first gay and lesbian resort, Cherry Grove, Fire Island,[39] or a section of Blackpool promenade taken over by gay men, or even a homophile Biarritz.

However, there were a number of reasons why a cabin at sea was not entirely heaven. First, attached to the job as it was, a cabin had all the insecurity of a rented flat; a gay seafarer could be evicted by those in charge at any time, particularly if he camped it up too much in inappropriate contexts. Secondly, he couldn't necessarily choose his cabin-mates, who might be homophobic. This mattered on long voyages, and swapping was not always possible. Thirdly, as we said above, a ship is actually a space that does not offer much privacy, to anyone. The lucky people aboard were those who did not have to share their cabin. The high premium on space, which led to the less prestigious workers being crammed in like sardines, meant that there was little opportunity for time alone. This resulted in a number of types of behaviour. Seafarers tactfully made themselves scarce when their cabin-mates wanted to entertain. They also got used to performing in the presence of an audience, and to *being* an audience. Frank remembers: 'One night my cabin-mate Judy had a gentleman visitor. I was on the bottom bunk and she was on the top bunk. If either of us met somebody compatible you'd put the curtains across, but then you would have to listen to everything all night. It was very rough one night, and the ship lurched to port and they both fell out of the top bunk. Then they started laughing. They could have killed themselves. But strangely, [his cock] was still in. I opened my bunk curtains and said, "I've heard of flying fucks in my time, but this is ridiculous". '

In addition, in the larger cabins on older ships, seafarers protected themselves from territorial invasion by arranging the furniture to indicate boundaries to where others were welcome or unwelcome, or to outline the social meanings of a particular space to newcomers. In some of the large older cabins of eight, ten or twelve, the gay guys pushed their beds closer. This was not to enable sex but simply to delineate a space that deterred ignorant straight people who might either unwittingly or deliberately trespass.

All the evidence from gay seafarers suggests that they constructed their shipboard world into a series of spaces that coincidentally enabled what Warren has identified as features of gay life ashore in gay-friendly cultures. These are home entertainment, cocktail parties and spectaculars, which she defines as large and lavish entertainments where people were exotically costumed, often as a fantasy character, dance to live music, and are offered elaborately displayed food.[40] Gay men used the ship as a site of conspicuous consumption where friends were routinely invited to their cabin home for drinks; where they drank in a sociable bar culture characterised by, as Warren points out, 'light conversation and heavy drinking'; and where putting on spectacular concerts and soirées of the sort described in Chapter 5 was a common part of a voyage's fun.

Freedom of sorts

A ship offered gay seafaring men many pleasures, and they made sure it did by setting up the arrangements they desired, wherever possible. The gay French philosopher Michel Foucault found the 1980s San Francisco gay 'community a heterotopia – a place of dumbfounding excess that left him happily speechless'. A heterotopia is not a utopia (an ideal place) but a place (*topos*) where arrangements are so different (*hetero*) that they highlight what the usual is like and offer the users fresh ways of seeing themselves, just as looking in the mirror can. Cemeteries and musicals are heterotopias.[41] A ship, particularly a gay-friendly passenger ship, was similarly a heterotopia that enabled gay men to think differently, and more positively, about their sexual orientation and what homosexuality means in different societies.

Warren points out that the gay world has two distinctions. 'It is almost universally stigmatized, and no-one is socialized within or toward it as a child.'[42] But on some ships these distinctions were much more complex. At least among the section of crew doing traditionally feminised work such as catering, homosexuality was celebrated rather than stigmatised. So ships offered men a space to develop a community which largely supported explorations of their sexuality. The main ways that gay sexuality was expressed was through relations with other seafarers; relations with passengers; relations ashore; and general participation in a community. Chapter 4 shows in more detail the kinds of relations gay men had with seafarers. And as the next chapter shows, the gay community – at sea as ashore – flourished and consolidated partly because it had a way of talking that helped it to define itself against the world.

As Ian, a waiter for P&O in the 1980s, euphorically summarises his ships as places of freedom: 'You couldn't ask for a better time, or a better place to come out. To come out in an atmosphere where you don't feel different, you feel one of the majority when you come out. You're part of something that's there and has been there for years and years, and it's just been waiting for you, and it's a really nice feeling.'

Notes

1. For an interesting history (that omits homosexuality), see Ward, C. and Hardy D. (1986) *The History of the British Holiday Camp*, Mansell, London and New York.

2. For some useful thoughts on refuge-style space, see Bachelard, G. (1969) *The Poetics of Space*, trans. M. Jolas, Beacon Press, Boston, MA, especially pp. 109 and 206.

3. *Titanic* was made in 1997 by Twentieth Century Fox/Paramount Pictures and directed by James Cameron. For an interesting analysis of gender in it, see Kramer, P. (1988) 'Women First: *Titanic* (1997), action-adventure films and Hollywood's female audience', *Historical Journal of Film, Radio and Television*, 18, (4), pp. 599–618.

4. Transatlantic air travel from the UK exceeded sea travel for the first time in 1957 when cheap tourist-class fares were introduced. Odgers, P. (1988) *The Hotel, Catering and Leisure Industry*, Gale Odgers Publications, East Sussex, p. 30.

5. For an entirely unusual view of the impact on passengers of such a voyage in 1948, see Armstrong, D. (2001) *The Voyage of Their Life: The Story of the SS Derna and Its Passengers*, Flamingo, Sydney, Australia.

6. See Walton, J. (1978) *The Blackpool Landlady: A Social History*, Manchester University Press, Manchester, p. 40. He refers to landladies who segregated single women and men on separate floors, kept an eye on engaged couples and by the

turn of the century had helped police Blackpool into an exemplary morality akin to that on ships before the Second World War.

7. The TV soap opera *The Love Boat* (1975) has its own website (see http://www.lovboatonline.com). Special Love Boat cruises are organised for fans (see http://www.lovboatcruise.com). See also Saunders, J. (1998) *Love Boats*, Llewellyn Publications, St Pauls, MN.

8. Ward and Hardy, *British Holiday Camp*.

9. That feeling could infect seafarers to some extent, although their lives were punctuated by the ships' watches (four-hour shifts) and mealtimes.

10. Walton, J.K. (2000) *The British Seaside: Holidays and Resorts in the Twentieth Century*, Manchester University Press, Manchester, p. 63.

11. Walton, J.K. (1997) 'Seaside Resorts and Maritime History', *International Journal of Maritime History*, IX (1), June, p. 136.

12. Shields, R. (1991) *Places on the Margin: Alternative Geographies of Modernity*, Routledge, London, pp. 83–6. Shields based much of his work on anthropologist Victor Turner's re-workings of Van Gennep's ideas about liminal zones. See, for example, Turner, V. (1979) *Process, Performance and Pilgrimage*, Concept, New Delhi.

13. See this discussion in relation to women in sea literature in Vlasopolos, A. (1994) 'Staking Claims to No Territory: The Sea as Women's Space', in Higonnet, M. and Templeton, J. (eds), *Reconfigured Spheres: Feminist Exploration of Literary Spaces*, University of Massachusetts Press, Amhurst, MA, p. 73.

14. See, for example, Abel, E., Hirsch, M. and Langland, E. (eds) (1983) *The Voyage In: Fictions of Female Development*, University Press of New England, Lebanon, NH, and Hanover.

15. *Now Voyager* was made by Warner Bros, in 1942 and directed by Irving Rapper.

16. Giddens, A. (1994) 'Men, Women and Romantic Love', in (no editor), *The Polity Reader in Gender Studies*, Polity Press, Cambridge, p. 243.

17. For a brief and accessible summary of this, see Lane, T. (1986) *Grey Dawn Breaking: British Merchant Seafarers in the Late Twentieth Century*, Manchester University Press, Manchester, pp. 6–16.

18. Dempsey, J. (1992) *I've Seen Them All Naked*, Waterfront Publications, Poole, p. 3.

19. See Shields, *Places on the Margin*, especially pp. 73–116, and Walton, *British Seaside*.

20. We mean 'carnivalesque' in the sense used by M.M. Bakhtin (1984) *Rabelais and his World*, trans. H. Iswolsky, Indiana University Press, Bloomington, IN. *Places on the Margin*, Shields, and Walton, *British Seaside* refer to it at length in relation to resorts. Its application to the high and low is best brought out in Stallybrass, P. and White, A. (1986) *The Politics and Poetics of Transgression*, Methuen, London.

21. Walton, 'Seaside Resorts', p. 136.

22. The classic example of this is a 1974 study by Dutton and Aron, who planted an attractive young woman who made eye-contact with some of the interview participants on the narrow and high Capilano Canyon Suspension Bridge. The men who had had the sexualised encounter attributed their heightened feelings to sexual arousal rather than to the fear felt by those other men who had not had that sexualised encounter.

23. Even if this is not true, the *belief* that it is true could act as a placebo effect. Certainly the rhythms bring on childbirth, which is why shipping lines decline to transport women beyond their seventh month of pregnancy.

24. Tourism sociologists have suggested that tourists' desires include the need for ego-enhancement and a cure for the sense of anomie, meaning a sense of absence, breakdown or confusion. Tourism expert Richard Sharpley summarises the need as being to 'be recognised, to have their ego or confidence boosted. Whilst on holiday, away from their usual surroundings and friends, people are able to act out an alien personality, similar to the king/queen for a day situation. ... However, it is more than an inversion of the normal and more than indulgence in ludic behaviour; the opportunity for ego-enhancement, for status enhancement links directly to the potential satisfaction of Maslow's concept of self-esteem needs. Equally, anomie as a tourist motivator can also be seen as resulting from the need for love and a sense of belonging.' See Sharpley, R. (1994) *Tourism, Tourists and Society*, ELM Publications, Huntingdon, p. 116.

25. Ward, D. (2000) *Berlitz Complete Guide to Cruising and Cruise Ships, 2001*, Berlitz, Princeton, NJ and London, p. 65.

26. Morton, H.V. (1945) *Blue Days at Sea*, Methuen, London, p. 122.

27. Ibid., p. 122.

28. Kern, S. (1992) *The Culture of Love: Victorians to Moderns*, Harvard University Press, Cambridge, MA, p. 26. He argues that travel has, since the nineteenth century, been associated with new places where lovers might meet in new ways. One of the key developments in the history of lovers' meetings was that a greater variety of places to meet developed in the twentieth century, especially for less upper-crust folk.

29. Warren, C.A.B. (1974) *Identity and Community in the Gay World*, John Wiley and Sons, New York, p. 39.

30. Goffman, E. (1956/1990) *The Presentation of Self in Everyday Life*, Penguin, London.

31. Warren, *Identity and Community*, p. 39.

32. Ibid., p. 43.

33. See, for example, the images in Gardiner, J. (1996) *Who's a Pretty Boy Then*, Serpent's Tail, London.

34. Newton, E. (1993) *Cherry Grove, Fire Island: Sixty Years in America's First Gay and Lesbian Town*, Beacon Press, Boston, MA, p. 43.

35. Warren, *Identity and Community*, p. 19.

36. Ibid., p. 37.

37 . Ibid., p. 39.

38. See Bachelard, *Poetics of Space*.

39. Newton, *Cherry Grove*.

40. Warren, *Identity and Community*, p. 55.

41. Miller, J. (1993) *The Passion of Michel Foucault*, Doubleday, New York, p. 26. See Foucault (1977) *History of Sexuality, Vol. 1: An Introduction*, Pantheon, New York, *Vol. 2: The Use of Pleasure* (1985); *Vol. 3: The Care of the Self*, (1986). Foucault was a part-time denizen of San Francisco sado-masochistic Fulsome Street and Castro Street bath-houses.

42. Warren, *Identity and Community*, p. 4.

Chapter 3

Speaking Gay Secrets

'How bona to vada you!'

Like most groups of people who spend a great deal of time together and also share some common ground, seafarers had developed ways of speaking that were unique to themselves. Dockers used a form of back-slang that involved inserting the syllable 'ag' before every vowel. For example, 'ship' would become 'shagip' and 'fuck off' would become 'faguck agoff'. However, gay men who joined the Merchant Navy had their own form of language, which was variously called Polari, Palare, Palari or Parlaree. As it was rarely written down, there were few, if any, spelling standards. Polari was a whole world in itself. Gay seafarers who had learnt it could while away hours, gossiping about who they fancied, who was doing what with whom, and who was the most well-endowed man on board. For many gay seafarers, Polari was a part of their everyday lives, a form of language that they took for granted. While it appears to have been most commonly heard on land in the more sexually oppressed period from the 1900s to the 1950s, it still appears to have been used by gay seafarers well into the 1980s. This chapter explores the history and development of Polari, how it was used by gay seafarers and why it was eventually abandoned by many gay men.

History and origins

Polari has a lengthy, tangled and illustrious history, stretching back to Thieves' Cant, a secret form of language that was used by criminals in the sixteenth to eighteenth centuries.[1] Also known as Pedlars' French or St Giles's Greek, Cant was most likely derived from what was called Elizabethan pelting slang and a form of it had been used in the eighteenth century by men who were collectively known as Mollies. The Molly subculture was based around clubs and taverns in London, where men went for the purposes of socialisation and to make sexual contacts with each other.[2] These men appear to have been early proponents of camp humour, sometimes dressing as women or enacting child-birth by using a pig as a stand-in for a baby. Some of their words concentrated on male–male sex: *riding a rump, the pleasant deed, do the story, swive, indorse, caudle making.* Others were less sexually oriented and were more likely derived from Cant, for example *flash ken*: house of thieves; *nubbing cheat*: the gallows; *mish*: shirt; *shap*: hat; *stampers*: shoes; *poll*: wig; *queer ken*: prison; *queer booze*: bad drink; *queer cull*: fop/fool. Although *queer* occurs in some of the phrases that the Mollies used, there is no evidence to suggest that it was used as a word to describe men who had sex with other men. However, it is possible that its use as a pejorative term may have originated here. A couple of Molly words *have* survived into the present day gay vernacular, possibly via Polari. *Trade* was (and still is to some gay men) a sexual partner, while to be *picked up* was to find a partner. The Molly lexicon at least tells us that cruising for gay sex is an age-old pastime.

During the eighteenth and nineteenth centuries, a number of words from Cant gradually found their way into a newer form of language, called Parlyaree. Used by 'grafters' (travelling circus and market people), entertainers, beggars and prostitutes, many Parlyaree words had Italian origins, although some words can be traced back to British English, Australian English, Spanish, Romany, Latin, French, Occitan (a Romance language intermediate between French and Spanish), Arabic and Shelta (an ethnic language spoken in the UK, with an Irish derivation).[3] Some Parlyaree words (for example, *manjaree*: food; *bevie*: drink; *nanty*: none) were derived from Italian via Lingua Franca: a form of language spoken in the ports along the Mediterranean coast and originating from the time of the Crusades.

Lingua Franca had a number of grammatical rules which gave it the status of a pidgin – a simplified form of language derived from two (or more) different languages. Some Lingua Franca words which appear to be at least related to Parlyaree are: *barca*: boat; *mangia*: food; *bona vardia*: all's well; *capello*: hood; *parlamento*: conversation.[4] Lingua Franca was almost certainly known to English sailors, who most probably brought it back to England with them.[5] In the eighteenth and nineteenth centuries, many wounded seamen, upon returning to England, were subsequently put ashore miles away from the place where they were to be paid. As a result, they were obliged to take to the roads against their will, acquiring the status of rogues and beggars as they made their way across the country.[6] Other retired sailors could have joined the travelling classes of showmen, players and pedlars in order to make a living.[7] The distinction between sailors and beggars is unclear when it is considered that an act of 1713 made wandering illegal, except for sailors. As a result, many beggars pretended to be sailors until the law was repealed in 1792. Therefore, in numerous ways, Lingua Franca words learnt by sailors would have entered the various versions of Parlyaree used by beggars, pedlars, strolling players and other travelling people.

It is difficult to cite a date (or even a decade) when Polari became something separate from Parlyaree, although lexicographer Eric Partridge places it to some time in the nineteenth century, writing that Parlyaree had become 'moribund'.[8] By this time, the strolling players and performers had been succeeded by those who worked primarily in music halls. And while many actors and dancers continued to work around the country and abroad, it was London, with its numerous entertainment venues, that became the base for Polari. As well as its theatres and music halls, London, like many large cities, became the home to gay men, who moved there for numerous reasons: anonymity, greater tolerance, a more cosmopolitan lifestyle, work opportunities, access to other men, etc. By the late 1930s, homosexual subcultures had begun to form in the UK's large cities, especially London. Dancers, known as *wallopers*, and singers, known as *voches* (voices), delighted in this language which they claimed for their own. While many of these *artistes* were gay, there were plenty who were not. For them, Polari, or *Palare* as it was more commonly known in the first half of the twentieth century, was simply the language of the theatre, with words associated with the stage, many originating from the older Parlyaree. Polari was especially popular with chorus boys, particularly those who were gay, and they adopted this form of language as their own. As John, a gay dancer, says: 'I learned "palari" when I was in the theatre, but it was a common language. ... It was common only among a certain class in the gay world. It was usually people like myself who were in the chorus, the common end of the structure, who used it.'[9]

The fact that Polari was based in and around London, the capital city, perhaps best explains why it had such a wide variety of influences and changed so rapidly. As well as being used by theatre people, Polari was influenced by the London-based rhyming slang. It is thought that rhyming slang had been developed in the early nineteenth century by Cockney navvies who used it as a way of mystifying the Irishmen who worked alongside them on the docks, canals and railway embankments.[10] Rhyming slang consists of replacing an existing word with a rhyming phrase or part of such a phrase. So the word *believe* is replaced with *Adam and Eve*, as in 'would you Adam and Eve it?'. Some common Polari words that were derived from rhyming slang include: *barnet*: hair (from Barnet Fair); *brandy*: bum (from brandy and rum); *hampsteads*: teeth (from Hampstead Heath); *irish*: wig (from Irish jig); *lucoddy*: body; *minces*: eyes (from mince pies); *plates*: feet (from plates of meat); and *vera*: gin (from Vera Lynn).

Other words were the result of more complex chains of rhyming slang. So *aris* meant arse because it is a truncation of *aristotle*, which rhymes with *bottle*, which is a shortened version of *bottle and glass*, which rhymes with *arse*. The word *plate* is rhyming slang for oral sex. One possible derivation is that *plate* rhymes with *fellate*. However, another derivation of *plate* is that the phrase *plate of ham* rhymes with *gam*, which is a truncation of the word *gamahouche*, a French-sounding word referring to oral sex.

As well as rhyming slang, Cockneys also used the less well-known back-slang, which involved saying a word as if it was spelt backwards. Some common Polari words that were created via back-slang include: *ecaf*: face (also shortened to *eke* or *eek*); *riah*: hair; and *esong*: nose. In addition to rhyming slang, Yiddish communities, living in the East End of London in the late nineteenth and early twentieth centuries, also contributed a number of words to Polari, including: *schonk*: to hit; *schnozzle/vonka*: nose; and *schvartzer homie*: black man. In later years, American airforce men, stationed in London during the last years of the Second World War, helped to add words such as *butch*: masculine, *cruise*: look for sex, *blow-job*: oral sex and *naff*: bad, to Polari's ever-expanding lexicon.

By the late 1960s, Polari had been popularised by the BBC comedy radio programme *Round the Horne*, which featured a couple of camp, out-of-work actors called Julian and Sandy, played by Hugh Paddick and Kenneth Williams respectively. With their catch-phrase: 'How bona to vada your dolly old eek' (how nice to see your pretty face), they quickly won over British audiences, becoming the most popular part of the show. Dave, a ship's waiter, said it was the highlight of the week for gay men ashore. The writers of the sketches, Barry Took and Marty Feldman, used a combination of Polari and innuendo in order to simultaneously draw attention to the fact that Julian and Sandy were gay, but also to ensure that they never had to state it explicitly. So when Sandy enthused about someone's *bona lallies* (nice legs), or Julian complained that 'trade had been a bit rough lately' (a reference to *rough trade* – a male sexual partner who became violent after gay sex), Polari was used as a way of filtering gay male desire so that naive members of the audience wouldn't understand every single joke. Innuendo was the most common form of British sexual comedy in the 1950s and 1960s, with the *Carry On* film series (also starring Kenneth Williams in camp or asexual roles) being the most popular form of this type of entertainment. Julian and Sandy used a combination of innuendo, euphemism and Polari in order to get away with saying the most outrageous things, without alerting the censors.

Julian and Sandy had a number of seafaring connections, suggesting that the writers were aware of the fact that homosexuality occurred on merchant ships. Their 'special friend' was called Jock – a sailor in the Merchant Navy who is described as a 'great butch omee, bulging lallies, eke like a Greek God'. Like his name (jock-strap, football jock, etc.), Jock is masculine, good with his hands (he can make ships in bottles), and plays rugby. He also has a disarming generosity which endears him to both Julian and Sandy – every time he comes into port he brings Julian a gift, while on Julian's birthday he presents him with a carafe of the appropriately named 'Merchant Adventurer'. Jock was representative of a particular type of man found in the Merchant Navy – the *trade omee*, who most likely had a wife or girlfriend back home and probably didn't consider himself to be gay, but was willing to have sex with other men (see Chapter 4).

And in a sketch called *Bona Sea-dogs*, Julian and Sandy make further reference to the fact that queer things can happen at sea. They describe how they got their *sea-lallies* (sea-legs), were caught in a storm (over the ownership of a pair of eyebrow tweezers) and were eventually 'picked up by the purser', in a lifeboat that was strapped to the deck of the *Queen Mary*.

Polari and the sea queens

Unsurprisingly, Polari was particularly popular in the gay Merchant Navy subculture, where it had been used long before it was publicised via *Round the Horne*. Some gay actors who, like Julian and Sandy were 'between jobs', joined the Merchant Navy as waiters or entertainers, sometimes just for a single voyage, to tide them over until their next role. As a result, they introduced other sailors to a large number of colourful Polari words and phrases. Polari was also common in the pubs around the East End dock areas of London, so seafarers were likely to have picked up words and phrases while on shore leave. Some Polari speakers have spoken about East End and West End versions of Polari, with the West End or 'shore-side' Polari being based on the simplified form of slang that Julian and Sandy used, associated with theatre queens and office workers who worked in the West End of London. The 'sea queens', however, used a more complex form of Polari, which was developed out of their contact with East End dockland communities, and possibly with languages used in other countries. East End queens elaborated on Polari, to the point where they could use it to confuse almost everyone, even the West End speakers.

Many of the gay seafarers were at least aware of, or used, Polari. Some of the words described different types of people, so a man was an *omi* or *homee* and a woman was a *palone*. A gay man was an *omi-palone* (a combination of man and woman) and a lesbian was a *palone-omi*. A young man was a *feely-omi*, while older gay men were called *antique hps* (the initials stood for *homee palone*). The police were referred to by a number of feminising terms: *Jennifer Justice, Betty Bracelets, Hilda Handcuffs, Lily Law*, while hairdressers were *riah-shushers* or *crimpers*. Other words referred to parts of the body (always useful when describing sexual activities or someone's appearance). As well as *ecafe, riah, esong* and *lallies*, there were *orbs* or *ocals*: eyes; *dish*: anus; *hearing cheat*: ears, *martinis*: hands (a *sweet martini* was the left hand, while a *dry martini* was the right one); *luppers*: fingers; *thews*: muscles (possibly forearms or thighs); *cartes*: genitals (*grande cartes* meant a big penis); *nawks* or *willets*: breasts. There were also plenty of words for clothes and make-up: *lally-drags*: trousers; *batts*: shoes; *fashioned riah*: wig; *groinage*: jewellery; *lippy*: lipstick; *slap*: make-up.

Common Polari verbs were: *vada*: to look; *charva*: to fuck; *troll*: to walk around looking for sex; *mince*: to walk effeminately; *cruise*: to look for sex; and *zhoosh*: to tittivate. Adjectives were mainly used to classify someone as good (*bona, fantabulosa, dolly*) or bad (*tat, naff, cod*), effeminate (*camp, queeny, swishing, screaming, dizzy*) or masculine (*butch*). If someone was available for sex and/or attractive, then he was *TBH* (to be had), whereas if he wasn't available, or was not worth having, he was *NTBH* (not to be had). Other acronyms included *VAF* (Vada! Absolutely Fantabulosa!) and *naff* (not available for fucking).

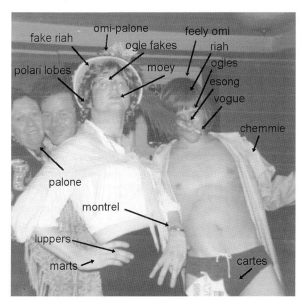

Many Polari terms refer to parts of the body or people. Picture courtesy of Bill.

While Polari mainly comprised nouns, verbs and adjectives (making it more akin to a lexicon than a language), it did contain some function words, which are more commonly found in distinct languages. *Nanti* was a standard negator, meaning 'no', 'nothing', 'don't' or 'none'. And *ajax* was a preposition meaning 'next to' (probably derived from the word *adjacent*). Pronouns in Polari were often reversed, so *he* became *she* and vice versa. *She* could be used to refer to a gay man, but was often extended, so that any man, no matter what his sexuality, was potentially a *she*. As with the feminising names for the police, Polari speakers had fun subverting the identities of the butchest or most important of men, including the ship's captain, by referring to them with female pronouns and names. Other Polari terms consisted of longer phrases such as *nada to vada in the larder*: small penis; *the colour of his eyes*: penis size; and *nanti pots in the cupboard*: no teeth. Many speakers did use Polari merely as a lexicon, replacing English words with the occasional Polari one (for example, *He's got a bona brandy on him!*). However, the seasoned speakers used it in more complex ways. For example, the phrase *order lau the luppers on the strillers bona* means 'go and play something nice on the piano', but is not a word-for-word translation.

Gay seafarers adapted or added new words to the existing Polari lexicon. So the word *lattie* (house) was used to create the phrase *lattie on water* (ship). Several seafarers we interviewed used the euphemism *do a turn* when referring to having sex with a man. It's likely that this phrase came into Polari via contact with actors where to 'do a turn' was to act on stage. The word *glory-hole* (which refers to a large hole drilled between two cubicles in a public lavatory for the purposes of sex) was also a slang term for the various compartments on a ship or for one or more rooms used as sleeping quarters for stewards. A *sea queen* was a gay man who was also a sailor, or one who had a particular liking for sailors. With several men sometimes sharing a cabin, privacy could be obtained by pulling a curtain across a bunk. This curtain, which was particularly useful when having gay sex, was known as a *trade curtain*. Finally, a cabin that was full of sea queens was known as a *fruit locker*: 'fruit' was a term for a gay man.

A number of Polari terms employed sex-as-food metaphors, so a *chicken* was a desirable young man, while the name for any kind of lubricant used to facilitate anal sex was *starters*. *Dish* referred to the anus, while *putting on the dish* was to prepare the anus for sex with a lubricant. Women were collectively known as *fish* (a particularly derogatory term relating to the smell of the vagina), whereas attractive sailors were *seafood*.

Polari was one of the ways that a distinction between different types of crewman could be delineated, marking the boundary between the flamboyant, camp seafarer and the more masculine men who may or may not have been sexually available. Mark, a waiter for eight years in the 1960s, describes how he'd be in his cabin getting ready for a party, with his *husband*, George, and his *sister*, Franny: 'I'd say to Franny, "what are you doing tonight, girl?" ... She'd say "What I'm going to do girl, I'm going to go round and dohbie [wash] the riah [hair], I'm going to do the brows, and then I'm going to put the eek [face] on for the Pig and Whistle." Well, my husband would understand that she's going to go round the cabin and get ready. He knows she's putting on make-up because that's "putting eek on" you see. But *he* wouldn't use it.'

So while many sailors knew Polari, it tended only to be used with any regularity by the camp gay men, not the *trade omees* or *husbands*. And it functioned as what the linguist Michael Halliday refers to as an *anti-language*, a form of language created and used by an anti-society – any group of people who are in opposition to the dominant or mainstream society in some way.[11] In the 1950s when Polari flourished, all gay men were, to an extent, part of an anti-society, but this was even more apparent in the Merchant Navy, where being gay could result in dismissal or transfer. While it was obvious to many seafarers that some of their number were gay, Polari provided a way of talking about other people *while they were present*, allowing a degree of secrecy. '"Nanti polari" meant shut up, somebody's listening', explains Dave. 'We'd be talking away, and someone would come past, a straight naff purser. "Nanti polari dear, nanti polari", your friend would say, and you'd look over your shoulder and there'd be someone ear-wigging [eavesdropping].'

Those who were not part of the inner gay circle would perhaps be aware of Polari. Some might know a few words, but they wouldn't be able to understand all of it. This was especially because some Polari speakers ad-libbed, changing words when they felt like it, in order to make the code more complicated. Martin remembers how one word was invented. 'One day we were sitting in the cabin and this thing transpired. Someone said, "What are we having for a bevvy tonight, girl?" because we'd have a cocktail before we went to the bar. ... We'd have various spirits left over. Passengers leave you a couple of bottles in the cabins when they'd left. And we had some vodka and some martini, and someone said "Oh I'll tell you what we'll do. Have some vodka and martini, we'll call it a vodka-tini." And of course that drink came out. I wouldn't say I invented it, but that's the way things came about, you know.'

Polari also functioned as a perfect initiation into the gay subculture in the Merchant Navy. According to an email exchange with a gay seafarer called Peter, who joined his first ship at the age of 16: 'Polari was very commonplace on board ships at sea. There were a lot of unfamiliar words to learn. The older queens looked after me and I was soon christened with a camp name. A lot of the older queens only spoke Polari.' These older, more experienced queens would 'teach' the language to the newer ones. In this way, Polari could almost be viewed as a 'family tradition'. It was handed down from generation to generation of gay seafarers, who were not linked to each other by blood ties, but by the unique status that their sexual identities gave them. Polari therefore acted as a focus of interest, by which the more established members of the gay subculture could impart knowledge to the newer seafarers, along with yarns about distant ports and practical advice on sea skills.

However, for Michael Halliday, anti-languages were used for much more than secrecy and group identification. They were also used in order to reconstruct the world, according to the values and world-view of a particular group.[12] So the word *bona* didn't just translate to the word *good*. It meant, very particularly, something that is good *from the perspective of a gay man*. Polari also allowed this anti-society to create words for experiences, concepts and points of views that didn't exist, or weren't often talked about in mainstream society. So there were words for different types of gay sex, or for different categories of people. The word *trade*, for example, sometimes referred to men who might be available for gay sex, but who wouldn't identify as being homosexual. But it could also mean any sexual partner, or even refer to the physical, fluid evidence of gay sex, for example, 'I was so surprised I almost coughed up last night's trade'. In other cases, Polari speakers borrowed English words and subverted their meanings. A good example of this can be found in Polari words that seemed to refer to familial relationships – a pair of *sisters* were two gay men who were the best of friends (or sometimes enemies). Sisters may once have been sexual partners, but now exist as rivals, as embodied in the gay proverb 'today's trade is tomorrow's competition'. A *mother*, on the other hand, would function as a mentor, introducing a less experienced gay man to the subculture. Again, a relationship with a mother is rarely sexual, although it may have begun as a sexual one. An *auntie* is usually a gay man who is older and/or unattractive, whereas a *husband* is a masculine sexual partner. A sexual encounter that occurs for the first time is sometimes referred to as a *wedding night*. Interestingly, as Peter notes above, being given a camp (or feminine) name is described as being *christened*. Maybe the name does, temporarily, become as fixed as one spoken over a church font by god-parents.

Camp names, as an aspect of language that was related to (or incorporated into) Polari, were a means of solidifying a new identity. They showed that someone had been accepted into the gay seafaring subculture. Martin describes the range of names he encountered on one cruise ship: 'You had

Many gay seafarers had camp nicknames, which helped to cement camp identities, especially when in drag. Picture courtesy of private donor (anonymous).

Prissie – she was a prissy queen; Mother who was one of the older queens – she was like a mother hen with all her young chicken queens who confided in her; Olga, because her grandmother was Russian, Lana Turner, who always wore sweaters and dyed her hair peroxide to convince us that she was a natural blonde; Mata Hari who was always snooping around at night looking for trade; Poppy, who used 'Californian Poppy' perfume by the gallon; Molly Brown, who got torpedoed in the war and still survives to tell the tale. Some of them, I didn't know their real names.'

This naming was almost always affectionate, although there was sometimes a sarcastic undercurrent present. A number of methodologies have been identified in the formation of camp names, many of which relate to an existing aspect of a person's identity. One of the most common ways was based on alliteration with the seafarer's 'real' name. So Jim would become Joan, or John Scott would become Sarah Scott. Another way was based on referring to a person's place of origin. So Scots Flo, Gwen from the Valleys and Anya from Aotearoa were from Scotland, Wales and New Zealand, respectively. This could be useful, particularly on ships where there was more than one Gwen or Flo. Other camp names were based on aspects of a person's personality, for example, Lazy Maisie, Mother and Dockside Doris. Physical appearance could also play a part in the new name that someone was given. Dave relates a number of people he worked with: 'There was always a Diamond Lil somewhere.[13] She always seemed to be the Queen Bee. The Black Widow: she used to wear black all the time. And there was Big Freda.' Some names referred to the movie stars that particular seafarers admired or emulated, often while in drag (see Chapter 5): Lana Turner, Carol Baker, Ginger Rogers. However, in other cases, names were simply assigned to a person because they appeared to 'fit' that person's camp identity: Tina, Hattie, Petunia, Peaches, Stella, Ella, Janet, Janice, Kitty and Ruby. Sometimes these names were preceded by the title Miss, for example, Miss Kitty.

Giving female names to gay men is not something which is confined solely to the gay seafaring subculture. Other gay subcultures based on land in numerous countries have also employed renaming techniques, and continue to do so. The tradition dates back at least as far as the eighteenth century Molly subculture in the UK.[14]

Polari could be a form of protection or secrecy for men who were covertly gay. However, for others who were camp and openly gay, their sexuality was obvious. So in that case Polari became more of a means of ritual insulting between rival queens. Faced with verbal abuse for much of their lives, because they were effeminate or different, some gay men had developed thick skins and quick tongues as a way of fighting back. As Frank, a steward in the 1950s and 1960s comments: 'Some of those queens were so sharp, you had to really think on your feet. They'd have a reply for everything. It became like a contest for you to think of something witty to say back to them. You had to learn how to do it, to save face.' Arguments, or mock arguments could be conducted between two or more queens, trading humorous insults for the pleasure of an audience, who were relieved not to be directly involved. While such arguments may have appeared aggressive or unfriendly to outsiders, it was sometimes the case that they were viewed as a performance or a game by those involved. It was a way of ensuring that they were the centre of attention, making others laugh, relieving boredom and letting off steam. In this sense, Polari is best considered in terms of allowing gay men to construct a humorously performative identity for themselves. Polari made people laugh.

Bricks in the ghetto?

However, as the twentieth century progressed, Polari gradually became unfashionable. Julian and Sandy had turned on audiences to the fact that a secret gay language existed. While the type of Polari that was used on *Round the Horne* was somewhat basic, it still exposed the secret. And once a code is cracked, it becomes less useful. However, that in itself wouldn't necessarily have caused people to stop using Polari – new words could have been invented to replace the old ones that had been discovered. The other blow to Polari was the eventual decriminalisation of homosexuality in the UK (although not in the Merchant Navy) as a result of the 1967 Sexual Offences Act based on the Wolfenden Report of ten years earlier. While gay men were still stigmatised and discriminated against in dozens of ways, they were at least less likely to face extortion claims or be sent to prison for having sex with men. As a result, there was less need for a covert way of speaking about subjects of gay interest. The Sexual Offences Act helped to pave the way for the Gay Liberation movement in the UK, although British gay men were also influenced by events in the USA.

However, some members of the Gay Liberation movement in the UK found Polari to be sexist, racist and ghettoising. It was viewed as aping heterosexual gender roles, with its emphasis on butch and femme. Feminist academic Mary McIntosh, while not explicitly against Polari, wrote of it in the gay magazine *Lunch* in 1972:

... camp is a form of minstrellisation ... parlare is a product of a culture that is deeply ambivalent and even while it celebrates effeminacy, 'obviousness' and casual promiscuous sexuality (precisely the elements that the straight world most abhors) can never really accept that these are good ... parlare itself ... expresses the ambivalence of the gay world about the gay scene. The terms of address that are distinctively gay are always used in a negative mocking way: 'Ooh, get you, Duchess'.[15]

In a follow-up article, writer Jonathan Raban wrote:

... the obvious trap facing any member of a recognisable minority is that his symbols will consume him; that his identity will disappear into the narrow funnel of his clothes and slang. He will become no more than a shrill mouthpiece for a sectarian lobby, determined, in the case of the homosexual, by a language of body parts and fucking. ... Isn't it time for everybody to tidy their toys away, to put the old uniforms in the trunk in the attic, or donate them to Oxfam, and to take a few, at least, of the bricks out of the walls of the ghetto?[16]

In the early 1970s, a number of people were sensitive about existing stereotypes of gay men as effeminate queens. They wanted to move away from anything that was regarded as camp – Polari was something associated with an older generation. The images of masculine gay men, including tough sailors, coming from America were viewed as sexier in any case. As a result, Polari was gradually eroded from the face of gay culture. However, while it became less popular in the gay bars and nightclubs of the UK, on the cruise ships it continued to be used well into the 1980s. Ian, who worked as waiter and barman throughout that decade, describes it as being a private gay language that was often used to talk about or make fun of the passengers, without them understanding. 'We'd use it to be really bitchy about the passengers, almost in front of them. We'd say something like "vada at the riah on that" about a woman's hair, and she'd be standing right in front of us. She wouldn't know what we were saying.'

Polari is still remembered affectionately by gay seafarers who were in the Merchant Navy in the 1950s and 1960s. Some continue to use it in their everyday conversations with friends. Others who were interviewed had difficulty remembering more than a few words. In the confined circumstances of the Merchant Navy, where homosexuality could be punished, Polari was a necessary fact of life for several decades. It became one of the more creative and subversive ways that gay men both protected and expressed their sexual identities.

It's understandable that the early liberationists wanted to place distance between themselves and a period where gay people had been treated poorly by society. And it's true that there are certain ways of using Polari that can display ambivalence, sarcasm, or downright rudeness. But in some ways it's a shame that Polari was so quickly discarded. When a form of language dies, a way of making sense of the world dies with it. In hindsight, Polari can be remembered as an important part of gay seafaring history. Above all, it was something that was a great deal of fun because of its association with secret knowledge and shared pleasures. It gave privilege and privacy in a situation where both were scarce commodities.

Notes

1. Lovric, M. (1997) *The Scoundrel's Dictionary: A Copious and Complete Compendium of Eighteenth-Century Slang*, Past Times, Oxford.
2. Norton, R. (1992) *Mother Clap's Molly House. The Gay Subculture in England 1700–1830*, Gay Men's Press, London.

3. Hancock, I. (1984) 'Shelta and Polari', in Trudgill, P. (ed.), *The Language of the British Isles*, Cambridge University Press, Cambridge, pp. 384–403.

4. Kahane, H., Kahane, R. and Tietze, A. (1958) *The Lingua Franca in the Levant: Turkish Nautical Terms of Italian and Greek Origin*, University of Illinois Press, Urbana, IL.

5. Coelho, F.A. (1880) 'Os Dialectos romanicos ou neolations na Africa, Asia e America', *Boletim da Sociedade de Geographia de Lisboa* 2, pp. 129–96.

6. Hancock, 'Shelta and Polari', p. 393.

7. Ribton-Turner, C.J. (1887) *History of Vagrants and Vagrancy, and Beggars and Begging*, Patterson Smith, London, and Salgado, G. (1977) *The Elizabethan Underworld*, J.M. Dent and Sons, London, p. 138.

8. Partridge, E. (1970) *Slang, Today and Yesterday*, Routledge, London, p. 249.

9. Porter, K. and Weeks, J. (eds.) (1991) *Between the Acts: Lives of Homosexual Men 1885–1967*, Routledge, London, p. 138.

10. Franklyn, J. (1960) *A Dictionary of Rhyming Slang*, Routledge and Kegan Paul, London, p. 5.

11. Halliday, M. (1978) *Language as a Social Semiotic: The Social Interpretation of Language and Meaning*, Edward Arnold, London.

12. Ibid.

13. Diamond Lil was a character created by the actress Mae West. She was, perhaps, representative of one type of identity that gay seafarers desired to emulate – a wise-cracking, self-assured adventuress who always got her man.

14. Norton, *Mother Clap's Molly House*.

15. McIntosh, M. (1972) 'Gayspeak', *Lunch*, 16, London, pp. 7–9.

16. Raban, J. (1973) 'Giggling in code', *Lunch*, 20, London, pp. 16–17.

Chapter 4

Sea Wives and Meat Racks

Straight people see gay sex as the core of the stigma that gay people bear. This means that every sexual relationship, however short, has a meaning for the gay man's identity, whether or not the rest of his community knew about it.[1] Each encounter could consolidate his view of himself, change his world-view and sense of possibility, and sometimes deepen his membership of the gay community.

Life at sea obviously creates particular kinds of relationships. So were they all along the lines of 'Hello sailor, goodbye'? Was there a gay equivalent of Jack Tar having a girl in every port? Could homoerotic love arise out of deep spiritual affinity between sea-brothers out on the deep? And how were these relationships different from relationships ashore?

Men at sea developed a range of different relationships with one another, not least because human company matters, particularly at sea and far from home. This chapter looks at why relationships happened, with whom, where and what kinds of relationship they were.

Ideal conditions

There were many reasons why relationships happened. Primarily, it was because there was such a plentiful supply of potential partners, and because the voyage, as we have argued in Chapter 2, was an exceptional situation. If people were gay, they could be in seventh heaven because there were so many men. And most of them, as voyages went on, might well be available.

So it's hardly surprising that thoughts turned to intimate encounters, and most of that intimacy was expressed sexually. If a ship's complement was as much as 99 per cent male then some of those relationships had to be between males. Chris says that the main thing to be understood about this period for gay men at sea is that 'it was warm'. Voyages were times when affections developed and other members of the crew looked after each other, in the absence of family and in the embrace of gay community that many were experiencing for the first time in their life. Bluebell, a sea queen for 33 years until 1983 makes the crucial point that 'affairs on ship could be very romantic',[2] not just casual sexual flings. Dave fell in love on several voyages. Some relationships were passionate, if not fiery. They grew and flourished from the soil of the camaraderie and live-and-let-live on ships.

Affinity with colleagues, loneliness, boredom and sexual frustration brought a readiness for contacts that might not be countenanced ashore. And of course some gay men had gone to sea precisely in order to meet as many gay men as possible. Some sailors chose a ship because of the possible sexual partners on it, as Martin, a steward for almost 40 years since the late 1950s, explains: 'There might be three ships in dock, I would be on one ship in the morning, working. And I'd walk into the pub at lunchtime and one of the queens would say to me, "Oh girl, we've got some fabulous omees on board." And I'd say, "Oh, I'm coming on there then, dear." Because I hadn't signed on yet. So I'd just take my book and say "I'm off, dear. Don't worry, I'm off." And my friend would say to the chief steward, "Oh, Martin's coming to join." I'd sign on to the ship because there's more talent on that ship. A girl's got to get her priorities right.' In periods of employment opportunity, the choice of available talent, not destination or vessel, could be the most important consideration when deciding where to work. Similarly, Robert, a purser, was thrilled to hear that he had been appointed to the *Chantala*. 'I couldn't wait to join her. I had heard many stories from two other gay pursers, who had served aboard these ships, about their sexual adventures with some of the cadets. Apparently, while only a few of them were gay, many of the straight boys would be quite happy to have their sexual needs taken care of after a few weeks, or days even, at sea.'

And sex between men also happened on ships because of the number of attractive, young, active, potential mates. Some gay seafarers could be surprisingly seductive. Men's natural attractions were enhanced by the tans that sunny climates brought. The white tropical uniforms, fashionable clothing bought in cosmopolitan cities and the relaxed demeanour of people working in the holiday industry could look spectacular set against the background of a blue sea, moon-lit deck, and palm tree-lined beaches.

One of the reasons sexual relationships occurred was not just sexual desire, but because they affected the identity of the gay men who engaged in them. Sex between two men, particularly if they were closeted, would have provided a form of intimacy unlike any other they had experienced. The gay stranger groped on deck, can reveal one of the most significant things about himself, that which his wife, family and school friends may never have shared: his sexuality.[3]

Because cruise ships were places where indulgence was elevated to a virtue, it is possible that the climate affected people's sense that they *could* or even *should* act with maximum hedonism and opportunism.

Crossing boundaries

So who did gay seafarers have relationships with? The most obvious potential partners were those who were the same as you – for example, those who worked or slept in the same area of the ship, had the same jobs or were equally as open about their homosexuality. Because most of the gay men on ship were stewards, so their most likely partners would be other stewards. And while this was sometimes the case, it's also been noted that for some of the queens there was the difficulty of like not attracting like. As Chapter 2 has shown, there were a number of *identity boundaries* between different types of seafarer on ships – status distinctions, for example between officers and stewards, age distinctions, such as those between older, more experienced staff and the much younger bell-boys, racial differences between the British workers and the large numbers of Asian employees, and gender differences, between those who were camp and those who were butch. Finally, there was a distinction between men who were openly gay, those who were closeted, and those who were married or did not consider themselves to be homosexual. So which of these boundaries was most likely to be crossed when relationships were formed on ships?

Stewards seldom had relationships with officers, because the physical space was constructed in order to curtail all fraternisation. Usually, seafaring personnel were expected only to socialise with those people who were on a similar level to them. As with most institutions, the chain of command meant that fraternisation between people who held different levels of power or responsibility was, to an extent, taboo. Robert, with the relatively high status of assistant purser, says: 'Of course you weren't supposed to fraternise with the crew anyway, you know, with the crew who are not officers. You had to be very careful.' However, after five or six years, he became frustrated with keeping his feelings constantly under lock and key. 'I got to the stage where I thought "Oh well, damn it, if they don't like it they can lump it." ' However, even then he had to be careful: 'Basically my relationships were with people ashore. Not that I had a lot of relationships. I had the usual "ships that pass in the night" thing, but that was all.' The fact that officers and lower ratings were supposed to be socially, not to mention sexually 'off-limits' to each other may have made such relationships even more attractive.

Sex with younger men on ships was also seldom possible, but for the very different reasons that they were treated protectively by their 'sea family'; their well-being was looked after, whether they wanted that or not. Bellboys, who used to run the lifts and help out in the dining room, were junior trainees, the youngest men in the stewards department, and aged 15–18. 'They were a no-go area to the rest of the crew, well-protected by the Welfare Leading Hand', says Frank. However, they could be quite deliberately tantalising and slip into your bunk to tempt you. Dave recalls a bellboy that he once knew: 'He was disappearing in civilian clothes every night, and we thought, "He's got some tart up there on F deck, some woman from Australia." But that wasn't it, we found out afterwards when he fell ill. He had a very severe cold, like a fever and he went into the sick bay. He'd also been working as one of the stewards in my saloon by then. So who should come howling down into my saloon but the Captain. "I say," he said to me, "Any sign of Smithy?" And of course, for a captain to talk about a bellboy like that. ... So I said "No, he's off sick sir." "Sick is he? Oh. Poor thing. I'll go and see how he is." Smithy was boffing the captain, who was about 50. He'd been having it off with the old man, going up to his cabin every night.'

Sex sometimes crossed racial boundaries, but not often because of the strict status divisions discussed in Chapter 7. The Goan bedroom stewards with whom many stewards had the most contact tended to be older family men, avuncular, plump and not very desirable at a time when James Dean-types were preferred. Occasionally someone might manage to arrange a meeting with a young Lascar kitchen boy or member of the engine crew, but Asian crew were pretty much out of bounds. The main inter-racial sex happened ashore, except in the case of men who were on duty when the ship was in a foreign port. Then partners, usually paid, came to them. This practice occurred as early as the 1920s and was still going on in the 1960s, according to Robert. A stewardess on the RMS *Alcantara* witnesses that in places like Cape Town, 'When the sailors or firemen couldn't get ashore these gay men used to come up the gangway ... and go down to the stokehole. They used to call them "dust-hole fairies". The men that they used to go and see had to be in duty while they were in port, so these gay boys had to come to them.'[4]

Many of the men whom we interviewed had relationships with masculine men who were known in Polari (see Chapter 3) as 'omees' or 'hommes'. These tended to be men who were not gay but heterosexual ashore. Lorri Lee, a sea queen who joined in the 1960s, says 'competition was very stiff if you wanted an homme'.[5] They were relatively scarce.

Dave agrees that you had to work quite hard to get the man you wanted. You didn't exactly have to be predatory, but determined. One young Elvis Presley look-alike, a pool attendant, was even offered a motorbike if he would agree to have sex with an older waiter.[6]

Why were some heterosexual men seen as potential gay partners? Seafaring life was an exceptional place where different behaviour could happen and people could find out about all their potentialities. People at sea were often cooped up for weeks at a time together during long voyages. For example, it was a long stretch between Colombo and Fremantle on Australia-bound vessels. It could be boring and lonely. In these circumstances men could develop affectionate feelings for their comrades. As Frank comments: 'Half the married men didn't even know if they were gay. They'd married very young, and the thing is, if a married man wants to go away to sea for three or four months, and leave his wife at home, then you have to question that. We used to call them sea gypsies because there's something wrong with people who run away to sea. They're hiding from something.' Classically, seafaring people assumed that anyone who was at sea had fled a problem. Newcomers were routinely asked: 'And what are you running away from then? Broken heart?' In this way the Merchant Navy almost had the feeling of the French Foreign Legion about it – but a lot more sybaritic.

So, some gay relationships were with gay colleagues, but others were with 'trade' colleagues who were heterosexual but available during the trip. The Polari term for a seafarer who engaged in gay sex without identifying as gay, was *trade omee*. Men who were straight might eventually 'give in' to what was sometimes called 'cabin fever', a seaborne counterpart to 'jail fever' or 'stir craziness', and turn to gay men as substitutes for women. Almost all passenger ships carried female nurses, stewardesses, laundresses, sales staff, social hostesses, masseuses, hairdressers, beauticians and, after the Second World War, entertainers and female pursers. But they were usually not sexually available. These women were not necessarily attracted to seafaring men. Many tended to view themselves as possessing a superior social status to most of the male crew. In addition, some female staff found men's promiscuity at sea to be antagonistic to their own preference for enduring emotional commitment, nor would they have sex with married men. Additionally, there could be a ratio of one woman to every 100 men. These women were often middle-aged and stereotypically seen by men as undesirable spinsters, not objects of allure. In any case women were officially stated to be off-limits while on ship, and their living areas were separate from men's living areas and policed. Female quarters were sometimes nicknamed 'Virgin's Alley', although some determined couples did manage to sneak into each other's rooms, or spare cabins, as well as meet in hotels when they got to foreign ports.

For all these reasons, women were unavailable and so there had to be a substitute: gay men. Married men, or those with established girlfriends

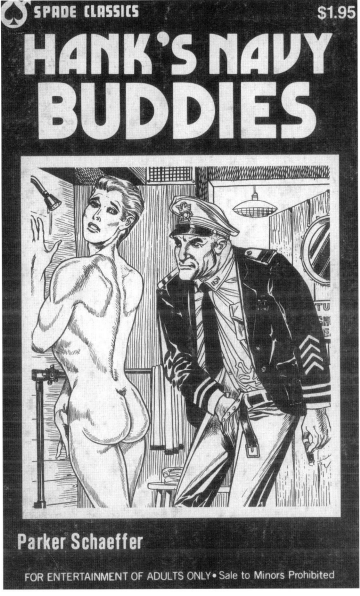

Butch and femme relations in the US Navy are pictured in this 1979 novel.
Picture courtesy of Star Distribution.

back home were sometimes the most willing participants in gay sex, as long as their gay partners could be relied upon to be discreet. Sometimes the seemingly heterosexual sailors were simply closeted, and a life in the Merchant Navy offered them the chance for male sexual contact on the world's oceans, hundreds or thousands of miles away from their families. They could blame it on the confined circumstances of being aboard a ship. For other married men who had been used to having regular sex with their wives back home, a sudden spell of enforced, institutional celibacy may have been harder on them than their single counterparts. Having gay sex was merely 'a tension release' or the next best thing to heterosexual sex when you were 'hard up'. Any kind of sexual release was termed 'getting dirty water off your chest'; it was like the contemporary advert for an analgesic: the slogan said it 'brought relief'. According to Frank, a steward for over 20 years since the 1950s: 'All these married men went to sea for three or four months to earn money to send the money home to their wives, but while they were away, *everything* happened. And then when they came home they were with their wives and children and that was it. They had their own friend back on board, they were two in a cabin, and that was it.' The potentially unequal relationship between butch married men and camp 'out' gay men was the subject of much of the stereotypical sailor-porn, as shown by the cover of *Hank's Navy Buddies*.

Oddly enough, some wives ashore could tolerate this kind of unfaithfulness. It didn't really 'count'. For some wives, a gay male rival for the attentions of their husband was much less of a threat than a female competitor. All the stories we have heard report that wives *were* prepared to be indulgent or forgiving.

An engineer with whom Geoff was involved was married to one of the dancers at the London Palladium. She viewed her husband's gay exploits at sea with a rueful shrug of her shoulders: 'She said to me, "I'd sooner Fred went with you, rather than go with another woman." ' And there was also no chance of their husband getting someone pregnant or marrying (although unofficial gay 'marriages' between men did take place on some ships). Similarly, a gay dancer describes the way he was accepted at his seafaring lover's home as a sort of junior, temporary wife: 'After the war I had another sailor, he was married, got two children, I was godfather to the second one. While his wife was pregnant I used to go to the house and cook the meals for them. She knew I was gay. She'd be more upset if it was a woman. She didn't see me as a threat. . . . The kids always used to call me Uncle Sam. . . . I used to spend quite a lot of time there and then eventually she was due to have her [third] baby. She had it at home. I said to him well I may as well come home and look after you lot, while she's up there. He said, would you? I said yes, certainly.'[7]

Gay men were also often seen as 'cleaner' alternatives when compared to female sex workers for straight seafarers. Sometimes this idea was based on absolute ignorance. Chris recalls: 'I always remember a Royal Navy matelot saying to me "We like fucking with the queers because we won't catch anything off them." It seems extraordinary now.' Before the 1980s, sex with a gay man, even unprotected sex, was implicitly viewed as a form of 'safe sex'. This was partly due to some people's assumption that it was women *per se*, rather than a minority of women (usually sex workers who were not in a position to insist on customers using condoms), who transmitted diseases, as if females were somehow innately ruinous and that men had no agency in the infection's transmission.

That's not to say that all heterosexual seafarers were prepared to have gay sex. Sexuality was fairly fluid for some men and more rigid for others. For some, their orientation at any one time could have been a response to location and opportunity. For others, who had a firmer gay identity, such fluidity may have felt like a betrayal, as their former partners went back to women once they became available. Additionally, some seafarers would have never been tempted to have sex with another man, no matter how sexually frustrated they became.

Bisexual or married men were sometimes believed to be secretly gay or in denial about their true sexuality. However, it is impossible to ascertain the proportions of butch or married trade omees that were truly homosexual, bisexual or just 'getting their rocks off'. Some men simply wouldn't have thought it important to place any label on their sexual behaviour. Others may have used the excuse of being at sea in order to justify having gay sex, after coming from the often homophobic social climate on land. Some may have been unaware of the firm demarcation of categories such as *heterosexual* and *homosexual* (and the term *gay* was rarely used by working-class homosexual men anyway until after the 1970s), so labels of sexual identity weren't quite appropriate to them.

Some of the younger seafarers were often surprised by the sudden attention they received from men whom they had previously never suspected might be interested in them. When Ian joined the *Canberra* as a waiter in 1981, he became friendly with an older married sailor and they often spent their evenings together, drinking beer and playing backgammon in the married man's cabin – a framed picture of the man's wife placed reassuringly by the bedside. However, after about a couple of months, one night his friend unexpectedly made it clear that there were other ways that they could spend their evenings together. Ian was shocked and fled, ending the friendship. When the ship returned to Southampton, the man's wife was waiting at the port to take her husband out for lunch. Ian was unable to understand why a man could be happily married, yet also want

The sexual identities of seafarers could often be fluid, as this picture illustrates (Winter 1957). Picture courtesy of Wayne Stanley, Athletic Model Guild.

to have sex with other men. 'Of course, if it had happened to me a couple of years later, it wouldn't have been a problem,' he admits, 'but I was very naive then.'

These then are some of the partners that gay seafaring men had, and the identity boundaries that were most likely to be crossed. The question was how to go about having some kind of relationship in the space allowed.

Your place or mine?

How were sexual practicalities carried out? What did camp stewards do to attract their butch colleagues, and once they'd established contact, in what places were sexual relationships conducted? How did the residential workplace with its dormitories, its grapevine of highly observant colleagues, and its odd nooks only known to old hands affect what happened?

A good number of sexual relationships developed through social contact between men in their working spaces, mess rooms or crew bar. It was at these moments that, as Chapter 3 shows, shipmates might talk to each other in Polari about who was fanciable: their dolly eek (pretty face), bona riah (nice hair), fabulosa ogles (fantastic eyes) and shapely lallies (legs). Dave, a waiter, spotted his love, a fellow waiter, in the dining room. It was the eyelashes that did it. Robert, who was a purser, describes how on his first voyage someone made a pass at him. 'One of the second cooks who was a Polish guy came up to me and propositioned me, just hitting on the fact that I was gay. It took me back a bit, not that it worried me, but I just had to be careful.' Once a member of the Asian crew who came into the office, ostensibly to discuss wages, brushed up against his body and made his interest clear. Some were very quick off the mark – and direct rather than full of seductive lines. Bluebell, a sea queen, describes sailors coming 'up to you at the beginning of a voyage and saying "You're mine for the trip".'[8]

Ashore a gay man might spot new potential lovers in a club. The nearest thing to this, and the main cruising spot, at sea was the crew bar. In the evenings after work during the voyage, many male staff used the ship's bar (known as the Pig and Whistle on all ships) as their place to unwind, especially the waiters who had been politely serving supper until nine or ten at night. Relaxation with mates was important after hours of high-adrenalin emotional labour spent making the passengers happy.

The *queens* (camp seafarers) often occupied a long bench in the ship's bar. This bench, for obvious reasons, was affectionately known as 'the Meat Rack'. The young queens made sure that they looked their best every night, not wearing full drag, but with a full face of make-up on, ready to flirt and bat their eyes at the more masculine sailors. Martin describes his tactics: 'I'd see someone I liked, and I'd say "Oh vada girl, I'm going to have him for trade." And you did. I used to have my blue eyes heavy with mascara and I'd sit there fluttering my eyelids like Bette Davis. Invariably I'd end up getting them in a matter of three months, I mean, in those days there weren't any stewardesses on the ships, it was just men.' Sometimes there was no cruising but a long-standing practice that some queens had of taking a partner because of his occupation. 'You might walk on a ship', says Martin, 'and say "I always go with the chip-pie", which was the carpenter, and he might come round later and knock on your door. I mean he might be married, he might be straight, but it wasn't "gay" [to him].'

Occasionally relationships simply grew out of proximity, which could bring affection or simply be convenient. Allan Bérubé noticed this same pattern in wartime: 'Buddy relationships easily slipped into romantic and even sexual intimacies between men that they themselves often did not perceive to be "queer".'[9] This was particularly the case in the two-berth cabins (knowingly referred to by some seafarers as 'married quarters'), after a few drinks. Geoff, a writer for P&O, remembers how on one voyage he shared a two-berth cabin with a married man who became his lover.

With cabins being shared, some courtships were often conducted under the cynical or supportive eyes of colleagues. Most gay seafarers describe listening, or trying not to listen, to someone having sex in the bunk above. However, when your own cabin wasn't available, other places had to be found, including foreign hotels, or the open deck in darkness. Dave says that a favourite place to have sex was in a spare passenger cabin. 'You'd bribe someone to give you the key. Another alternative was to borrow a cabin from a friend who was on duty, or to tell your cabin-mate to make himself absent at a certain time. The point was to do it out of sight of officers.' But Allan Bérubé recounts a story which shows that even Naval officers were able to look the other way. Robert Gervais was on late watch on his destroyer when his 'lieutenant came by . . . both of us looked down at number two turret there and two guys were having sex. You could just see it in the moonlight. . . . He looked at me and said "Gervais, would you go down there and tell those men to move underneath the turret out of sight of the bridge." Not get their names or stop what's going on or bring them up to the bridge! . . . I thought "You old son-of-a-bitch! You're not as bad as they think you are."'[10]

Because Bill was himself an officer he found that sexual encounters had to be carefully managed during his time at sea in the 1970s. 'I think a lot of the stewards or the pantry boys could be openly gay and they could get away with it. But a few of them got the vibes. There was one of them who must have heard a rumour about me and he tried it on with me one night. You had to get rid of them pretty quick, because if someone's caught in bed with you, then it was a sackable offence.' Bill's first experience of gay sex was with the third engineer. 'I told him to apply for a job in the company I was in, and he came up for an interview and got it. I fucked about with him a bit in the cabin, trying to grope him and that, but he was always very worried in case we got caught, so it wasn't until afterwards, when he was in Aberdeen for a job, that we got it together.'

However, sometimes seafarers were prepared to take risks, especially if alcohol had been involved. Frank remembers a fling he had with an officer. 'I ended up rather the worse for Cuba Libra's in the officers quarters. When I sneaked back to my cabin afterwards I only had one of my own flip-flops on. I didn't know who the other one belonged to. I felt like Cinderella. Luckily Prince Charming returned mine two days later.'

Types of sex

Studs and queens

So what forms of sex occurred between men? Most of it took the form of the more traditional, 'vanilla' (that is, penetrative but not 'kinky') sex. 'There was sucking, fucking and rimming [licking the anus] says Chris. In the 1950s and 1960s some of the more extreme forms of gay sex had not yet been popularised and appeared not to happen often, if at all on cruise ships. Chris continues: 'Fisting [putting a fist up someone's anus] wasn't even thought about in those days, it just didn't exist. The nearest thing was when somebody stuck a finger up your arse. And tit work [pulling and biting someone's nipples, sometimes using clamps or clips], that didn't exist either, it wasn't even thought about.' The use of sexual props such as cock-rings, dildos and leather harnesses wasn't popular either, although such sexual toys just about existed by then. Had they been found by officers, they would have been somewhat incriminating, hence the use of other objects such as pepper-mills (see p. 103 below).

Most of the sex happened between two people as the close conditions on board ships didn't facilitate threesomes or group sex. That's not to say that group encounters never happened, but they were relatively rare. As a number of gay seafarers attested, group sex was more likely to occur ashore, in gay saunas, private rooms of clubs or male brothels (see Chapter 6).

Stereotypically, the acknowledged distinction between queens and the married or otherwise 'straight' trade is that the queens were passive sexual partners, getting fucked or 'servicing' their trade orally. That is, the usually straight man got a version of sex similar to conventional hetero-sexual behaviour: he penetrated a 'woman' or was sucked by 'her'. Importantly, this didn't require any change in his view of himself as a man. Sexual roles were strongly linked to gender roles. Indeed, some men may have believed that taking an active, penetrative or dominating sexual role with another man increased their own sense of masculinity.

'If you took it up the arse you were bitch and if you gave it you were butch, and you were more masculine if you gave it', says Chris. Queer theorist Tom Waugh refers to this sort of relationship as the *stud/queen binary*, a defining paradigm of 1960s constructions of queer masculinity.[11] The brooding, inarticulate, masculine stud is the object of desire, the one who is looked at, the silent, ambivalent, muscular guy posing in a jockstrap for 1950s beefcake porn, or film stars like James Dean in *Rebel Without a Cause* (1955), Joe Dallesandro in *Flesh* (1962) and Marlon Brando in *A Streetcar Named Desire* (1951). The queen, on the other hand, is talkative, gesticulating and humorous. He is a male Blanche Dubois, openly and flatteringly desiring 'masculine' men.

Before Gay Liberation in the 1970s, the stud/queen binary was particularly true for gay men from working-class backgrounds. The queens were outrageous, effeminate and 'obvious', while the studs were so butch that they often appeared to be heterosexual.[12] Their masculinity was so absolute, so assured, that it didn't actually matter if they had gay sex. The label of homosexuality, almost always linked to effeminacy, simply couldn't be pinned on to them. The relatively low social status of working-class gay men meant that they could have as much sex as they wanted and it wouldn't matter – their reputations weren't wedded to the higher echelons of the establishment. Middle-class gay men, however, tended not to be classed within the stud/queen binary, which is why so many of the officers on the ships tended not to participate in camp activities or have as much sex as the stewards and waiters – they had different sorts of reputations to think about.

While some of the men we interviewed agreed that the masculine or married men were only interested in their own orgasms and wouldn't be passive or reciprocate during gay sex, Frank claims the opposite: 'They'd have every kind of gay sex, it wasn't a sort of thing where they'd say "I don't do that" – when they were away at sea they'd do *absolutely every-thing* and then say "Oh no, please! I'm not gay but don't hurt me! I'm not gay." And then they'd go home to their wives and sometimes they'd invite their friends home for the weekend, to stay with their wives.'

Robert also notes that straight men were more sexually versatile than they are stereotyped to be. He had an 'affairette' with a Scottish man, Dennis, while he was on the *Chantala*. 'I was sun-bathing on deck and he was painting the railings while dressed in a dirty white boiler suit – open to the navel. I was watching him out of the corner of my eye and became much excited when I saw that he was sporting a very noticeable erection. Taking the bull by the horn, so to speak, I said "Would you like me to take care of that for you?" "Och! I thought you'd never ask," he replied. Dropping the paint-sodden wad he was holding in his fist (that's the way they paint on a ship – or did then) into the pot he walked over and knelt down so that his crotch was in my face. He took out his dick and waved it teasingly in front of my face. "We're going to have to be quick," he said "the Mate will be up to check on me at anytime." So I proceeded to give him one of the fastest blow-jobs I've ever given anyone – not that it would have taken too long anyway as he was in dire need of relief. That was the first of about two dozen times that I had sex with him. He wasn't gay but was a very willing and responsive lover. He was always happy to bring me off orally with a suck like a vacuum cleaner!'

Frank tells an apocryphal story about an incident involving a loudly heterosexual married man. The ship was anchored off Gibraltar when a launch arrived to take a crew member ashore for hospital treatment. 'It appeared that he had a very large peppermill stuck up his arse – desperate times and desperate measures. Of course most of the crew were looking over the side to see just who it was. They did cover his face to save the poor chap a great deal of embarrassment. He was probably the one who was decrying all the gays on the ship. I always wondered just how he explained the situation to the wife and family back in England. The ones who shouted the most were the ones with something to hide.' One aspect of conducting one's sex-life on board a ship was that privacy became a luxury that was sometimes dispensed with.

Safe sex?

One of the things that made gay-friendly ships in our period heavenly was that it was a particularly happy time in the history of curing sexually trans-mitted diseases. Between the 1920s and late 1970s, and particularly after the 1940s, the discovery of medications for sexually transmitted diseases had made them a much less serious issue than they had been for sailors in previous centuries. Sexually transmitted diseases such as syphilis were relatively rare; though no less fatal if neglected. Gonorrhoea was easily and quickly treated by penicillin. AIDS was simply not yet a concern.

'In those days,' says Chris, using cockney rhyming slang for *diseases*, 'coughs and sneezes didn't exist, and it was just the culture – "There's a lot of gays [in the Merchant Navy], you get your dick sucked, don't you?"' Men didn't worry as much about using condoms, or 'French letters' as they were known, with gay crewmates. None of the seafarers who were interviewed said that they used condoms for anal sex before the late 1970s.

And looking after sexual diseases was a routine part of seafaring culture, like dealing with sunburn, stomach upsets due to foreign food, and scalds or mangled fingers caused by kitchen accidents. Diseases, if they occurred, were just viewed by the men as an acceptable occupational risk. Short-arm inspections were routine after ships left foreign parts; newcomers on the ship often wondered why so many men were queuing up outside the doctor's cabin. Robert, a purser, acknowledges that sexually transmitted diseases were 'very common, particularly NSU (non-specific urethritis), and regarded as an occupational hazard. A few days after we left Mombassa, our first port of call in East Africa, each voyage the doctor would have a line of crewmen outside his surgery who had suddenly found themselves going through the roof as they pissed what felt like broken glass. On cargo ships the Chief Officer would deliver a handful of condoms to each man's cabin before we got into port. There was no stigma to having an STD, although one would be subjected to a certain amount of ribbing. It was difficult to keep hidden the fact that you had a dose of the clap when your shipmates could hear your cries as you took a leak!'

The kinds of VD adverts that appeared in the Seafarers' Union journal, *The Seaman* (and not other trade union journals). Picture courtesy of RMT.

If the ship didn't have a doctor aboard, or if you were too busy – or not too ill – you'd wait until you got home. 'It was the case that when you got in [to your home port], you go to the local hospital for a check-up', says Dave, a steward in the late 1950s and early 1960s. 'There wasn't anything dangerous, the worst was a few jabs of penicillin and you were up and running again.' Geoff agrees: 'I can't recall anyone having any sexual diseases. Perhaps people kept it quiet. It didn't enter one's mind. I suppose we were just lucky, I mean, syphilis and gonorrhoea were about, but you never worried about it.'

While he was aboard the *Kenya*, Robert found that he had pubic lice. 'The first time I ever got crabs (or mechanised dandruff as it was known) I was 17 and I went down to see the ship's doctor for some medication. He was often a bit drunk – he hardly needed to use anaesthetics as he could almost put you out with his breath! He gave me some lotion and told me to apply it twice a day. I applied this stuff on myself and that evening I happened to be dancing with the ship's nurse. We had to attend the dances and dance with the passengers. "What's the matter with you?" she said, "you're moving very funny." And I said, "This damn stuff the doctor gave me for crabs, it's burning me to pieces." She said, "Well maybe you didn't dilute it properly." I said, "What do you mean, dilute? He never said anything about dilute." "You're supposed to do it, one part to twenty parts water," she said. Well it got rid of the crabs, and a few layers of skin. So it worked.'

The relationship

What kinds of gay relationships happened on ships? Some were stable for the duration of the trip, some endured beyond and a very few became partnerships that lasted over a decade. The main categories are 'marriages', casual and secret encounters, and 'affairettes', as described below.

'Marriage'

While some relationships were brief or recreational, others had a high emotional content and a level of commitment that was intense, routine and styled on domestic monogamy. By their existence they implicitly and publicly refuted the damaging image of gay people that Allan Bérubé notes: '"perverts" obsessed by sex who could not love and were not worth loving.' Such a powerful stereotype robbed many gay men and women of the self-esteem and mutual respect upon which they could build long-term relationships and reinforced the notion that they were condemned to a life of loneliness and one-night stands.'[13] Established gay partnerships, squabble-filled though they sometimes were, cemented the shipboard gay community and allowed new understandings of what homosexuality meant.

Carol Warren identifies three models of long-term sexual relationship or 'marriage' within gay communities ashore. These are 'a faithful marriage modelled on that of heterosexual couples, a marriage with an open "arrangement" and a marriage with a three-way arrangement'.[14] In most cases, men on ships tried the first model. Martin describes his relationships with butch crewmen as being similar to a heterosexual marriage, with him taking the role of a traditional 'suburban housewife'. He and his husband often worked different shifts, but would arrange to meet up in the ship's bar after they had both finished, much as the straight man may have routinely met up with his wife in the local pub near closing time. 'On the passenger ships, they didn't stock spirits in the bars to begin with, so us queens would have a pint with a dash of lemonade in it. And if your husband had finished work before you, he'd have your pint lined up at the bar for you, as the bar might be closing by the time I got off.' Martin's quarters were used as a day room while his husband's cabin was where they spent their nights. 'If he was on watch you might make some

Camp seafarers provided services both domestic and sexual. This drawing, by Bryon Fear, is based on a photograph, taken at a shipboard fancy dress party courtesy of a private donor (anonymous).

sandwiches, I used to sit there knitting and making pots of tea, and I'd do his ironing for him and things like that. It was all quite camp really, you were sort of like an unpaid wife, the only payment we got was cock – not that we were complaining, it was lovely.' A popular drag costume for some seafarers was as a maid – at one party some men donned maid's outfits with the name 'Gypsy Tea Rooms' on their hats.

In that period, many married seafarers were used to having their wives (and before that, their mothers) do all or most of the domestic chores back home. They had their meals cooked for them, their clothes washed and ironed, and their spaces kept spic and span. On ships, as in the army, the domestic needs of the personnel were catered for. So meals were centrally prepared, cabins were cleaned by lower-grade personnel and laundry was tackled by the ship's laundry staff. Unsurprisingly, some seafarers were not used to carrying out other daily domestic routines. So one of the advantages of taking up with a sea queen, as well as the sex, was that the level of domestic service they received was very high. They got personalised attentions, such as uniforms being hand-pressed to taste. The standard was so impressive that an officer's wife might compliment her husband's steward as being such a good 'replacement' for her. Indeed, when one officer was ill ashore, his visiting steward was so concerned by the wife's standard of nursing care that he moved in, so that the job could be done 'properly'. Domestic abilities could therefore be one of the areas where rivalry between a gay seafarer and the wife of his sexual partner was expressed, even at a distance. High standards were one way a gay steward might demonstrate his 'superiority' to the 'real' wife.

As many of the more openly gay seafarers were bedroom stewards, kitchen staff or waiters in any case, they were accustomed to preparing food, tidying cabins and making everything look nice and presentable. The care-taking aspect of such relationships often balanced out in different ways, with the butch married men often being fiercely protective of their male 'wives'. 'I was in London, in the East End, with my boyfriend,' recalls Martin, 'and these three young fellas, they'd be called louts nowadays, shouted at me, "Hey! You bag!" and all that. So my fella walked up to them and said, "Hey listen, that's my missus you're talking to. Piss off if you don't want to get filled in." He was quite big, my boyfriend, in more ways than one. And these lads were terrified and they ran off.'

Long-term or intense relationships were sometimes marked with an unofficial ceremony with wedding rings being exchanged. Weddings between crewmates were conducted onboard, usually in secret – the penalty for being found out could be instant dismissal. 'I was on a cargo ship,' says Geoff, 'and one of the catering boys and one of the engineers put on a marriage ceremony. They were caught and asked to leave.'

Martin was more fortunate in that he was never penalised for his relationships. In his experience, a 'marriage' was often acknowledged by many of the crew, with the partners receiving nothing more than good-humoured ribbing or sarcasm. 'They'd say to him "Your missus is in there looking for you." ' 'If two people were getting together,' says Dave, 'there'd be all sorts of people coming up to you saying, "Congratulations on your wedding and marriage" and all this nonsense. It was very nice.' Couples would often wait until they could both get jobs on the same ship, so they could be together.

As in every marriage, in shipboard 'marriages' there were arguments, separations and divorces, particularly resulting from possessiveness. Domestic rows sometimes took place very publicly in corridors, and in one story, in the passenger's dining room. Break-ups could even be noticed by the captain if the forlorn party took to drink or violence to ameliorate his loss. And senior colleagues, as Chapter 7 shows, could be helpful in enabling the unhappy pair to move to new homes on the ship.

Casual and secret encounters

A good proportion of the sex on board ships occurred secretly and briefly. As Bérubé noted with wartime relationships too, if you were on the move, it made sense not to put yourself in a position where your heart could be broken[15] – and anyway, temporary thrills could add to the attraction. Such relations were, in Warren's terms, more like the relations between a producer and a consumer, more objective than the closer, primary, almost familial liaisons described in the previous sections.[16]

Discretion could be an important aspect. Chris, speaking of the late 1950s and early 1960s says, 'Most gays in this culture, kept their mouths shut. They didn't rush around telling everybody. And I only found out gradually that other people, other deck crew, would do a turn as well.' It was a gentleman's agreement between queen and trade – gossip would only have lessened the chances of it happening again. The nominally heterosexual men had their masculine reputations to uphold, and some may have felt guilty or confused after enjoying sex with another man.

'People used to wake you up in the middle of the night, people you'd never expect,' remembers Frank. 'If people knew your cabin and what time you finished duty, plus your cabin-mate was on a different shift to you, someone's hand would come up.' 'If someone came to your cabin, you knew what they'd come for, and that was that,' Geoff explains. There was often no need for words. 'And strangely enough, it happened more often than you would think. Particularly when you're stuck on a cargo ship, or sometimes, a passenger ship. The assistant chief steward had the cabin next to mine. He was a nice, good-looking guy: straight, and he mixed with straights although he didn't mind gays. And then one day he said to me "Hey Geoff, come in the cabin", and I popped in there, and he'd got a big stiffie, a hard-on. He promptly wanted me to suck him off which I did. He said "I don't want to fuck you, I won't fuck you." But had I played my cards right he would have fucked me. And now this happened occasionally, not a lot, not infrequently, occasionally.'

However, for inexperienced, naive, shy or closeted seafarers, especially officers, the unspoken nature of gay sex in the Merchant Navy meant that sex could be a furtive, frustrating affair. Alan, who was a 16-year-old apprentice radio officer in the 1950s, found himself in a sexual relationship with another apprentice called Jack, who was the same age as him. The sex was composed of 'a quick wank – it was almost like playing doctors and nurses. By that I mean that it was an undirected sexual exploration. Very much "dick-centred" with no purpose beyond that in mind.' However, Jack was sharing a cabin with another apprentice, and it became obvious to Alan that they had talked about him because the other apprentice wanted to 'play doctors and nurses' with Alan as well. The other apprentice wasn't gay, he just felt jealous at being left out. So Alan's sex-life at sea was simply a continuation of the encounters he'd had as a schoolboy: occasional bouts of mutual masturbation with no real emotional attachment. In the eight years he was at sea, he had no long-term relationships with any men, other than these furtive encounters. 'That isn't all that I wanted, but it was all I got, because I was too shy to say what I wanted. I was too scared to say it to the wrong person.' Fear of exposure, ridicule and dismissal meant that Alan didn't venture out of the closet very often.

The most closeted seafarers were known as *Black Market* or later, when the word 'queen' was used more often, *BMQs* which stood for *Black Market Queens*. These were men who were not open about their sexuality. They were available but they would do it very covertly. It didn't imply that they sold their services and they seemed to have only had occasional relationships.

Several of the gay seafarers who were interviewed spoke of *phantom gobblers* or *phantoms*. Martin describes what they did: 'On the cargo ships, you'd always get a phantom who may be a black market queen or some bold queen, and when the fellas were sleeping she'd go round and lift the sheets and give them a blow job, and that was called a phantom gobbler.' They only appeared infrequently and Chris thinks it may have been the way some men dealt with their reticence. The identity of the phantom gobbler was generally known, but wasn't often made public.

Christmas party. Flirtations between men were common, although they didn't have to lead to anything. Picture courtesy of Bill.

'People knew, we knew who it was, but people didn't say. They just enjoyed the pleasure until someone caught them at it,' says Frank.

Clearly, the phantom gobbler would have to be careful about who he offered his services to, lest he pick an unwilling partner. 'He'd get a black eye once or twice but it still didn't stop them,' says Frank. But mainly they were welcome nocturnal visitors and their semi-anonymity added to the frisson. Perhaps some crewmen were secretly grateful that the phantom gobbler existed, affording them the occasional sexual release. They could pretend to be asleep during the phantom's ministrations, so that they could disown any responsibility of actively participating in, or enjoying, gay sex.

Flirtations were another kind of relationship. Many didn't get anywhere but they were part of the fun of the trip, unless they brought trouble from a jealous partner. By comparison to these little encounters, however, there were the most common forms of relationship: short-term affairs.

Affaires

What was more usual for many gay men in the Merchant Navy was neither long-term relationships lasting many years, or the odd unspoken brief encounter, but a series of short-term sexual relationships, *affaires* or *affairettes* between seafarers. These could last for anything from a few days to the duration of a voyage or several voyages.[17]

With so many attractive, young, potentially available men present on every ship, it could be quite difficult to maintain a long-term relationship, especially if partners were posted on different ships. There were just too many other distractions, particularly on the vast passenger ships that contained a large stewarding workforce, most of whom would be gay. 'With up to a thousand men onboard in those days, you could get a sore dick,' says Chris, who had as many as three lovers a night. 'There weren't long-term affairs, it just wasn't the atmosphere for it. It was too easy to fall over and have someone else.' Dave agrees, 'The crew used to change every couple of months, especially if you were cruising for two or three weeks somewhere, you'd get new people signing on, so there was always new talent coming on board.'

In these types of relationship the grapevine was important. A seafarer who was young and cute, or butch and muscular, could easily find himself the centre of attention, as the older, more sexually experienced guys fought over him. Sex could easily become a contest – who could be had, and how many men could you get? Some queens didn't like to see anybody else enjoying themselves, or worried that they were getting old and past it. Sex was a way of validating their own attractiveness. It kept things from getting boring and allowed gay crew mates to inhabit a constant soap opera. 'Once you set sail, that was it. It could be a month to Australia,' says Dave. 'People would pass from hand to hand, so to speak.'

Seafarers nursed secret crushes, or were devastated when their current partner moved on to someone else. The jealousy was particularly bad whenever someone new came on board. 'We used to get some of the lads straight from sea-school,' remembers Ian. 'They were only seventeen or eighteen, and if someone had them first, it would cause problems.' Rivalry over new partners was not uncommon. On the face of it, this sexual competitiveness was no different from what happened in shore-side gay bars. 'If you're the new face in a bar, then it's no different from a new face walking up the gang-plank. They'll get lots of offers from people to show them the ropes,' says Ian. 'A couple of times, I've warned new people coming on, I've just said, "you know, be careful", because there's some queens who are a bit ruthless. And some were very ruthless.'

Unsurprisingly, the concept of relationship counselling wasn't common in the 1950s and 1960s, and in any case, gay relationships simply weren't supposed to happen on the ships. If you didn't have friends to talk to, then you were supposed to sort out your relationship problems yourself and just get on with it. In any case, there was a masculine culture of not exposing feelings or seeing emotional problems as resolvable through discussion. There was no 'ship's counsellor' or mediator who could help to solve problems, although a ship's nurse, doctor or sympathetic parental figure might be approached. If a relationship blew up in someone's face when they were on a long voyage, it could be difficult to create emotional distance between them and their ex-partner. For some, it felt as if the only place they could go was over the side. Others, however, confided in those gay colleagues who liked to play an agony aunt role.

'My god, they used to be territorial,' remembers Frank. 'And not always the prettiest got fought over. The jealousy was frightening. There was one who sailed on a cargo ship, he murdered his lover because he found him in bed with someone else. So sadly he went to prison in Australia.'

Carol Warren noted a pattern in the gay men she studied that is relevant to men on ships: '... cruising and its outcomes provides one of the bases for sociability itself – the telling of sexual anecdotes'.[18] Because of the gossip and the fear that their latest partner would be taken away from them, some queens were all the more careful to keep their latest partner under wraps, and woe-betide anyone who spread gossip about them. Frank recalls how once he had been sharing a cabin with a very good-looking young man called Joe, although there had been nothing sexual between them. 'Joe was very friendly with a chap called Keith, who had subsequently bought him a watch. And it transpired that someone had told everyone that Keith had bought Joe this watch. On a ship they can't wait to gossip. So Keith thought that I had said something about the watch, which I had not. It turned out that Joe had been bragging about the watch himself. I was asleep in my cabin and Keith came in and grabbed my throat. Luckily the people in the next cabin heard and they dragged him off me. I'm always more sinned against than sinning.'

As the above paragraphs show, sexual predatory situations developed on ships, whatever people's sexual orientation. Having said that, however, the idea of the queen as always-predatory should be dispelled. 'I think that out of all of them, there's only been two that I really wanted,' discloses Frank. 'There was a Scottish boy who lived in the next cabin along from me. He was very nice but he was straight. He used to masturbate six times every day, very highly sexed. And you can imagine this, you're next door – every night. I was tempted, but I got to the stage where I didn't want to spoil the friendship with him.' And there was often a tension over whether to be mates or lovers. Sex 'upped the ante' and created intensity, not least because it was so associated with roles and identity.

But for all that we have described sexual connection and intimacy on ships, a surprising number of men did not have relationships with men on ships, but ashore. For example, one waiter was 'married' to a postman, whom he missed. On ships, some gay men found not their soulmate for life, but friendship – and lots of sex.

Many ways of loving

Gay relationships at sea ranged from casual flings to 'marriages'. They could take place with other members of the ship's complement, sometimes across identity boundaries such as status, age and ethnicity, but most likely across gender, with queens having straight trade as partners. And the triggers ranged from romantic desire to sexual lust to pent-up physical need to simple availability: a happy coincidence of the time and place being right. Often these relationships took place within the context of friendliness of affinity between members of the same team.

In answer to the questions at the start of this chapter we can offer the following summary. Despite the stereotype that gay male relations are sexual and casual and even exploitative, the stories we have heard suggest that there was friendship, and even tenderness and romance. It was not a case of 'Hello, goodbye, whatever your name was.' Certainly some men had a lot of relationships, because they were making hay while the sun shone. But this was often not callous or cavalier, but simply taking jubilant advantage of a long-awaited freedom, in a culture that was similar to the wartime spirit of 'live-for-today' described by Bérubé.[19] Some men did have a 'girl' or boyfriend in several ports. Interestingly, they did not usually return to them for repeat visits. Sometimes love *did* grow out of friendships, only sometimes between men who shared cabins. That affection had many forms, including brotherly support. It could be familial. Occasionally the more romantic love was only expressed after they had stopped sailing together. Space and distance enabled expression.

What is remarkable is that situational bisexuality was accepted. Sociologist Georg Simmel argues that secret and stigmatised communities, such as gay ones, often need members to be loyal and committed to it, in order to keep the secret.[20] By definition, bisexual men on ship were only *partially* committed to the gay community, though often party to its secrets. But the 'full-time' gay members of that world did not treat them with the hostility that we might expect 'part-timers' or 'traitors' to face. Maybe this was because 'trade' men, particularly those in the catering department, were primarily part of an equally important community: that of their (denigrated) gang on the ship. And perhaps it was also because lower-grade staff such as stewards shared a common enemy: the officer class who could clamp down on gay activity. And maybe, too, they were just too desirable to ostracise.

Of the loving and sexual relationships that did occur on ships, the differences between them and those ashore in the UK were as follows. They were frequently observed, despite the fact that some seafarers tried to keep them as tightly guarded secrets. Some seafarers couldn't help boasting about their latest conquest to their friends, while in other cases, it was obvious when two guys were going with each other. The time spent alone together in each other's cabins, the grunts and groans that could be heard through metal bulkheads that conducted sounds disturbingly clearly and the way they acted around one another provided all-too-obvious clues. With everyone living in such close quarters, gossip could spread quickly, and some men liked nothing more than figuring out who was available and who was having sex with whom. With everyone potentially available to everyone else, this multiplied the chances for intrigue and jealousy onboard the ships; in that sense they are similar to the sex that takes place in other institutions, such as boarding schools or the armed services. In the case of stewards, relationships were conducted within a largely benign and supportive context, in the kind of intensive *gay* community that would not exist ashore in the UK for another few decades. Gay relationships were seen as normal, not shameful or even unusual. However, for officers, it was different. Their relationships were often covert, difficult to sustain and usually far less frisky and parodic than those of the queens. The point was that the field was so big: a ship could be full of hundreds of men willing to have a gay relationship of one sort or another. No wonder, then, that long-term, monogamous relationships could be difficult to maintain in an atmosphere of unprecedented temptation.

Many of these relationships on passenger and cruise ships happened in a resort-like space surrounded by people in vacation mood, so they had a special frisson. And they felt temporary, which added additional spice to matters. On top of that, they occurred in an atmosphere that was often carnival-like, irreverent and transgressive, as described in Chapter 2. Queens could have relationships in female clothes and in 'feminine' ways. In their spectacularly camp identity they could be worshipped by the sea-borne equivalent of Stage Door Johnnies, not rejected as dirty degenerates. That were, in their parlance, 'fantabulosa'.

For many gay people afloat, sex was fun and extremely welcome when the opportunity presented itself. But friendship and self-respect were also important. In any case, there were plenty of other diversions for gay seafarers to indulge in, as the following chapter reveals.

Notes

1. This is argued by Warren, C.A.B. (1974) *Identity and Community in the Gay World*, John Wiley and Sons, New York, p. 70.
2. Kris Kirk, and Heath, Ed (1984) *Men in Frocks*, Gay Men's Press, London, p. 32.

3. *The Sociology of Georg Simmel*, ed. and trans. K.H. Woolff, see Simmel, G. (1950) Free Press, Glencoe, IL, p. 369.

4. Interview M0097, by Sheila Jemima, Southampton City Heritage, Oral History Section.

5. Kirk and Heath, *Men in Frocks*, p. 31.

6. Story from Sheila Jemima to JS, 27 July 2002.

7. A dancer (unnamed) (1991) 'A Dancer's Life', in Porter, K. and Weeks, J. (eds), *Between the Acts: Lives of Homosexual Men 1885–1967*, Routledge, London and New York, p. 105.

8. Kirk and Heath, *Men in Frocks*, p. 32.

9. Bérubé, A. (1991) *Coming Out under Fire: The History of Gay Men and Women in World War Two*, Penguin, London, p. 188.

10. Ibid., p. 190.

11. Waugh, T. (1996) 'Cockteaser', in Doyle, J., Flatley, J. and Muñoz, J.E. (eds), *Pop Out: Queer Warhol*, Duke University Press, Durham, NC, p. 54.

12. Newton, E. (1993) 'Role Models', in Bergman, D. (ed.), *Camp Grounds: Style and Homosexuality*, University of Massachusetts Press, Amherst, MA, p. 43.

13. Bérubé, *Coming Out under Fire*, p. 18.

14. Warren, *Identity and Community*, p. 72.

15. Bérubé, *Coming Out under Fire*, p. 119.

16. Warren, *Identity and Community*, p. 112.

17. The length of a voyage varied. The shortest ones were two-day mini-cruises, then there was the three-week hop from England to New York and back, while longer journeys, such as the trip to the Antipodes or the Far East could last several months.

18. Warren, *Identity and Community*, p. 71.

19. Bérubé, *Coming Out under Fire*, p. 98.

20. Simmel, *Sociology of Georg Simmel*, p. 348.

Chapter 5

Sequins, Satin and Stilettos

Camp sites

'Camp ... is one of the ways we have managed to make sense of a world which at best tolerates and at worst exterminates us ... one of our most fearsome weapons ... and one of our most enriching experiences.'
Andy Medhurst[1]

Classically, 'the sailor' in gay iconography[2] is uniformed in masculine style: dazzlingly white trousers are revealingly tight round the thighs; his glistening chest is muscled and hairy. Maybe he's even tattooed with a swallow, a symbol associated with gay sailors. Gay images of a desirable US sailor show him in a pert white hat, a brooding slash of hair falling down over smoky eyes. He gazes out with gravitas – and can clearly pack a punch.

However, a passenger ship was precisely the place where many gay men could be the opposite: be-frocked, be-wigged and be-jewelled. In fact, such floating hotels provided a space where the more camp gay men could 'become' the kind of girl that such a butch sailor might fancy.

Passenger, and particularly cruise, vessels were almost a gay space waiting to happen. They were situations of spectacle and carnival where clothes mattered to almost everyone and where trying on other people's identities – sanctioned by numerous fancy dress parties – was usual. Passengers obediently packed the garb that the etiquette books recommended,[3] and critically taking note of other people's frocks (and affairs) was a major pastime aboard. The poem, 'A Cruising Sidelight' published in the journal of the UK seafarers' union indicates this:

Mary had a little dress,
A dainty bit and airy;
It didn't show the dirt a bit
But, gee, how it showed Mary![4]

The cover of one of the US gay porn novels about sailors, 1987. Picture courtesy of HIS Surrey Books, New York.

The opposite? Cross-dressing on ship in the 1980s. Picture courtesy of private donor.

Recreational clothes weren't important to just the passengers. The ship's complement, on duty, was in ceremonial dress too. All the crucial and minute gradations of rank and job were evidenced by the tightly regulated uniforms, from the embroidered baton on the sleeve of the ship's orchestra conductor to the miles of gold spaghetti worn on a commodore's sleeve.

What might we mean by 'camp'? Camp is a concept that is extremely difficult to define, as its meanings have changed over time, but some modern theorists have come up with a range of ideas. In 1966 Susan Sontag described it as a 'form of aestheticism', claiming it was playful, detached and apolitical.[5] For Philip Core it was 'the lie that tells the truth',[6] while for Andrew Ross in 1993, camp was something that 'challenged ... legitimate definitions of taste and sexuality', but it was also 'tied to the capitalist logic of development that governed the mass culture industries'.[7] For Scott Long, camp was a 'moral activity' which allows gay men to 'parody the forces of oppression',[8] whereas Moe Meyer redefines camp as 'political and critical' and a 'solely queer discourse'.[9] Andy Medhurst disagrees, saying that some camp queens could be 'frighteningly reactionary'.[10] Whether camp is viewed as political, apolitical or both at the same time, it certainly appears to have been used as a framework which allowed seafaring queens to construct themselves and their view of the world, based on ironic, mocking and self-mocking humour.

If camp was a theory, then drag (or aspects of it) could perhaps be seen as one of its practices. When seafarers dragged up they not only put on feminine clothes, but they adopted or exaggerated gestures, mannerisms, speech patterns and behaviour that were a way of affecting a whole identity. When we refer here to drag in reference to seafarers, it involved dressing in female clothes. However, more recent ideas about drag see it as involving the wearing of any form of clothing to create a new identity. Drag does not have to be cross-gendered, so a gay man who puts on a military uniform to go to a nightclub could be wearing 'army drag'. However, Andy Medhurst sees camp as 'above all, the domain of queens. It is a configuration of taste codes and a declaration of feminine intent.'[11]

Some writers see camp as more political than drag. Carol Warren argues:

[Drag] is always a parody and an exaggeration of all the things that imply theatrical or pin-up femininity in our society: long ball-gowns and gloves, towering

Comical drag: Elder Dempster crew and passengers enjoy a show where cross-dressed men do not attempt to pass as gay. Picture courtesy of The Cowden Collection.

and elaborate coiffures, glittering jewellery, colourful and heavy makeup, deep cleavage, or lots of leg showing. . . . Drag is unserious and fun, or it becomes a way of life, and therefore an identity. Whereas transsexuals and transvestites wear female clothes because their very self-image depends on it, gay people get into drag to celebrate the ritual occasions of the gay world, like Halloween.[12]

Camp can take many forms, so while we'd argue that all seafarers who put on a frock were being camp to some extent, they would not have all affected the same camp identity. A seafarer posing as a haughty dowager duchess would possess a different identity from one with a nickname like Dirty Gerty. Both would be camp, but in different ways.

Donning fancy dress for special events had been a normal part of shipboard life since before the start of the twentieth century. Fancy dress was worn by passengers and crew at parties that were designed to pass the time; by passengers and crew during the Neptune ceremony, a theatrical initiation rite which took place when the people crossed the equator for the first time; and by crew who were part of the foo-foo bands (informal groups of seafarers with some musical talent and instruments, who had a pantomime performative style). In all three cases, cross-dressing occurred. Photographs and histories of liner life show that at parties, men might dress as anything from princesses such as Cleopatra, to milkmaids, nurses and housewives. Status, and sometimes race, as well as gender were

Dressed up for a shipboard party. Picture courtesy of Ian.

changed. In initiation rites, an officer would be garbed in King Neptune's robes and some men might be attired as mermaids, as photographs and scripts attest. Shipboard photos show men wearing a cocktail frock with hob nailed boots or a flowery summer dress with a beard, deliberately not seeking to pass themselves off as women. Such comic dress was akin to the kind of radical drag that was used in the 1970s by Gay Liberation activists as a political statement, a rebuttal of the usual accoutrements of femininity. For example, at the 1971 feminist demonstration against the Miss World beauty contest, members of the Gay Liberation Front (GLF) protested at stereotyped gender roles: 'One guy was dragged up as Miss Ulster swathed in bloody bandages. Others were attired in parodies of Miss World outfits like Miss Used, Miss Conceived and Miss Treated, they paraded on an alternative catwalk outside the main entrance to the hall.'[13] Carol Warren argues that though comical, radical drag has a deeply serious intention: to shock the straight world, to revolt against the fact that the straight world has power over the gay world.[14] However, the goals of the men who played in foo-foo bands appeared not to be plausible impersonations of women but comical parodies of feminine stereotypes. They did not, apparently, have a radical intention.

Clothing is a key form of communication. On ships it allowed people to manage the impressions they made on others, and conveyed how they wanted to be treated (which might have been quite different from the way they were normally seen on land). It was a particularly urgent requirement for voyages on passenger ships which, as temporary situations, were governed by uncertainty and established rituals. People on ships needed particular clothes for security. The right garments (or lack of them) could be a key factor in determining whether someone was found attractive. So it's not surprising that clothes mattered on board a passenger ship. Nor is it surprising that people used clothes in this situation to try on new identities. The weekly fancy dress parties were an opportunity for people temporarily to claim to be anybody or explore alternative aspects of their usual selves. So, where better for a wannabe female impersonator to go than a place where he could finally get into the glitziest of frocks, and find men who wanted to get into what lay beneath them.

For British people living in the 1950s and 1960s, apart from ships, the only other places where cross-dressing was sanctioned were the theatre (particularly pantomime) and seaside resorts, such as Blackpool, which had a 'May Queen' carnival that involved dragging up.[15] Significantly, these resorts were also sites of recreation and spectacle. As a writer on cross-dressing, James Gardiner observes, 'just one of the symptoms of the rampant homophobia of the 1950s was the virtual disappearance of drag acts from the theatres and music halls. The *Soldiers in Skirts* found alternative jobs, frequently as sea queens; the more talented discovered there was still a place for them in pantomime.'[16] However, many drag queens also worked on the gay pub drag scene, as Kirk and Heath offer in their different view. Men who'd been in revues such as *Forces Showboat*, *Forces in Petticoats*, *Showboat Express* and *Misleading Ladies*[17] became the stars in some of the East End pubs that seafarers frequented (because they were the first ones that were encountered when they left the ship). An example of such a pub includes the Round House at King George V dock, near the site of the current City airport, remembers Chris, a steward.[18]

The shipping industry offered slightly more regular employment, where camping it up was an amateur pleasure. Models for camp queens were available in the literature of that period, such as 'The Queen is dead' in Hubert Selby's 1957 novel *Last Exit to Brooklyn* and Devine and other queens in Jean Genet's *Our Lady of the Flowers* (1963). Camp behaviour on ships appears to have become more popular during the 1960s and 1970s. In the early 1960s Chris recalled camp guys wearing just feminised versions of male clothes, for example a shirt tied at the waist. 'Basically cross-dressing did happen, but to a lesser degree. They used to dress quite effeminately, you know, scarves round the neck and their shirts tied up in the front to show their midriff.'

Not every gay man who worked in the Merchant Navy wore drag or camped it up. Some were not even out, as previous chapters have shown. But for anyone who wanted to explore the more feminine and performative aspects of his identity, a ship was an ideal place in which to do so, and that included the men who considered themselves to be heterosexual.

Three situations for cross-dressing

For the men who wanted to put on women's clothes there were three cross-dressing situations on ship, each associated with place and context. In descending order of intensity and performativity, they were: first, public events such as shows and parties; secondly, semi-public flauntings in working areas such as showers; third, private behaviour in cabins, a situation that could exclude heterosexuals.

Shows

In the postwar decades, ships' shows, also known as 'concert parties', were the main space where gay seafarers could turn drag performance into

Seafarers might wear the most glamorous of dresses at concert parties. Picture courtesy of private donor (anonymous).

a high art. Wearing tiaras, false bosoms, sequins and stilettos was *de rigueur*. Comedy and musical numbers, which were often parodies, comprised the main features of these shows. It is here that the sea queens could become arch pantomime dames, brassy chorus girls, grand divas, raunchy comediennes and classic thespians for their audience. Allusions to popular culture, such as current or camp movies, were common. Ian recalls: 'We rewrote *The Wizard of Oz*, just put modern songs into that as well. Lots of camp numbers, lots of referrals to life on the ship, slagging off the passengers, and the officers.' Interestingly, drag queens also used their performances in order to make fun of the ship's 'untouchables' – people they wouldn't normally dare to insult publicly since, under any other circumstances, it would have resulted in a reprimand or dismissal, as Chapter 7 shows. However, the humorous and artificial nature of the performance sanctioned such open displays of rudeness. Drag queens are *expected* to be caustic and insulting. They can therefore get away with saying what no one else dares to say, perhaps because they are considered to be at the bottom of the gender hierarchy.

Many of the drag acts were inspired by real-life actresses and singers. 'You'd have idols,' says Martin. 'Barbra Streisand had just come in then, the queens doing drag would be taking off Barbra Streisand . . . you might get queens miming to her.' Replication of larger-than-life stars was a key feature, as was an odd silence by the performers. Queens moved their lips in time to the divas and camp radio entertainers who were such import-ant models for gay men in covert times – men like Kenneth Williams and Stanley Baxter, says Frank. 'We did all those new revues that had been in London, miming to them all. If any new show opened on Broadway some-body always bought the LP. It was very difficult to play records onboard ship as it was a different electric supply and you had to get a 60 cycle pulley to slow down the turntable. If it was rough weather you couldn't play them at all. I always had about 100 LPs to take on a four-month trip. Then, fortunately, audio tapes became available.'

Subverting existing songs, making camp meanings out of heterosexual musicals like *South Pacific* and *Seven Brides for Seven Brothers*, express-ing identities through shared jokes, *being* a plausible imitation of a movie or musical idol and admiring their colleagues' ability to impersonate women, were ways that some gay men not only proclaimed but explored their identity. Such behaviour also enabled the gay subculture to create and establish a community based around shared knowledge.

The musical content of the shows varied, as did the sophistication of the humour. Geoff remembers that on his P&O ships in the 1950s such con-cert parties 'were mainly drag things' which did not include much singing but 'little sketches'. Chris, a steward, ship's writer and storekeeper around the turn of the 1950s remembers them as drag shows: 'sort of mimed basi-cally, to the old Ethel Merman songs, that sort of thing. Very clever, not tacky at all.' As James Gardiner points out, 'the 1950s saw the emergence of the most glamorous dames ever seen, still playing for laughs, but look-ing gorgeous'.[19] They were a far cry from pantomime dames of the Cinderella's Ugly Sisters sort, played since the 1880s 'for laughs by fre-quently straight actors presenting grotesque caricatures of womanhood that had little to do with attempting plausible impersonation'.[20]

Shows were non-professional events organised by seafarers. They could be presented as simply light-hearted entertainment but actually functioned as a key place of camp self-outing. And such outing often happened. Companies differed in their arrangements but there was usually at least one show a week on a voyage, often at weekends. Sometimes they were fairly improvised events, with not much time for rehearsal. Passenger shows were more usual on long trips like those to Australia when there was time to rehearse and present something of a higher standard than that which would have been accepted if it was just performed for other col-leagues. But as Ian remembers from the 1980s, 'We did about two big shows a year, for the crew, but the passengers used to come in [too].' There was usually no formal stage with footlights. Sometimes the stage could be little more than a curtain in the mess room or old flags.

Sometimes the curtain was makeshift, and little more than a bed cover. Picture courtesy of private donor (anonymous).

On this Cunard ship, the curtain was made from an old White Star line's flag. Picture courtesy of the Oral History Unit, Southampton City Council.

As shipboard entertainment became more sophisticated, crew shows were able to borrow stage and fancy curtains. Picture courtesy of Ian.

These shows had grown from older traditions. The ribaldry and the delightedly risqué tone were akin to the troop shows put on by and for service personnel in the Second World War. These shows routinely had men taking female parts. The slot for shipboard shows existed because of the enduring emphasis on self-entertainment aboard the ships. These shows were an institution derived from the established tradition of sailors making their own entertainment (dancing hornpipes, playing instruments picked up in foreign countries, etc.), and an *outré*, below-stairs descendent of the older tradition of concert parties above stairs. They had a connection with the seaside tradition of pierrots, black and white minstrels and concert parties. From at least the early nineteenth century passengers on ships had entertained each other with highly ritualised – and predictable – extracts from middle-class appropriations of High Culture ashore. They might involve a classical piano recital, a poetry recitation, drawing-room songs such as 'Come into the Garden, Maude' (sung without any *doubles entendres*), extracts from Dickens, an occasional comical monologue taken from P.G. Woodhouse and ending with the National Anthem. Such events were, of course, attended in evening dress. The main difference between these older shows of the nineteenth century and the drag shows that were typical of the mid-late twentieth century was that the former were respectable and the latter were iconoclastic: they referred to images, such as stars, and were enjoyed *because* they were disreputable.

There was an additional touch of history. By borrowing from the tradition that such shows were for charity (and taking a collection), gay seafarers established their shows as being socially useful, and not just an opportunity for a public romp in petticoats. Ian, a waiter from the 1980s, remembers: 'We used to charge other crew members to come and see and put all the proceeds to the RNLI.' The Royal National Lifeboat Institution and seafarers' orphanages were the two most popular charities on ships. This move demonstrates how much gay performers were aware of the boundaries within which they could work. Additionally, shows were also diluted for the passengers' edification. 'The crews got the dirty version while the passengers got the cleaned-up one,' Lorri Lee recalls, of her days on the Royal Mail *Andes* to South America in the 1960s.[21] Public nudity or portrayals of gay sexual acts would not have been acceptable, even as part of drag or camp performances. And if there was one thing gay seafarers knew, it was where the line was drawn and how to respect that line.

Semi-public flauntings

The more frank material was permissible at private shows, where those 'below stairs' could let out their feelings about those 'above'. Ian points out that such exclusive performances had a more carnival-like nature in that the 'low' seafarer asserted the power to lampoon the 'high' (passengers and officers) – hidden parts were revealed and ideas of 'proper' behaviour challenged. This was made easier by access to new technology during the 1980s: 'We also made videos and little mini films which we used to show in the crew mess. [They were] things like "the life on a ship". And [we'd] rip the passengers off, slag them off, and be really outrageous. We used to make all these videos and show them to the crew, that was great fun.' These private shows were less polite than the public *Wizard of Oz* performance described above.

These public but crew-only events were part of the underground subculture of the ship where workers refuted the lowly status ascribed to them. Sometimes this was achieved by replicating the elite's behaviour, in sophisticated private *soirées* and parties. However, this was often a non-parodic emulation of the more well-to-do passengers' High Culture. The hallmark was the serious wearing of elbow-length gloves, rather than clown's red noses and bosoms made of rolled-up socks. *Soirées* appear to have included mainly gay people, unlike other events where quite a lot of straight people joined in. They were exclusive. Such *soirées* didn't involve on-stage ritual and comedy, although dressing up and acting female parts sometimes occurred. Martin, a steward, explains: 'There were some [gay

Seafarers could look like the aristocracy. Picture courtesy of private donor.

men] we'd call blasé queens, that are more upmarket than the common ones. ... They would have parties, and you were usually sent invitations. ... It was called a *soirée* then, you see, and you were invited to different *soirées*. ... If you were in with the in-crowd you went to the in-parties.'

Even some parties were themed and ritualised. Frank, a steward, remembers a special, regular kind of party they had on the *Canberra* in the 1960s. Some of the gay stewards that he knew lived in a cluster of six cabins, organised so that they could finish work late without disturbing each other's sleep. The cabins were collectively known as Quality Street, which was also the name of a Thackeray novel and a new brand of mixed chocolates, with a crinolined lady escorted by gallant officer in tight breeches on its packaging. *Soirées* were held there regularly. 'It was called the Fortnightly Club. They'd have a party every fortnight, and have a theme with all six cabins open. Music in only one cabin and even once they had a masked ball, with printed invitations, also a fancy dress party

THE FORTNIGHTLY CLUB

present

— THE NEW AUTUMN HATS —

at Renées Boutique, Quality Street

Doors Open 11.30 p.m.

Cabaret 12.30 p.m.—Vicky   R.S.V.P.

An invitation to a *soirée*. Note that Renée's Boutique was likely to have been a nickname for someone's cabin. Picture courtesy of private donor (anonymous).

with everyone taking hundreds of photographs.' Some parties had the invitations printed in French, adding to the theme.[22] Exclusivity was most important in these parties – you could only invite two guests from the crew.

In comparison with this opportunity to dress in finery, there were the fancy dress parties that women as well as men attended. Bill, an engineer in the 1970s, says: 'We had quite a lot of parties in the bar when you went to sea. Particularly, if you had wives on board, officers' wives, they'd get a bit bored. Sailing slowly in the Pacific for five weeks, you've got to do something. Socialising, entertain yourself. So there were a few. Once I got dressed up. I've always been sort of receding so once I got dressed as a Buddhist monk, but another time I just got dressed up in drag. Just a wig and a bit of skirt and oranges for boobs and what-not. I borrowed the officers' wives' clothes.' Ian, who was a P&O waiter in the 1980s, remembers: 'We used to have these crew discos once a fortnight, and everyone would just dress up and do really outrageous things.' In fact, the fun felt almost uninterrupted, or so people's memories now have it. 'It was like a non-stop party all the time, it was like New Year's Eve every night. And I felt really happy and comfortable. It's a great time of your life, in your early twenties.' Many seafarers, looking back, wonder how they had the energy to be up half the night. 'Youth was the key,' says Ian.

```
                 THE FORTNIGHTLY CLUB

A club has been formed,with the intention of entertaining,with the
title "The Fortnightly Club",the following rules have been decided

1-There will be eleven members
2-Subscription will be £I sterling,payable bi-weekly
3-A party will be held bi-weekly in peaks 132,133,135,136,137.
4-Each member is allowed two guests,one of which must be changed
5-Every party must be original.
6-Drag will not be worn.
7-Every member will see that all guests are attended to,and that
all is left clean
8-One musical gramaphone/taperecorder will be used at limited volume
in peak/132/133
9-Parties will oficcially end at 2a.m.
1o- any money spare from party expensez will be used for a large ball
to be used at Xmas


Any queries or suggestions should be adressed to The Secreetary,peak
133,and will be raised at the first meeting.
...........................
               A MASKED BALL
To be held  in Quality Street on Tuesday 24th October.


3 cases Allsops lager @ 1/5 per bottle..................£3..12..0
3 bottles gin @ 25/3 per bottle........................£3..15..9
2 bottles scotch @ 31/3 per bottle!!!!!...............£3..2...6
24 bottles tonic water @ 9d per bottle...............  ..18..0
6 bottles ginger ale,6 bottles soda...................    9..0
I bottle fruit cordial................................    5..0
33 invitation cards...................................   10..0

                                    Total     £I2.12..3.
```

The rules of The Fortnightly Club were strictly formalised. Picture courtesy of
private donor (anonymous).

There was also the bar scene, described in Chapter 4, which was at the
opposite end of the spectrum to *soirées*: based less around formal rituals
and somewhat bawdier. Here there was a different level of performance,
one geared to replicating heterosexual courtship. The queens used to get
made up at night to go to 'The Pig and Whistle'. '[They were] not necessarily in full drag but you always had the full face on, which we used to say
was the full eke,' says Martin. The queens would use the opportunity to
eye up and flirt with more masculine seafarers.

Formalised shows, parties and pub displays were not the only situations
where camp performances took place. Some men 'performed' more informally off-stage. A ship can be imagined as a cluster of minor and major
theatrical spaces: for example, a vegetable-cleaning area of the kitchen
and the first-class dining room respectively. Some camp men made use of

Toned-down navy drag. Picture courtesy of Ian.

many of these 'theatres', decking themselves out for masculine eyes to consume in areas of the ship that were off-limits to passengers during working hours. Queens delighted in wearing pink frilly negligees and furry slippers, with rollers in their hair, to the communal early morning showers. They vied with each other and flaunted themselves for the firemen to whistle at and relish. Every opportunity to camp it up was taken. Martin recalls: 'I used to walk about with make-up on all day.'

Private performances

Even in private it felt to some seafarers as if the show never stopped. In the Merchant Navy a ship's cabin was not a particularly private space and it could be used both to conduct a relationship and to prepare for more

Masks added to the pleasure of secrecy. Picture courtesy of private
donor (anonymous).

public camp performances. For some, the cabin was a place where they
performed wifely roles, in drag. As Martin said in Chapter 4, a queen
might, in his cabin, wear feminine clothes to perform the role of good wife
for his man: serving food and then serving him. It was only slightly over-
the-top that 'Carol Baker' went to bed with 'rollers in ... fluffy slippers
and painted toenails', as Martin remembers.

Cabins were also the place where camp men performed together as
stereotypical women, gossiping and dolling up together. Martin explains:
'You used to sit and drink pots of tea together and have drinks together
and pluck each other's eyebrows or do each other's hair or swap drag.
"What are you doing tonight, girl?" and all this carry on.' In the larger
multi-occupancy cabins it was the same. 'All the queens would be in there,
fighting round, trying to get ready for the saloon, because you used to put
semi-make-up on for the saloon evening at night, you always had a bit of
blusher on, your eyes done.'

So being camp on board the ships could be a round-the-clock affair as
well as episodic. It was presaged by the older forms of cross-dressing, such
as public shows, which had not been organised for gay ends but had
created a context where camp flouncing could be assimilated as relatively
unexceptional. 'Carol Baker' was so confident that the ship offered her
space to be feminine that when 'she joined the ship, the only men's gear
she had was a pair of shoes and a pair of jeans', says Martin.

There could be lots of hilarity between friends. Picture courtesy of private donor.

The attraction of cross-dressing

Most people 'perform' chosen identities, particularly when in the presence of others: we act rather than just *be*. Queer theorist Judith Butler has talked extensively about gender as performance in the sense that it expresses a *fabrication* manufactured and sustained through bodily signs such as acts, gestures, talk and behaviour.[23] So what some gay men on ships did was construct an alternative identity for themselves, based around feminine ways of behaving. It's not that the identity was 'false'. It's just that it was the conscious product of observation mixed with a more natural, unconscious form of self-expression. The camp persona was created deliberately from a range of possible self-presentations. And passenger ships were a great place to find glamorous female role models, as Chapter 7 describes.

Most of our interviewees focused on describing what happened when people cross-dressed, rather than on *why* they enjoyed it so much. And so sometimes we have had to infer or guess about this from understandings of gay men in other situations, such as those investigated by theorists on camp, Andy Medhurst and Esther Newton.[24]

Performers

One of the main reasons why men, particularly in the pre-Wolfenden period, enjoyed cross-dressing was that it was a public and celebratory statement of gay identity, a rebuttal of enforced masculinity and heterosexuality. On ships, cross-dressing was a clear and permitted statement that you were (or wore) what you wanted to be. It was a claim that could not be made easily or publicly at that time on land, as Chapter 1 showed.

Camp was a means of self-exploration, however unconscious. Dragging up, and seeing so many camp role models in front of them, men could explore possible other identities and do so in a light-hearted and supportive context. They weren't exactly acting as women when they dragged up, but as something that is gendered differently from men *and* women, although there are similarities with both. For example, there's an element of bawdiness and aggressiveness in many drag performances which is very unlike stereotyped female gendered performances. Cross-dressers who are transvestites tend to act more traditionally 'female'. What drag queens tend to do is exaggerate, parody, combine or even subvert traditional gender roles. Why do so many drag queens choose to be very powerful, fabulous, glamorous, dramatic women rather than more ordinary ones? In appearing hyper-feminine, they draw attention to the fact that it is a *performance* – no woman can be *that* glam for real, therefore it must be drag. It could be argued that drag queens, in taking on female roles, are associating and identifying with another oppressed/powerless minority group. But if that is so, then why do they choose to adopt the personas of the most powerful, extreme women: wealthy members of the royal family, film stars, or rapacious bad girls who use men in the way that men traditionally use women? Sex, too, should not be ignored. One of the bonuses of being dressed as a woman in public was the fact that it helped to attract new lovers. Your goods were on view.

Camp men on ships were not dressing as any old woman, but as glamorous, seductive and exceptional women: the sort who could have scores of heterosexual men queuing up. In order to attract a hyper-masculine sailor, you need to become hyper-feminine. However, the odd thing about all exaggerated gender roles is that they can become camp because they appear so studied and unreal – even the ultra-butch ones.

So the different dressing-up opportunities or roles offered a range of possible selves for example, a refined duchess, a glamorous film star or a foul-mouthed, hard-as-nails man-eater. Reviewing a range of camp colleagues, Martin recalls 'There was Carla, she was going with this wealthy man in the UK and he came down in a Rolls Royce. We always used to call her ... "Piss-elegant Carla", but it was a term of endearment, believe it or not. You met all sorts.'

While cross-dressing was an exploration of self, it could easily be disguised or justified as entertainment. The seriousness of a man's intention to dress as a woman could be covered by the excuse that it was just for the concert party. So the process of cross-dressing, with its private goals and satisfactions could be enjoyed legitimately; the drag queen was camping charitably, not selfishly. The entertainment was undoubtedly needed: Chris points out that: 'You were there [on the same ship] for three months, basically, away from home. And when you finished in the evenings, six and eight o'clock in the evening, then of course you made your own entertainments. But it took a camp form.'

Acting as an entertainer – on or off stage – brought the additional bonus of attention and appreciation, even notoriety. As Esther Newton points out: 'The drag queen looks in the mirror of the audience and sees his female image reflected back approvingly. It is through the process of group support and approval that the drag queen creates himself.'[25]

Frocks, particularly spectacular ones, also brought a respite from the conformity imposed by the shipping line. If the function of uniforms is to impose uniformity, a company identity, hierarchy and some semblance of masculinity, then to cross-dress was a riposte to all that an employer required. Most uniformed workers make creative adaptations to their

Group support was part of the joy of dragging up. Picture courtesy of private
donor (anonymous).

uniforms to express individuality, but camp seafarers went many stages
further than most in making this crucial assertion. When a uniform is
worn, a role is adopted – a person impersonates the worker that he or she
is being paid to be. But when someone wears his own choice of clothes,
then he is showing his own personality – the person he most desires to be.
It was even more fun to make your own from unpromising material, and
queens often showed incredible amounts of creativity and skill in putting
together quite sophisticated outfits using various odds and ends that they
had scavenged from around the ship. Bluebell, a sea queen for 33 years,
remembers: 'One time I needed a new outfit and one of the queens cut out
the lining from the lounge curtains to make a gown for me. She dyed it
green so they never managed to trace it.'[26] Martin notes that 'some of the
queens could make drag out of tablecloths and other bits and bobs. It's
surprising what you can make out of whatever's lying around.' Huge
amounts of effort were put into this work: 'That's all you did prior to parties ... all that work that went into those costumes, I mean cotton wool
and heaven knows what,' says Frank.

A further pleasure was that the lavish and over-the-top clothes were a
reparation for the greyness and restriction that was typical of pre-
Wolfenden Britain, especially for working-class men. Martin underlines
this: 'I mean, in the UK if you wore a pink shirt I think you'd have been
arrested, but when we went to sea, certain things were normal. So we'd

People made fancy dress clothes out of all sorts of materials that were lying around. Picture courtesy of Ian.

wear pink shirts and white flares and that carry on. And you'd back comb your hair and tease your hair up ... like Connie Francis, the old star.'

There was particular pleasure in being waged for entering a frock-wearing world from which men were usually barred. Dave recalls walking 'on board this ship, the *Himalaya* in Tilbury. I said "I'm joining". They said "Oh yeah right, what are you coming [as]?" "I'm a steward." They said, "Right, go forward, that way. Go into peak six, seven or eight", because that's what the cabins were called, "peaks" – right up in the sharp end. "Look round any bunk that's not occupied and take it. Make sure there's no bedding on the bunk or anything in the locker." Well, I walked into this peak. There were about six bunks – a couple of beds that were made up and a couple that weren't. I looked around the lockers, and the locker by the porthole was shut. From the bottom was about a foot of white tulle and two pairs of silver high heel shoes sticking out. I was so naive. I thought "My god, I've come into the women's quarters." So I fled. After I'd come out again, I looked back and I thought "No, just a minute, this *is* number six." So anyway, I was just unpacking my stuff and this great tall elegant thing came swishing in and said "Oh, hello darling. Are you new? Mm? First time at sea? My name's Janet. That's my locker." And I said "Oh I see, you've got this" [pointing at the tulle sticking out of the locker]. "Oh yes, couldn't get my dress in, dear." And I thought "This can't be bad. I'm being paid for this." '

Camping it up, that rebuttal of prescriptive uniformity, was a way of relatively powerless workers achieving a sense of agency in relation to many aspects of shipboard life. A man who created a feminine and larger-than-life identity for himself could feel that he had a hand in what happened him while onboard; he was not just what his employer wanted him to be. And as well as rebutting rules, camping avoided the potential abjection that went with a service-related job. Waiters and stewards who dressed and acted like movie stars or famous singers found a way to avoid the misery and anger that can come from waiting on people who didn't respect or even notice them. To be a queen was to invert the social understandings about status and state that lower-ranked staff, rather than passengers or officers, were the significant figure in the landscape. Of course, this was a denial of the actual enduring power relations, but if enough people on a ship acted camp, then the critical mass could create a feeling of personal power, although, ultimately, replacing one form of prescriptive behaviour and power roles with another creates another (alternative) hierarchy. What happened to the closeted men who couldn't join in, or the ones who were uncomfortable with it, or the ones who tried but just weren't very good at camp repartee? Being an outrageous queen was a way of acting anti-dependent, so much above the petty and mundane that you didn't have to care if you hadn't got a man. Of the many outrageous queens Chris remembers, 'there were some who didn't care a damn'. Their acid tongues could terrify men – and impress those who didn't have their courage.

There are a number of other ways that camping could help gay men feel a sense of agency. Film and television can make some people feel like passive viewers, people who cannot interact with the distant, glamorous world on view. One exception to this is that women can buy make-up recommended by actresses with the promise that wearing it can transform them into glamorous film stars, as feminist writers on film stars, such as Jackie Stacey show.[27] On a passenger ship, where so many of the famous travelled, the waiter who wore clothes or make-up like a movie star had a sense that he was the same as – or even better than – them, not like a passive member of a cinema audience who never got behind the celluloid. As Loren Lorenz, 'the first drag stripper in England', says of a friend who first shipped out at the same time as her, on the *Orion* in 1950, he 'thought he was going on a pleasure cruise and took a huge trunk of clothes with him. In fact we ended up in the utility gang – all we were doing was scrubbing floors and cleaning lavatories',[28] but putting on shows made it fun. The fantasy play compensated for the actual lowliness of the job.

Because mainstream society regulates gender roles and insists that people should identify with one gender or another, conflict can arise. It meant, Newton argues, that gay men who wanted to dress in drag, needed to find a community. Membership of the shipboard gay community allowed female impersonators to find a form and an audience.[29] The community could socialise alternative expressions of gender, rather than requiring them only to exist in private. That is, camp men no longer had to feel peculiar or out of line in wanting to look like women. They were part of a large number and so their desires came to be seen as ordinary and indeed, resolvable, at least temporarily. Instead of being forced to choose between gender roles and being cast as suffering from a form of pathology, drag queens could feel that they had just been in a wrong situation before. Tellingly, Mick Belsten, a seafarer and Gay Liberation Front (GLF) activist, became less shy and sought company the more he dragged up. GLF historian, Lisa Power, remembers that he hung out with the GLF 'Queens of Colvillea' living in Colville Terrace, Portobello, West London, but only rarely cross-dressed. Once, he 'had these beautiful roses in his hair and looked amazing. It was the first time I'd seen him in drag, he'd had a lot of problems with it. He supported it but was very hesitant about doing it himself.'[30] Mick stayed at drag queen Bette Bourne's house then moved house again. 'He got more and more into drag and feminism, it was a big thing for him.'[31]

Although dragging-up was part of Mick's feminist affinity with women, some men were less empathic towards females and had developed a more polarised way of thinking about gender. Cross-dressing could be some men's way of dealing with the anger they felt at not having the same sexual access to men as women did. They often felt that masculinity was imposed on them; they were not born with it. Parodying women could act as a form of retaliation as well as a restitution of a lost 'right'. The people we spoke to frequently referred to the pleasure of borrowing women's clothes from passengers, officers' wives and female colleagues. This doesn't seem to have been brought about by need so much as the pleasure of hijacking someone else's frocks or make-up. One gay man went so far as to 'cheat' a woman passenger out of her fancy shoes by submitting to her sexual desires. Martin remembers one of the queens had the nickname of Prissie: 'He was very glamorous as a man or a woman. He'd seen this female passenger at the table, who fancied him. He wanted a nice pair of shoes to go to a party. So he went up [to her cabin] and "slipped her one" and grabbed the pair of shoes on the way out. He said he'd borrow the slippers that night for the ball.' However, women's giving of clothes could also signify a bond between them and gay seafarers, as Chapter 7 shows.

Pains of performing

Were there no pains among all these pleasures? Although we have described the benefits of being able to perform, theatrically and ordinarily, as 'women', there were also some difficulties. One of the drawbacks of being very camp was that a person could feel confined to a role and that there could be no fluidity in how they were then seen. Camp is a metaphor for speaking (or shrieking) loudly about gay sexuality. Queening very publicly can then make it hard to take a step back into 'quieter' homosexuality or even heterosexuality. However, this would have been less of a problem on a ship, with its temporary community, than ashore in a job where one's colleagues remained static. Seafarers could move in and out of their camp personas. The large number of camp seafarers who are now straight is evidence of this. The gay seafarers we interviewed for this book were concerned that their photographs of camp shipmates did not appear in the book, for fear of outing their ex-colleagues who are now living traditionally heterosexual lives.

As discussed earlier in this chapter, some of the drag queens took on identities of wealthy, titled or famous women. There is no evidence about how a working-class boy who impersonated a movie star such as Carol Baker dealt with the more humble reality of who he 'really' was. Some may have over-stretched themselves and then taken a tumble back in non-performative spaces where a catering minion is just a catering minion, no matter how glorious his self-image. It may be that the queens were not desired on ship as much as they believed a glamorous 'star' of their status should be, because they were, finally, just colleagues. As Peter Bailey, who has studied the history of barmaids' glamorous sexuality, argues, one of the properties of glamour is distance. 'Distance not only sustains and protects the magical property that is commonly recognised in glamour, but also heightens desire through the tension generated by the separation of the glamour object and the beholder, a separation that also functions to limit the expression or consummation of desire.'[32] However, a ship allowed no such separation between the gay catering staff, who were all quartered tightly together.

And how much was the freedom to mime and mince across the high seas a limited licence? Certainly the shipping line and its agents, the officers, controlled when and where campness happened, as Chapter 7 shows. As Chris recalls: 'If you were a bedroom steward you didn't camp your tits off [all day long], you kept within your parameters. When it was off parameters, in the ship's quarters, then it didn't matter.' But perhaps it did matter. Perhaps it was seen as a threat to heterosexual norms. That's why the parameters were implicitly understood by all parties.

Maybe the emphasis on camp, which offers only one set of personas, actually *reduced* gay men's ideas of the range of identities that were open to them? When asked whether it was always the gay guys who did drag, or was it straight ones as well, Chris replied that in his experience it was always the gay guys – 'that's what gays do'. However, not *all* gay guys did it. Camping was *some* men's main activity and form of self-expression, but it was not performed by every gay man in the Merchant Navy, particularly those who were less open about their sexuality, or those who were officers or engineers, where a more masculine role was expected. It appears from our limited evidence that the pleasures of camp dressing outweighed the pains for performers. And such performative cross-dressing seemed largely to delight those who experienced it.

How did camp work for audiences?

Just as gay men were performing both on and off-stage, so their audiences viewed them in on and off-stage positions, from the flattering spotlights to the stark, exposing daylight of the deck. Some of those 'audiences' included more covert gay men. They could gain pleasure – and an understanding of how they too might be received by the straight world – through watching cross-dressed performers. It was a way of experiencing gay sexuality as a vicarious pleasure. Chris says that he loved watching but didn't take part. 'I was just in the audience. I enjoy it, but it's never been my scene.' Some gay men, while still not performing, got even closer by becoming involved in the back-stage production of camp spectacles. Geoff, with his skills as a writer, delighted in designing and printing the invitations for camp concert parties. He participated in the charade by proxy, dressing up other men: 'I used to go and watch, or help, I'd always do the make-up and stuff like that.'

Those 'performances' that took the form of camp banter with passengers in the dining room or allowed non-performers limited inclusion (for example, through lending props), were an enjoyable disruption of routine for 'audiences'. Camping added fun to the day, and for some passengers, this brush with the forbidden was something that was delightfully risky yet also safe. The ship's function as a liminal zone meant the cross-dressing could be enjoyed without being taken seriously. However, while this may have worked well for voyeuristic passengers, it usually diluted any overt political impact that camp could have made.

Coupled with the pleasure at witnessing transgression was the thrill of privilege at feeling temporarily part of a secret community, viewing a world to which the audience *might* belong, or would never belong to. Kirk and Heath suggest that for land audiences the enchantment may partly be because 'men went home feeling more "masculine" and the women more "feminine" [but] more likely it was just that in those days of relative inno-cence ... people could allow themselves to be amazed and indulge in a healthy dose of voyeurism without being obliged to feel guilty about it. Besides, it was on the stage so it was "safe".'[33]

Gay seafarers report the delight with which female passengers and crew joined in the masquerade, lending the props that denoted femininity. Martin remembers the loaning that some queenly bedroom stewards man-aged. 'Some of the passengers, the wealthy ones, they'd all [loan make-up]. It wasn't Estée Lauder, but another well-known firm. [It was] good make-up. We'd use their mascara and their best blusher and their lipstick.' Perhaps the fact that the tales can be remembered indicates the riskiness involved and the unpredictable 'audience' reactions. Frank recalls one pas-senger's reaction to the illegitimate borrowing by his friend, Miss L. 'Miss L was in a cabin and she thought the passengers had gone to dinner, so she tried on Madame's mink coat, with earrings as well, and was posing in front of the mirror. Then she heard the toilet flush. Madame came out of the toilet and there Miss L was, standing in the fur coat and earrings. And she [the passenger] said "Oh dear, it looks better on you than it does on me." '

One by-product of the female audience's role as dressers and wardrobe mistresses might be that in lending femininity they discovered that they owned something that someone else wanted to borrow. It could give a sense of their value as possessors of such accoutrements, even if their gender was then parodied.

From this story of both performers and their audiences we get a sense that both parties got quite a lot of what they wanted. The shipping line got relative industrial peace and did not have to provide entertainment for off-duty residential workers. They got a crew who focused their energies in a non-risky way: rehearsing, costume-making, and performing accept-able kinds of gay sexuality in safely ritualised ways which limited out-breaks of anarchy. Conversely, camp men got their chance to flaunt and flout without major social problems or risk of the attacks that might take place ashore.

The rights and rites of drag

So what role did clothes, hairstyles and make-up play in gay shipboard company? The stories that were related to us reveal that cross-dressing was one of the main ways that gay sexuality was expressed, 'off-stage' as well as in shows. It was performed most often on passenger ships, where ceremonial dress etiquette (uniforms and 'correct' evening wear) and play-ful transgression (fancy dress parties) were a key part of social interaction. And how did gay men wear camp clothing? The proportion of gay men who did so wore it with varying degrees of bravado or discretion, depend-ing on what they could get away with – sometimes a tricky judgement to make. The degree of camping up was drastically affected by location, and also by company. Cross-dressing for seafarers was a group activity, not a solitary one – an expression of collective pride and a sense of their right to 'be' female.

Where did they get their drag from? The men's stories show that the process of preparing, including borrowing from women, was a key part of the annexation of another identity. Buying, particularly commissioning, a frock was an act of commitment and determination. So was bringing drag from home. By contrast, borrowing a dress was playful, provisional and perhaps a more unconscious assertive attack on women's presence on the ship and females' unquestioned right to frocks. It could be an assault on compulsory masculinity but it didn't necessarily involve Gay Liberation ideas about the distorting effects of rigid gender roles on both women and men.

As for their reasons for wearing drag, it was clearly part of some men's expression of the kind of person they wanted to be, perhaps in the face of limited options. It was a way of performing a particular gay identity. It brought some gay men pleasure and the space to explore who they were or might become. It was fun, recreational, a highly creative act and an overlooked expression of working-class male talent in drama, dressing, needlework and imagination. It complemented the interior design skills some gay men applied to their cabins, as we saw in Chapter 2.

And what happened as a result of wearing drag? It brought men who were homosexual the pleasures just listed, as well as strengthening a sense of gay identity, rights and community, not least because camping so visi-bly outed and consolidated gay culture at a time when it was still hidden and nascent. The daily sight of stilettos and eye-shadow, the flouncing and take-offs of female movie stars, meant that straight people on the ship had to face the existence, varieties and scale of gay sexuality in life. And that involved understanding that heterosexuality was only one mode of sexual expression. By witnessing camp performance and making choices – not necessarily freely – about how they wanted to perform their own sexu-ality, covert gay men learned from these models and anti-models. Perhaps all parties learned with wonder just how much subversion a society would and would not permit around sexual orientation. The extremeness of a camp voyage highlighted the boundaries (and the flexibilities) that were not usually so evident because camp was normally confined to theatres and homosexuality to public silence.

In short, camping was one of the main things that made ships heaven – for some. Clothes were the props that enabled men to go far in exploring what life beyond the narrow streets of compulsory heterosexuality could mean. And clothes were the metaphor, too, for a different way of behaving: yet another reason for discarding uniform trousers to see what lay beyond. And this was enacted within the oddly safe space of the gay-friendly passenger ship. As the next chapter shows, going ashore offered other ways to learn about camp and express gay sexuality, as long as care was taken. Land was not necessarily as safe.

Notes

1. Medhurst A. (1997) 'Camp', in Medhurst A. and Munt, S.R. (1997) *Lesbian and Gay Studies: A Critical Introduction*, Cassell, London and Washington DC, p. 275.

2. Bentley, K. (2000) *Sailor: Vintage Photos of a Masculine Icon*, Council Oak Books, San Francisco, CA and Tulsa, OK.

3. The significance of clothes on ships has been discussed by Jarvis, A. and Raine, P. (1984) *Fancy Dress*, Shire, Princes Risborough, and by Charteris-Richardson, C. (1998) *Tired Feet and Glamorous Nights: The Fashion Travel Connection in the Inter-war Years*, London College of Fashion, MA thesis.

4. *The Seaman*, 12(68), 3 February 1937, Warwick Modern Records Centre MSS 175a/4/1/27.

5. Sontag, S. (1966) 'Notes on Camp', in *Susan Sontag against Interpretation and Other Essays*, Farrarr, Straus & Giroux, New York, p. 279.

6. Core, P. (1984) *Camp: The Lie That Tells the Truth*, Delilah Books, New York.

7. Ross, A. (1993) 'Uses of Camp', in Bergman, D. (ed.), *Camp Grounds*, University of Massachusetts Press, Amherst, MA, p. 74.

8. Long, S. (1993) 'The Loneliness of Camp', in Bergman, *Camp Grounds*.

9. Meyer, M. (ed.) (1994) *The Politics and Poetics of Camp*, Routledge, London, p. 1.

10. Medhurst, 'Camp', p. 281.

11. Ibid., p. 278.

12. Warren, C.A.B. (1974) *Identity and Community in the Gay World*, John Wiley and Sons, New York, p. 107.

13. Power, L. (1995) *No Bath but Plenty of Bubbles: An Oral History of the Gay Liberation Front 1970–73*, Cassell, London, p. 167, quoting Peter Tatchell.

14. Warren, *Identity and Community*, p. 109. See Laud Humphreys' 1970 study

of an American city, *Tearoom Trade: A Study of Homosexual Encounters in Public Places*, Duckworth, London.

15. Walton, J.K. (2000) *The British Seaside: Holidays and Resorts in the Twentieth Century*, Manchester University Press, Manchester, pp. 161–2.

16. Gardiner, J. (1996) *Who's a Pretty Boy Then?'*, Serpents Tail, London, p. 107.

17. Kirk, K. and Heath, E. (1984) *Men in Frocks*, Gay Men's Press, London, p. 32.

18. Although it was not a gay pub, it was gay-friendly, run by a buxom, warm, heavily made-up landlady whom gay men liked.

19. Gardiner, *Who's a Pretty Boy Then*, p. 107.

20. Ibid., p. 107.

21. Kirk and Heath, *Men in Frocks*, p. 31.

22. The use of French added an additional touch of glamour and sophistication to the procedures. Unsurprisingly, Polari, the camp form of language used by gay seafarers, also had a number of French words within it: *bijou* – small; *maquiage* – make-up; *nanteois* – none, *bevois* – drink.

23. Butler, J. (1990) *Gender Trouble*, Routledge, London, p. 136. See also Butler, J. (1993) *Bodies that Matter: On the Discursive Limits of 'Sex'*, Routledge, New York.

24. Medhurst, 'Camp', and Newton, E. (1998) 'The Queens', in Medhurst and Newton, *Lesbian and Gay Studies*, taken from Newton's (1972) *Mother Camp: Female Impersonators in America*, University of Chicago Press, Chicago, IL.

25. Newton, 'The Queens', p. 47.

26. Kirk and Heath, *Men in Frocks*, p. 32.

27. Stacey, J. (1994) *Star-gazing: Hollywood Cinema and Female Spectatorship*, Routledge, London.

28. Kirk and Heath, *Men in Frocks*, p. 24.

29. Newton, 'The Queens', p. 47.

30. Power, *No Bath, but Plenty of Bubbles*, p. 221, quoting Cloud Downey.

31. Ibid. p. 222.

32. Bailey, P. (1990) 'Parasexuality and Glamour: The Victorian Barmaid as Cultural Prototype', *Gender and History*, 2(2), Summer, p. 153.

33. Kirk and Heath, *Men in Frocks*, p. 19.

Chapter 6

Ho Land! Ho Freedom!

'What's to be done ashore?'

For seafarers of any sexual orientation, ports were ostensibly places of pleasure and freedom after the confinement of the ship and the routine business of regular work. They were also spaces where seafarers faced and reworked the complexities of their own foreign and sexual identities. If

The pleasures of arriving at foreign ports after long voyages – Alan arrives in Sydney harbour, 1962 on the *British Kestrel*. Picture courtesy of Alan.

you were a masculine gay man on ship, what kind of gay man could you be on land? In addition, foreign ports were places of education in which seafarers could learn that the repressive sexual climate in the UK was not typical of all countries.

A few days' stop-over offered the chance to meet new people and an escape – or obligatory foray – from what could be the claustrophobic and intricate (although also reassuringly familiar) relationships that could develop as a result of working and socialising with the same people every day for weeks. Away from regulation and the officers' gaze, the lower ratings were free to enjoy themselves in a new environment. Sometimes this was a place with an established gay subculture, offering 'a network of sites at which homosexual desire could be expressed'.[1] Sometimes there were places that had a sex industry[2] that catered for a variety of tastes, especially in the well-colonised eastern and African ports.[3] As theorists studying the concept of space have argued, places constitute what occurs socially.[4] Therefore, what gay men did in port didn't just happen coincidentally. Nor could such things have happened

Waiters from the *Oriana*, sight-seeing while on shore leave in Suva, Fiji (1960s). The man in the centre just needs a jacket to complete his uniform. Picture courtesy of private donor.

just anywhere. Ports like Port Said, Durban and New York caused and enabled particular practices.

The limited amount of time that the ship was in dock sometimes contributed to an atmosphere of hedonist consumption and partying, touring bars and clubs, spending wages on souvenirs and presents, or visiting sex industry workers. It also justified caution, which was expressed in some seamen's tendency to visit, mob-handed, the same places on each trip, and often just to settle in the first pub beyond the dock gates. As Tony Lane, an historian of the Merchant Navy remarks, 'It is surprising how *in*curious most seamen are. ... Going ashore is less an "expedition of discovery" and more a search for a substitute for the Saturday night out.'[5] Most relationships had to be contingent, although a surprising number of men returned to familiar women in a kind of serial monogamy.[6] Many seafarers discovered what it was like to be the new boy in town during shore leave, that fantasy 'sailor' figure of much gay porn, such as *San Diego Sailor*[7] and *Seafood Platter*.[8] Shore leave was a time of enormous sexual opportunity that had to be taken advantage of in a relatively short period of time.

Away from the ship, gay seafarers, particularly those who were not 'out' on their ships, could afford to be much bolder than normal. In many cases, the consequences of their actions needed to be considered only in the short term – as soon as their shore leave was over they could escape. The culture of bar-hopping, which many sailors engaged in, also lowered some inhibitions. Alcohol particularly helped those from ships where such beverages were scarce to act with more courage than usual.

The time spent between voyages also allowed seafarers to touch base with contacts back home, as well as sample the growing underground British gay subculture. And they enriched it with the information they brought back with them, particularly from North America, Australia and the Middle East.

The British scene

Public places

What pleasures could Britain offer a gay seafarer when he docked? Although homosexuality was illegal in the UK up until 1967, it had not stopped the rise of a number of discreet gay bars and pubs, particularly in urban areas, for those who wanted to socialise in commercial places rather than just go home. In some cases private membership was a necessity, while in others, the distinction between gay and straight was less obvious. In particular, many of the pubs in the London docks, such as the Marquis of Granby, had drag shows and were used by both gay and straight seafarers, as well as dockers and others who lived in the area. The Ken and the Round House were also popular seafarers' pubs, conveniently positioned outside the dock gates. Later on, quite a lot of the West End queens and the shore-side people filtered into the Ken and the Round House, says Martin. 'Some arrived in sports-cars, but our only form of transport was high heels.'

Sea queens actually lived near these pubs, so 'performances' happened informally as well as formally. Historians of gay cross-dressing, Kirk and Heath, record that during 'periods ashore [between ships] ... which queens called "on the beach" ... they followed the Sea Queen's Credo ... that it was a queen's entitlement to live where the sailors lived. [Lorri Lee recalled] "We never wore drag in the pubs ... but certainly we were very noticeable, particularly on the days that a ship was coming in and everybody knew that there would be a big Sea Queen reunion at the local. We all wore our fluffy bunny-wool sweaters or whatever was all the rage at the time. Most of us had plucked eyebrows and teased-up, back-combed hair ... although we never wanted to be women, we *did* want to be a little bit more than men. ... By the sixties Stella Minge's place was in full swing. She had a bawdy house where you could rest for the night with a sailor on your arm – using a room there was far better than staying at the Seamen's Mission and having the bother of throwing your plait out of the window and getting your sailor to climb up it. Stella's was an amazing place, with parties every night; you'd see yards of seamen staggering there from the pub with crates of beer. The neighbours used to hate us."'[9]

Jack Robinson, a ship's catering worker, describes what he found in the early 1940s, and the difficulty he and his shipmate-lover, Bobby, had in feeling that this was a place where they could be gay on *their* terms. He went to 'the Railway tavern, an offbeat pub with a three-piece band, piano and drums, singers lining up to give a turn. "They're all queer," said Bobby. "Look at them. Some of them are dressed as women. Let's piss off. This place makes me nervous." We stuck around and enjoyed the entertainment but the situation was unreal, false. It seemed a mild sort of madness and something we would never understand. There were other pubs, lively joints where the East-Enders had a knees-up every night of the week, but most of them finished up with some kind of female impersonator on the mike. That's the way they seemed to like it, so we ... took a bus up to West End, a different London altogether.'[10]

Other British coastal cities also had pubs that were frequented by gay seafarers, including Liverpool's Royal Court and the Magic Clock in nearby Hood Street. A heterosexual ex-AB (Able-Bodied Seaman), Don

Trueman, remembers the Royal Court pub, next to the Royal Court Theatre. 'The gay guys used the little back room, the snug, we were in the public bar, we'd blow them kisses from time to time. They'd walk through the public bar to the gents and we'd say "Nice arse" or something and they'd say "Ooh, thank you" but they wouldn't follow it up if you weren't serious. They'd flash their tackle [penises] in the gents – you could tell what they were by the way they were standing at the stone. People in the dancehalls nearby would get passes out and come in for a drink. If girls came through the snug bar instead of the public bar the gay guys would spit at them and call them names like "slut" – because the girls were potentially taking away the men that the queer guys might have got.' The Juniper Berry and the Horse and Groom in Southampton were also popular pubs for gay seafarers.

Because of the secrecy in which the gay subculture was conducted in the 1950s and 1960s, gaining access to gay pubs and private clubs wasn't as easy as today. Information about local gay venues can now be obtained via a plethora of sources: listings magazines, the Internet, telephone switchboard facilities, or just by walking down certain streets and noticing the openness with which many urban gay and lesbian establishments announce their existence. But for people who hadn't already made contact with other gay men and lesbians, discovering that this hidden 1950s/1960s subculture even *existed* could be difficult. However, the Merchant Navy had a culture whereby information about what pubs to go to in foreign ports was routinely shared. Individual sailors passed on information to each other about different bars, clubs, cottages[11] and cruising grounds. The lone, inexperienced gay man may have found it difficult to summon up the courage to step through the doors of a gay club for the first time. However, as part of confident group, entering the gay subculture with friends was much easier.

Going ashore also provided a chance to meet up with friends from previous voyages. 'We'd arrange to meet in the gay bars in London, and then go to the shows together or some camp revue,' remembers Dave, a steward at sea from 1956 to 1963. 'It was good, the shows seemed to be in our grasp, they're a bit expensive now.' *Hello Dolly* and *Gyspy* were particular favourites. Robert, a purser from 1957 to 1968, remembers that in the early 1960s the A&B (Arts and Battle-dress) was an example of one of the more discreet gay London clubs. Located on the third floor of a building which occupied the south corner of the Leicester Square end of Rupert Court, Soho, it was reached by climbing a steep flight of stairs and then knocking on the door to gain access. In the absence of an International Spartacus Gay Guide, the A&B implemented its own guide in the form of a visitor's book where members could record details of other gay establishments, meeting places and cruising areas that they had visited all over the world. They could also warn of places that were dangerous and therefore to be avoided.

Other gay pubs in London included the Blue Posts at the other end of Rupert Court, The Salisbury on St Martin's Lane, which was the setting for the pub scenes in Dirk Bogarde's movie *Victim* (1961), and the Rockingham, which was often frequented by closeted MPs, senior officers in the armed forces and other public figures. One notorious establishment was on the King's Road, Chelsea and was called Le Gigolo, a popular drinking place for gay artist and film-maker Derek Jarman in the 1960s.[12] It looked like an ordinary coffee bar from street level, but there was a dimly-lit bar in the basement, along with a dance floor that was some-times used for anything but dancing. 'I was taken there by the Third Engineer [on a cargo ship in the early 1960s],' remembers Robert. 'It was very crowded and hot, and when I went on to the dance floor, I discov-ered that it was not so much a dance but more of an orgy, and the further one got sucked into the heaving mass of bodies, the more overt the sexual activity became. In no time at all I found my trousers round my ankles, and my dick in someone's mouth, all the while trying to fend off others who were anxious to stick their dicks up my rear end. I couldn't spend more than half an hour on the dance floor, it was almost difficult to breathe and the crush was frightening. One had to literally fight one's way out. I developed a way of simplifying my exit. I would just say "Excuse me, I'm going to throw up!" and the crowd would part like the Red Sea!'

Robert describes how he was arrested twice during police raids on vari-ous gay establishments in London, even though none of the patrons was doing anything more illicit than having a drink. On the first occasion he had to appear at Bow Street Magistrates Court after being kept in a cell with a dozen others overnight. He was fined and the magistrate told him to seek medical treatment. On the second occasion he and the other cus-tomers were released with a 'warning' by the police after it was discovered that one of those who had been arrested was the son of a cabinet minis-ter. As was often the case, someone 'at the top' had pulled strings to ensure that the incident was covered up.

Being gay while on shore leave in the UK could mean an interruption to your career, through arrest. Don Trueman recalls that in a police raid on an underground lavatory in Liverpool[13] eight stewards from one Cunard ship were arrested. The leader of the group, Jimmy aka The Queen of the Pacific, put on a good show at court, and Don and his brother seafarers, who were friends of Jimmy, went along for the performance. 'Some were found guilty and sentenced to six months, others were remanded. Jimmy used to really wind up the coppers and he said "Come on, now, we'll have to see that queer doctor at Walton [prison]. I hope he'll put some Vaseline on his finger when he inspects me." Jimmy was often arrested for cottaging and he'd relish confrontations with authority. For example he'd also taunt the police with, "You don't have to hit me with that truncheon but you could do *something* with it."'

Domestic life

In comparison to this public culture where performance helped you get by, private family homes were a more complex affair, and home towns were places where many gay seafarers felt they could not be 'out'. This was true to such an extent that in the 1960s and 1970s some gay stewards on leave in British cities would avoid places where they might accidentally meet each other, in case their own gay identity was revealed.

So not all seafarers returned to their families during shore leave in the UK. Some stayed in seamen's hostels, rented rooms or borrowed space for those few days. Many tended to think it was not worth having their own place as they were away so often. Gay seafarers would sometimes use the fact that they didn't earn much money as an excuse to share a bedroom with each other, something which parents or hotel clerks would innocently condone – an excuse for proximity that led to further intimacies. As Bérubé points out, in the war 'the differences between cruising and wartime hospitality became blurred as strangers invited servicemen into their homes for the night'.[14]

Family members could be surprisingly accommodating. Jack Robinson describes a youthful encounter in the late 1930s with one of the Campello brothers, all seamen on Cunard's *Queen Mary* and therefore home in Liverpool once a month. The first time they got together was one early wartime evening: 'I walked Tony home after the all-clear sounded. His mother was expecting us. Tony's room looked extra bright – fresh flowers on the side table and a flimsy nightie on each pillow. She watched her son strip down to his girl's panties and slip on a nightie as I washed at the handbasin. The boy slid into bed. I slipped off my scarlet trunks, hesitated for a moment, saw the expectant look in her eye and thought "What the hell!". She held back the covers for me and I pulled the support from my stiffened penis. "Good night," she said as I got into bed with a big hard-on. Tony was in my arms before she went out of the door. . . . Tony's ship would dock every few weeks so I knew we'd be able to see each other from time to time.'[15]

Abroad

One of the benefits of joining the Merchant Navy for gay men was that it afforded them the opportunity to sample the gay subcultures of other countries, where attitudes towards homosexuality were often more equivocal than in the UK They could be treated like a normal person, albeit a tourist to be relieved of money, or welcomed, or even, in the USA, as just another member of the community.

Far-flung places could prove to be eye-openers for many gay seafarers. 'Most of the trips I did were to the Far East,' says Geoff, a writer, steward and purser with P&O from the 1950s. 'There weren't gay bars as such, but people were so understanding. It wasn't like in England where you had to be on your guard every moment. People just accepted you for what you are. Everything was so natural.' 'There used to be bars in Japan full of very feminine boys,' remembers Chris, 'but the whole culture then, even worldwide, was a certain degree of discretion. The only place where I didn't find discretion was when I used to meet the Royal Navy in the China Flea Club in Hong Kong [in the late 1950s]. I was 19 and all those bloody sailors, they all wanted to fuck me. So I let them!' There was a bit of foreign trade available too. Dave says: 'As I recall, certain young Aussie stevedores were not averse to the odd dalliance in a sea queen's cabin (or two!), just to break up the working day. They were also good for purchases of stolen booze at bargain prices, and always enjoyed our parties!'

Frank, a steward from the 1950s to the 1970s, found that even in nominally heterosexual places, men from other countries were not as shy as those back home. He and two of his friends had gone ashore to a beach bar in Athens which was full of dancing heterosexual couples. On the next table there was a number of Greek students, one of whom took a fancy to Frank, grabbing his hand and kissing it. However, as many other gay seafarers have discovered, being the new person on the scene can make them extremely popular. 'Then someone else came over to ask me to dance. The one who was kissing my hand said something to him, and suddenly all the tables were over-turned. My God! They started fighting. We had to creep up and out of the way while the place was in an uproar. The one who had been kissing me eventually followed us back to the docks where the tenders were waiting. We said goodbye and there was a great deal of tongue wrestling and it was all very wonderful. Anyway when I got on to the launch, some of the passengers were there, they must have been out for the evening. It was very quiet. My friend said to me, "You know when you said goodbye to that vision you were right at the side of the coach full of passengers", and so all the passengers had seen and heard everything. I blushed so much. I couldn't wait for that particular cruise to be over.'

The gay subcultures in other countries were sometimes much more vibrant places than in the UK, and it was often in an overseas city port that seafarers realised, sometimes by accident, that there were whole cultures based around homosexuality. On radio officer Alan's first voyage, at the age of 16, his ship docked in Rotterdam and the first bar that he and his mates went into was called Danny's, a place which had a lot of gay staff. 'The waiters were young men, and they had make-up on, but not female make-up. They wore a scarf, like a shawl, over their arms. One of them kissed me, which gave me a hell of a thrill because to be honest, I hadn't even identified them as gay. I wouldn't have identified anybody as gay, because it wasn't a concept I was aware of. I knew I fancied men, but I wasn't able to talk to anyone about it. I wasn't aware that there was anything special, it was just me.' Ian, a waiter with P&O, also remembers how he was introduced to the gay bars and clubs in Australia, in the early 1980s, as a naive first-timer. 'It was nice being chatted up – the first time I had sex with a man was in Sydney. I'd met him in a bar. He chatted me up and I went back with him to his hotel room and that was really nice.'

Sightseeing and friendship

As with ports in the UK, shore leave in overseas cities also allowed seafarers to see the sights, take in a show, buy new props and glamorous gowns for future drag and revue nights, and catch up with old friends. Queens flocked to the Manhattan stores or Singapore dressmakers where they could find the most modern and outrageous frocks. Fashionable props as yet unavailable in the UK were bought to bring home. For example, in the early 1960s Dave had orders to bring home some goods coveted by British gay men. They were copies of the long-playing record of the musical *Gypsy* and bottles of Old Spice aftershave lotion, because it had been seen on a gay man's dressing table in a movie.

'We went to the opera in San Francisco and many other cities if time permitted,' says Frank. 'We could visit friends and go to all the parties.' Indeed, many of those who were interviewed said that they still kept in touch with friends they had made in ports all over the world. They got to know other countries almost well enough to feel as though they half lived there. (Indeed, some later lived in those countries when they left the sea.) In particular, visiting gay seafarers became acquainted with red-light areas such as Kings Cross in Sydney and 42nd Street in New York. This wasn't particularly because they were interested in sleazy milieux, but simply that gay life then seemed to be linked with the downtown areas offering a wide variety of paid sexual services.

Wharf angels and container queens

For those who were in a relationship with other seafarers who weren't on the same ship, then shore leave could be the only chance to meet up with their partner. However, unless two ships were docked in the same port, it would have been extremely expensive to pay for a commercial flight to meet a loved one somewhere else. 'In the 1960s I had a relationship with another purser from another ship,' said Robert. 'It was a long-distance relationship because the only time we saw each other was in port or when we were on leave together. And I had one on-going relationship in East Africa who I used to see regularly when I got out there. It was funny, a lot of the crew had boyfriends in each port, not only the gay guys but the straight guys. They had this sort of bush telegraph. They knew when the ships were coming in and they'd all be standing down the dockside when the ship docked.'

Greeting the sailors as they disembarked was part of the routine of the sex industry and of local people's relish of the novelty and opportunity that a ship from another, more developed, country could bring. Frank notes the acceptance of gender diversity: 'Some girls came down for the boys, and some boys came down for the boys. You were lucky if you were chosen.' The females were commonly known as dock rats or wharf angels. These partners, both male and female would be sneaked on board and virtually live in the cabins of their boyfriends for the duration of the ship's stay in port. Some were paid in presents, others, like the shipgirls or seagulls referred to on p. 11, were simply fascinated by seafarers.[16]

Martin, a steward for about 40 years since the late 1950s, elaborates on the relationship between the queens and the wharf angels. 'Some of them were in the same league as us. They were like prostitutes, but they didn't take money. They just liked the cock side of things. Some of them were fabulous. One came to me one day and said, "Have you any tampax?" And I said, "I've run out at the moment, dear." I thought she was being camp but she was for real. They treated you like women really.'

Ian notes that necessarily it was not uncommon for seafarers to have one-night stands while ashore, particularly after the 1970s as stop-overs became more and more brief. 'A lot of the turnaround ports, we were only in overnight, and a lot of people did go out and have trade for one night, pick someone up, and go back to their hotel with them.' Ian notes that in the 1980s there was also a group of older gay seafarers who were known as *container queens*. Rather than bearing the expense of booking a hotel room, or taking a new partner back to their cabin on the ship, the container queens would simply pick up a local fellow and go with him to the containers on the quayside, where the business of sex could be dealt with quickly.

Another aspect of being ashore was that it could sometimes reveal a side to colleagues that had previously lain dormant. This was especially true of officers, who were more likely to play down their sexuality while onboard, as the following story demonstrates. In 1957 Robert became friendly with another purser called Kenny who was a year older than him. Their positions meant that they couldn't frequent the ship's public rooms, so they spent a lot of time drinking in each other's cabins. Kenny was very attractive, extremely well-hung and had a reputation with the ladies. There was unfriendly rivalry between him and another purser in their efforts to have sex with the female passengers. Robert often wished that Kenny was gay, although he never made any advances towards him, and nothing sexual ever happened between them.

After about a year, the friends were separated. Kenny went to work on a cargo vessel and the following year Robert joined another cargo ship. During a stop-over in Nacala, a small port in Mozambique (or Portuguese East Africa as it then was), Robert encountered a Portuguese port official called Pedro, one of about half a dozen Europeans living in Nacala. As the ship was in dock for three days, Pedro offered to take Robert to his bungalow for dinner one evening. After the meal, Robert asked Pedro if he could use the bathroom. Pedro said it was through the bedroom, so Robert got up: 'As I passed through his bedroom I could not help noticing a collection of photographs on his dresser. I stopped to look at them and was struck by one large framed picture of a very handsome-looking woman in a tight-fitting sheath dress with long black hair. To my astonishment I realised that I was looking at Kenny in full drag. The photo was even signed "To Pedro – with love from Kenny"!'

When Robert got back to the lounge, he couldn't stop himself from saying that he'd seen Kenny's photograph. Pedro was very forthcoming and told him that he had a sexual relationship with Kenny, who was totally passive sexually. Robert was amazed. About a year later he met up with Kenny again when their ships were in London and told him about Pedro. 'We both had a good laugh about things although we never did have sex together. I suspect that was because I had always seen him in my fantasies as a top man rather than a bottom.'

Freaking the normals

Not all of the ports that gay seafarers passed through were gateways to exotic and gay-friendly cultures. Some of them were more pedestrian, and in such cases a queen would simply have to be creative and provide the entertainment for herself. Given that some queens relished trouble and deliberate confrontation with straightness, ports could be used as an enjoyable opportunity to affront others or to assert gay identity. Martin relates an anecdote that could have acted as a precursor to the film *Priscilla, Queen of the Desert*. His ship had docked in an unfamiliar Welsh port, not the most cosmopolitan of places. He and his friend, Gerty G-String, took a look round, realised that there was only one bar in the village, and decided to make the best of it. First of all, they spent some time getting ready for their night out. 'Gerty used to wear a crushed velvet blue jacket and King Charles shirts, plus a full face of make-up. She also had masses of bleached blonde hair. I was darker and smaller, and I'd got my eyes blue with eye shadow and back-combed my hair.'

The two seafarers may have been the height of 1960s camp fashion, but small-town Wales had never seen the like of them before. As he tells it, it was a confrontation of butch versus femme, backward versus sophisticated. They sauntered into a pub which was full of big, butch Welsh miners – and were greeted with a stunned silence. 'It looked as if we'd just come off a space ship. Everything just stopped.' Martin went up to the bar and said to his friend 'What are you having, girl?' The barmaid was so shocked that she was shaking as she poured their drinks. However, the pair simply stood their ground and gradually people's conversations continued as normal. 'You'd have thought that aliens had arrived in Wales that day,' Martin laughs. 'It was quite a hoot really.'

Some queens found that they attracted negative attention from other seafarers. However, once again, brazening it out was sometimes the best course of action. Geoff was in Singapore in the 1950s and had been performing in a drag show called *Tilly's Boyfriend* at Connell House, a Merchant Navy hostel that had its own stage. Afterwards he and one of his friends had a bit to drink and decided to go outside in full drag. 'When we went outside, there were some Australian sailors, in those days when they went ashore they had to wear full uniform. "Look at those queers," they were saying to each other, and I could see there was going to be a problem. And this chap came over to me. I was standing in the middle of the street, wearing all this drag and feeling very bold because I'd already had a few drinks. "Get back to your Sydney!" I said, and he just sort of fled. It pleased me immensely.'

Robert describes another instance of drag which took place in Mombasa and in a more high-powered setting. 'Every year there was a ball in aid of the Red Cross which took place in the grounds of Government House, hosted by the Governor General of Kenya. The catering staff and food for the buffet were usually supplied by our shipping company. On once occasion, [our] second chef, known as Francesca, was among those deputed to organise and run the buffet. He arrived at Government House wearing a wide-brimmed ascot hat, high heels and a figure-hugging green satin dress with a fishtail. The fact that he had also had quite a bit to drink only added to the occasion – drag queens are gifted in the art of repartee when stone cold sober but are mistresses of the art when fuelled by alcohol. You may imagine the sensation he caused standing behind the buffet tables as various Colonial Officers, farmers and their wives presented their plates only to find that they were being served by a man in drag! It was the talk of the town (and I suspect the Colony) for years afterwards.'

Clearly, if a man had the guts to walk around wearing make-up and/or drag, he was often more than likely to be able to handle confrontation. While such acts of defiance were not overtly political in the way that the Gay Liberation Front of the 1970s or various queer activist groups in the 1990s used drag performance, it could be argued that anyone who publicly refuses to conform to gender and sexuality norms by dragging up is making some sort of political statement, as well as enjoying a particular personal pleasure and testing his power against society.

While some queens may have appeared effeminate, they were tough cookies, enjoying the attention they received from strangers and revelling in the outrage they created. 'The Queen of the Pacific' commanded respect because he could fight and entertain. Straight ex-shipmate Don Trueman says admiringly: 'There were two things he said he liked: fucking and fighting. And he could do both well. He said, "You had to learn to fight if you were gay," and developed martial arts skills. According to legend, he beat a stevedore with a docker's hook on New York docks, after another stevedore threw him a hook to defend himself. He went cottaging, not because it was convenient at a time when people didn't have their own flats, but because he liked the sheer excitement, particularly in downtown New York where he was likely to be threatened. "Half the excitement was in the risk. It was all part of the game." '

Paying for sex

Stereotypically, a group of sailors (of any sexual persuasion) having a night out on shore leave in a foreign port would be expected to indulge in lots of drinking and then a visit to a brothel. Loneliness, pent-up sexual energy and the desire to make the most of their brief time ashore meant that seafarers were often expected to use prostitutes (referred to hereafter as sex-workers). Unsurprisingly, brothels flourished in many port cities as part of the sex industry, particularly those in less-developed countries serving people from the developed world. A visit to a brothel was trans-actional sex which wouldn't result in anyone having to make a long-term commitment – an important factor for those seafarers who had wives and long-time girlfriends back home. While some seafarers would have become attached to sex-workers, the fact that they could only visit them while their ship was in dock meant that such relationships weren't likely to become too intense. In the sex industry, ships were viewed as containers of fresh potential clients – in some ports there would be a welcoming com-mittee of representatives from the local brothel.

Robert describes the typical refrain that clamoured in the ears of anyone walking down a gangway, particularly in Africa and Asia. Whenever he came ashore in Egypt he would almost always be approached by a man who would ask 'Hey English, you want my sister?' When Robert answered in the negative the man would simply change tack and ask 'You want my brother?' Making offers as people left the ship was a routine that continued in the port, where seafarers report that everyone seemed to know that you were off the ship that had just tied up. Jack Robinson describes the familiar chorus that greeted him and his gay lover after they docked in Naples and walked up the Via Roma in the mid-1940s. Hungry street urchins yelled:

'Hey mister! Wanna jig-jig? Fucki-fuck? Wanna sell food?'
'Mangiare! Mangiare! Food! Food!'
'... Two cigarettes ... fuck my sister...'
'Wanna small boy?'
'Piss off.'
'Wanna big boy? Mangiare! Food! Wanna screw?'[17]

Away from the United Kingdom, other cultures often had a very different attitude towards homosexuality. For some people it was a crucial money-making opportunity, with necessarily few overriding moral or ethical issues attached. Hunger took priority over niceties.

Many seafarers' attitudes towards sex-workers were influenced by British racial attitudes of the times. Some saw sex industry workers, because they were foreign and in an inferior position, as barely being humans worthy of respect.[18] Others were more aware about their relative privilege as well-paid whites, while still paying for sexual services. Jack Robinson, sailing on the *Empire Pride* as chief night troop cook in 1945 illustrates this. 'Through the Red Sea we went, across the Indian Ocean and then tied up in Bombay. It was dreadful. The caste system disturbed me ... as we walked the foul pavements in Grant Road I wondered what caste the 'peg boys'[19] belonged to. No one would marry outside his caste but who would marry a peg-boy?

'You like a nice clean boy, sahib?'

'Piss off!'

'Very young, very clean . . . Only two rupees . . .'

Was he in the merchant caste? And the boy sitting on the greasy peg . . . what caste was he? Female ratbags sang little snatches of bawdy songs they'd learned from British troops, reached out with skinny brown arms from the cages they were kept in and tried to do business with any passer-by.' But his mate Buck whizzed Jack away in a gharry to the last word in luxury, the Taj Mahal Hotel. There Buck got cold English beer and 'Bobby and I . . . settled for a tongue bath by a gorgeous boy with kohl-darkened eyes, ruby red lips and a diamond pin in his handsome nose. He said his name was Prince Bubbles, but we didn't quite believe him.'[20]

Some of the seafarers we interviewed saw no harm in occasionally using prostitutes when they were offered to them, whereas others said they would never have offered anyone money for sex. Others accepted that prostitution occurred, but money didn't directly come into the equation. A night out, a lavish meal ('big eats') or a present may have been acceptable exchanges in some cases.

The strong association of seafarers with sex industry workers – be they exploitative Maggie Mays, stereotypical Whores-with-a-Heart-of-Gold[21] or simply poverty-stricken women, often wives of seamen who hadn't left enough money behind – may be an exaggeration and a sexualisation of a more complex, intimate, less commercial encounter: hospitality humanely offered to ready strangers. The sexualised story fits the myth of sailor as adventurer. However, a proportion of the gay seafarers who were interviewed *did* describe encounters with both male and female sex-workers. Sometimes very young, inexperienced or closeted sailors would end up at a female brothel, usually having being talked into it by friends. Bill, an engineer from 1974 to 1980, often passed through Korea and was initially surprised at how the women started chasing him whenever he got off the ship. It was an established tradition that seafarers went with the women for a few dollars and pretended that they were rampant with them, even if they weren't. Going with a female sex-worker could sometimes be a good way of establishing a 'heterosexual' identity although it could also have the reverse effect. Another informant told us that on his first voyage, he went with a female sex-worker because it was 'the done thing'. However, it was an awful experience and she ended up slapping his face. The experience helped him realise that he definitely preferred men – and after that his relationship with female sex industry workers changed.

'They didn't appeal to me, but they used to love me because I'd talk to them, and they got on quite a different level with me. With other men it was no chat, get straight into bed, but with me I didn't want to get into bed, so I'd talk to them.'

Male sex-workers were not as common, but in some cities gay brothels did exist. Robert once visited one in Barcelona while he was drunk. He remembers that it was a large house at the docks end of the Ramblas, an area where some of the more camp gay men could be found seated in ladies hairdressing saloons. The brothel, he found, 'had several floors and one entered via the basement into a sort of large reception area where a number of men, including some British and American sailors in uniform, were being entertained by a number of very handsome boys of various nationalities.'

'A man of about 30 came up to me and after offering me a drink asked me what I was looking for. I told him that I preferred young men without body hair. He told me that I had come to the right place and asked me if I was ready to "view" what was on offer. I was very excited by this time and followed him through a curtain to a short passage with a door at the end, which had a small window set in it at eye level. He told me that this was a one way mirror and that I could see the men, but they could not see me. I looked through and was amazed and delighted to see about a dozen young men – all naked, standing in a semi circle. My guide started to tell me about each man – where he was from, how old he was and what he would or would not do – passive only, active only, versatile and so on.'

Robert wanted to purchase a German man he had seen in the reception area. However, he was told that the man had already been taken for the night by two American sailors. So instead he opted for an 18-year-old Arab who did not speak much English but was perfectly capable of performing sexually. The cost of the experience was about £15 (a sum that would have bought a new record player in the UK, and comprised three-quarters of a British agricultural labourer's weekly wage).

On another occasion, in the 1960s, Robert had gone with two of his friends to the Rainbow in Mombassa. 'It was late in the evening and very crowded when we got there. We ordered our beers and then I heard one of my friends order me a 'special', but he wouldn't tell me what it was. We were seated at a table with a long tablecloth that reached the floor. After about ten minutes I became aware that someone was unzipping my fly. I went to look under the table but my companions stopped me and suggested that I relax and enjoy. It immediately became apparent that someone was very expertly giving me a blow-job. I was so excited that I came in no time at all. As soon as I had finished a young African man came out from under the table and at my friend's prompting I gave him two shillings as a tip. In those days it mustn't have been more than the price of a beer!' Another establishment in Japan, called Eve's Bar, offered a similar 'special' which was only available while standing at the counter of the bar. Tiny curtains would open, a hand would come through and a mouth would administer oral sex. 'Both males and females were available, and it was fascinating to watch a sailor standing at the bar, glassy eyed and legs trembling, and then collapse across the bar after reaching a climax,' remembers Robert.

In Singapore, Geoff found a subculture of male sex-workers who dressed as women and were known locally as Kai Tais. They plied their trade to closeted gay and bisexual men on Bugis Street. While in Hong Kong, Geoff was in one bar that was well-known for its gay male prostitution. He got to know the workers quite well and one of them asked him why *he* didn't also charge money for sex. 'It doesn't work like that, my dear,' Geoff replied.

Historically, servicemen have been suppliers of gay, usually rough, paid sex. For example, guardsmen were particularly associated with male prostitution in the mid-twentieth century, while Donaldson notes that sailors in the past have been stereotyped as sexually casual, easily plied with alcohol and willing to do almost anything for money.[22] However, none of the seafarers we interviewed were aware of any sailors who took money in exchange for sex, despite the reputation that some stewards had of being prepared to do anything for a pecuniary incentive. This was partly because, for them, sex was more important than being a means to a financial end and partly because prostitution was often seen as shameful. Additionally, some catering workers were already making money in tips as well as in wages, and some were involved in systematic scams, such as selling off stolen goods from the ships' stores and short-changing drunk passengers. Paid sex may not have seemed a culturally acceptable way of earning extra money.

America: Gay Liberation and bath-house culture

After the Second World War, for the ships that stopped off at American ports there was a new culture awaiting British gay seafarers, one that was far from being about sex tourism in a climate of colonial relations. New York and San Francisco had long offered facilities to visiting seafarers. As early as 1927 'whenever the fleet comes into town, every sailor who wants his dick licked comes to the Times Square Building. It seems to be common knowledge among the sailors that [1 Times Square] is the place to go if they want to meet fairies,' complained Mr Farley, whose newsstand was in its basement.[23] Since the end of the Second World War, many of the gay Americans, whom Allan Bérubé has described as serving in the military,[24] had been settling in cities such as New York, Los Angeles and San Francisco, and large gay communities had quickly grown up in these places. As in the UK, American attitudes towards gay men were not particularly tolerant from 1945 to 1970. After the war, homosexuals, particularly those in the armed forces or government, had been judged as security risks, potentially being open to extortion. In addition, the defection of British gay spies Guy Burgess and Donald Maclean to the Soviet Union in 1951 had further linked homosexuality to communism. American gay bars, like those in the UK, were routinely raided by the police. Gay men and lesbians were stigmatised by society.

Then, on the night of Friday, 27 June 1969, the Stonewall Inn, a gay bar in New York, was raided. The patrons decided to fight back. The gay bar culture joined forces with gay activists, and this paved the way for the emergence of an organised Gay Liberation movement. More than any other occupational group in the UK, seamen had a greater chance of happening to be in New York on that night. Those on the transatlantic runs from Liverpool or Southampton to New York were therefore in a position to understand the new climate in North America. Many British seafarers had been visiting New York for years and were already happy to import its culture, which they labelled 'Cunard Yanks'. They enlivened life in the UK with clothes and styles from Manhattan, and an appreciation of jazz and black culture that they brought back from Harlem on vinyl. For Jack Robinson, sailing on the *Tyndareus* in the early 1940s to the sounds of Glenn Miller and Twelfth Street Rag, part of the pleasure of the trip would be in acquiring the radical new alternative to button flies. 'I hoped to visit America, to buy some modern clothes like the zip trousers, jacket-type shirts and colourful gear that only US servicemen and seamen wore.'[25]

In the 1970s, North American gay subcultures in metropolitan areas experienced a kind of 'Golden Age' associated with hope, freedom and a new definition of gay identity which focused upon masculine 'Marlboro Man' imagery, as physique magazines illustrate. Many British gay men were amazed during the 1970s and 1980s when they crossed the Atlantic to America and Canada and found a dynamic, vibrant and political gay scene.[26] The North American gay subculture, being more advanced, complete and self-promoting than the British gay subculture, provided a political and cultural template for British gay men.[27] The Americans had shown that by uniting they were beginning to achieve economic and political power – for example, gay men and lesbians were winning political office. 'Gay is good' went the West Coast slogan: a motto that could be proclaimed on ships, even if the lifestyle changes were not compatible with a ship's conservative social structure.

Although it is hard to tell from the limited evidence available whether Gay Liberation politics had any effect on sexual identities in the British Merchant Navy, there are several reasons why it probably didn't. First, most UK passenger ships only went to New York, not the West Coast, so gay seafarers encountered only one version of the movement. Secondly, as Lisa Power notes, closeted gay men – as many seafarers were – felt frightened by the Gay Liberation Front (GLF). Its blatant vociferousness could undo the limited gains made. Managing social relations in an intense residential job is a feat and GLF politics would have affronted some straight colleagues if imported onto the often-conservative ships. Thirdly, the GLF was associated with student politics, and at that time very few working-class people went to university. This meant that the majority of seafarers, despite the occasional students doing summer vacation jobs on ships, were unfamiliar with the alien culture of student protest meetings, for instance those at the London School of Economics or those opposing Miss World contests as denigrating. They were still buying the very physique magazines that GLFers were burning in 1971 on the grounds that such magazines were part of the role-playing that 'cripples the ability to form balanced relationships and ... destroys the emotions in wasteful fantasy'.[28] And although some of the lower deck crew were of a class that might be expected to make political protest (for example, the demonstrations against the 1971 Industrial Relations Bill had GLF members involved), service workers on ships tended to be entrepreneurial and individualistic, not collective in consciousness.

Fourthly, the permissiveness on some passenger ships was such that some gay men may not have felt any need to join protest parades, even if they had been ashore and had enough leave time for such activities. Finally, some gay seafarers would have found it difficult to side with the GLF's protests about masculinity's destructiveness. For example, the articles in *Achilles Heel*, the liberationist men's movement magazine that ran from 1978 to 1981, stressed that men's estrangement from their emotional selves was a heavy price to pay for the privileges of living as men in a patriarchal society.[29] As writer Victor Seidler argued soon afterwards: 'If we live in a "man's world" it is not a world that has been built upon the needs and nourishment of men. Rather it is social world of power and subordination in which men have been forced to compete if we want to benefit from our inherited masculinity.'[30] Nevertheless, there was at least one gay seafarer prominent in the Gay Liberation Front, the late Mick Belsten.[31] He was living ashore at the time.

For many gay men, the over-riding ethic of the time was sexual self-fulfilment.[32] With Gay Liberation the concept of gender deviance had been removed, provoking a sense of pride in gay men. Gay sex was no longer considered something dirty and shameful, and as a result a bath-house culture had emerged in America. While the more overtly political and confrontational side of Gay Liberation may not have always engaged the average gay seafarer, the resulting sexual openness that Gay Liberation afforded in the USA, was something in which they were able to share.

Bath-houses had been popularised in books such as Armistead Maupin's *Tales of the City* (1978) and Larry Kramer's *Faggots* (1978), or films such as *The Ritz* (1976). They were often explicitly targeted at gay men, offering a paradise of hedonism and sexual opportunity. Many bath-houses were more than just places where sex could be obtained – they could function as social clubs or places of entertainment. Bette Midler famously began her career by performing at The Continental in New York. Some saw it as an unbelievable Wonderland. Frank says of San Francisco: 'The Club Baths was the best one, and then there was Ellis Street and some on the Castro. The Everard was another world to us from England.' At a famous New York bath-house: 'We entered the changing cubicles and a small waist was really necessary for changing into the smallest towel. The enormous Roman pool had the most beautiful men there leaning over the rail watching every new face entering or swimming nude. The steam room was dimly lit and could maybe hold about 30 people. The large chain on the door heralded new trade. Daisy chains [group sex] were everywhere and every type of aperture appeared to be filled with something. I lost my friend for hours and required a rest. The only place for peace and quiet was the cubicle for changing. Later on, turning a corner there appeared to be steps leading to another room filled with dormitory beds and sleeping cubicles. In charge of this section of the building sat a large, burly policeman with a gun who was getting a blow-job from a kindly customer. I thought "God this is living".'

As the bath-houses were places where semi-public and/or group sex occurred, they could often afford some embarrassment when visited with seafaring friends who were also colleagues. The darkened corridors and vapour-filled steam rooms could sometimes mean that you didn't know who you were having sex with until afterwards. Frank was ashore in San Francisco and one of his friends paid an embarrassing visit to a bath-house. 'He was in the Turkish bath and pleasuring this gentleman orally, and in the heavy steam, somebody came behind him and started to rim him. It was one of the stewards from the ship. He said, "you dirty bitch", and of course he couldn't wait to tell everybody back on the ship what had happened.'

Ian tells another story about a visit to a bath-house in San Francisco: 'I'd gone with my friend and he said, "I'm going to have some trade," so I said,

"I'll just sit at the bar." I didn't like those sorts of things. Anyway, I sat in the bar and there were television screens showing gay porn, and then I suddenly realised that I wasn't watching a porno film, it was showing what was going on in the steam room. And it suddenly showed my friend's face on the screen. It was so embarrassing, I couldn't tell him what was happening. I did afterwards of course. We laughed about that for a long time.'

The bath-houses flourished during the 1970s, but many were closed down in the 1980s due to concerns about AIDS. As Frank says of his trips to the American bath-houses, 'Many of the guys who did everything in there, they aren't with us any more. It's sad.'

Gay pornography

As well as being places of sexual opportunity, stop-overs at distant shores afforded gay seafarers the chance to purchase gay pornography, which could have functioned as a useful stand-in for sex with a partner during periods at sea when none was available. While heterosexual imagery abounds in the media, gay pornography was one of the few ways that gay sexuality was acknowledged or validated. At a time when, in many parts of the world, homosexuality was unmentionable or scorned, seeing pictures of desirable, naked men, or reading about men having sex with each other *and enjoying it*, was more than just a turn-on; it was a potentially liberating experience, providing people with sexual role models who didn't care what society thought of them – a long way from the usual representations (or non-representations) of gay men found in the 1950s, 1960s and 1970s mainstream media: victims, sissies and depressives.

Bringing gay pornography on to a ship was always risky as it could have resulted in embarrassment or even dismissal if found by the wrong person. Bill says, 'When I was in the States, I started going round those bookstores and magazine stores. On the quiet I bought a couple of magazines and had a wank over a few of them. I took them home with me, concealed.'

The laws in the UK governing pictorial or photographic representations of the naked male image were somewhat strict. Geoff remembers that the nudist magazine *Health and Efficiency* was about the nearest you could get to pornography. However, overseas there was a lot more on offer, particularly coming from America after the 1950s, which was gradually becoming more daring. 'Physique' magazines were pioneered by amateur photographer Bob Mizer, who had formed The Athletic Model Guild and started a mail order business in 1948. By 1952, Mizer's magazine, *Physique Pictorial*, could be found on sale in Europe as well as across America.

Robert describes his first encounter with such pictures: 'On our third night out from London I was having a beer at the bar when a Second Chef came up to me and said, as he handed me a book, "I hear you like Agatha Christie – have you read this one? – I think you'll enjoy it." I took the

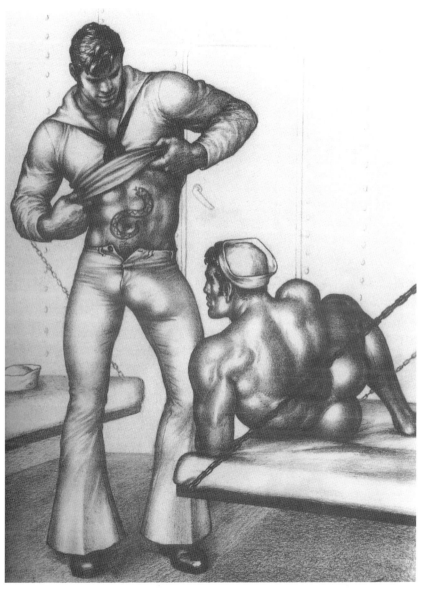

Images of seafarers preparing to have sex like this one were popular staples of erotic gay artists. Picture courtesy of the Tom of Finland Guild (1962).

book and it fell open to reveal two or three gay pornographic photographs. Completely flustered, as I had never seen anything like them before, but at the same time excited by them, I closed the book – but in doing so managed to let the photos fall to the deck. As I hurriedly retrieved them I was aware that several of his companions were watching me with some amusement. I tried to give the book back to him, saying that I had read it (I think it was *Murder at the Vicarage*) but he said, "Never mind, hang on to it anyway, I'm sure you'll enjoy reading it again." I returned to my cabin, where for the first time in my life I wanked off fantasising over hard-core porn pictures rather than advertisements from mainstream magazines!'

F. Valentine Hooven, a writer on gay sexuality, notes that by the end of the 1950s so many battles had been lost by the American censors that even gay-oriented physique photos were tolerated, as long as they were seen to have some redeeming social value.[33] This usually meant that the implicitly gay magazines had to stress the importance of good grooming, exercise and body-building, while at the same time showing lots of muscular men in posing pouches. *Physique Pictorial* paved the way for a number of similar magazines: *Tomorrow's Man*, *Vim*, *Trim*, *Grecian Guild Pictorial*, *Adonis*, and *American Manhood*. The physique magazines became more daring over time, graduating to showing men wrestling, or naked from behind. The emphasis on body-builders and the importance of physical fitness gradually decreased, until by the 1970s gay magazines had started to feature a range of different body types in more sexually explicit and full-frontal poses. The magazines also showcased erotic drawings by artists like Tom of Finland, Etienne (later known as Stephen), Art-Bob (possibly a pseudonym of Bob Mizer), Bob MacLane, Steve Masters and Harry Bush. Sailors were a recurring theme of both the drawings and photography in these magazines.

However, physique magazines were not the only source of pornography available when docked in a foreign port. As well as offering access to sex-workers, some dockland pimps also had photographs or 'dirty postcards' to sell, and it was also possible to buy written pornography. Geoff remembers that some of the earliest examples (of heterosexual erotica) were called Port Said Bibles – pocket-sized booklets that had been printed in Paris. In 1961, H. Lynn Womack had successfully sued the Postmaster General for seizing copies of his physique magazines. A year later he founded Guild Press, a mail-order book service which offered erotic novels for a gay male readership. Other publishers followed suit and the availability of gay erotic novels started to pick up pace in the USA in the mid-1960s, with 30 gay paperbacks being published in 1965 and over 100 in 1966.[34]

(c)

(b)

(a)

Gay porn: (a) *Sailor's Hunky Trucker* (1976), courtesy of Surree Limited Inc, (b) *Lusty Seaman* (1972), courtesy of Parisian Press, and (c) *A Sailor Coming Out* (1972), courtesy of Parisian Press.

With titles like *Reform School Punks*, *Biker in Bondage*, *Lusty Seamen*, *Campus Gang Bang*, *Trucker's Stud Son*, *The Cops are Comin'* and *Hayloft Cousins*, these novels explored and exploited common themes associated with masculine occupations and same-sex institutions. In not showing pictures, the books were able to be much more explicit in their *descriptions* of gay men having sex than the physique magazines of the time, leaving little to the reader's imagination. And as the 1960s progressed, the books focused less on social realism and more on sex. As writer Susan Stryker explains, 'most gay paperbacks published after 1965 were sheer sexual wish-fulfilment fantasies'.[35] These novels were very seldom about queens; they do not offer role models to camp seafarers. But they do reveal the extent of the interest in a type of overt macho virility.

Worldly wisdoms

While life on the passenger ships could be a liberating and exciting place for gay seafarers, it could also be a restricted, repetitive and regulated existence, occurring within the context of long working hours, carrying out the same daily routines and meeting the same people. Shore leave therefore functioned as an important kind of holiday from the norm and a learning experience for all seafarers. For gay sailors it could be a chance to explore further their sexual identities, in a much wider, more unpredictable context. The ship itself was a liminal space, where identity boundaries could be transgressed, romances could occur and a party atmosphere reigned, but the employees of the ships were responsible for creating and maintaining such an atmosphere, devising shows to entertain themselves and passengers, while ensuring that their behaviour didn't attract too much negative attention from officers. During the short periods of time when they were free to explore a foreign city, however, the main people they had to consider were themselves.

Frequently, they returned to the ship with a knowledge of different shore societies and a new position from which to view themselves and their sexuality. Knowledge gained from gay colleagues could be used ashore to locate the subcultures in different port cities. Time spent on land could provide opportunities to catch up with friends, spend a night of passion with a long-distance lover, or secure a one-night stand. In particular, stop-overs in American cities like San Francisco and New York exposed British gay men to a more open subculture than they had experienced back home, introducing them to bath-houses and bookstores where gay pornography could be purchased.

Partnerships in less developed foreign ports were not simply an early form of sex tourism. Eastern acceptance of gay activity was welcomed, not crudely exploited. Middle Eastern countries, argues Mary McIntosh, made a 'radical distinction between the feminine, passive homosexual and his active, masculine partner. There, however, neither is thought of as having been "born" homosexual.'[36] This relaxed attitude was lapped up appreciatively, as a better approach to sexual relations. Several of the men we interviewed retain a respectful bond with that part of the world which opened their eyes to the different possibilities in relationships.

Moving between foreign ports meant that British gay seafarers were likely to be more sexually sophisticated than their shore-side counterparts. Their travels and experiences in other countries offered them new perspectives on sexuality, whereas for much of the 1950s and 1960s the British model involved scandal, secrecy and shame. With exposure to different cultures and viewpoints, seafaring gay men were in the advantageous position of seeing a much wider range of attitudes towards sexuality, allowing them to take pride in themselves and cheerfully reject the restrictions placed upon them by British society.

Perhaps this goes some way in explaining why gay seafarers were not seen to be traditionally involved in the Gay Liberation movements of the 1970s. In choosing a life at sea, they had implicitly rejected the hegemonic social values imposed on them in the UK. In many ways they already *were* liberated. There wasn't a crying need for Gay Pride marches or demonstrations on ships because gay men were already accepted by much of the straight crew and passengers, as we will see in the following chapter.

Notes

1. Houlbrook, Matt (2001) 'For Whose Convenience? Gay Guides, Cognitive Maps and the Construction of Homosexual London 1917-67', in Gunn, S. and Morris, R.J. (eds), *Identities in Space: Contested Terrains in the Western City since 1850*, Ashgate, Aldershot, p. 169.
2. We use the semantically neutral terms 'sex-worker' and 'sex industry', rather than 'prostitute' and 'prostitution', with their associations of 'bad women'. These terms are now conventionally used by people in the industry to refer to a structured service in which the workers who have direct physical contact are one part of a supply side. Although these are anachronistic terms, because neither the seafarers whom we interviewed, nor the people who offered to sell sexual services to them in the 1950s and 1960s would have used them, this is an important distinction to make.

3. For a summary of the sex industry's operations, see Seabrooke, J. (2001) *Travels in the Skin Trade: Tourism and the Sex Industry*, Pluto Press, London, and Weitzer, R.J. (2000) *Sex for Sale: Prostitution, Pornography and the Sex Industry*, Routledge, London.

4. For a summary of these arguments in relation to gay space, see Houlbrook, 'For Whose Convenience?', p. 166. He particularly uses Michael, K. and Pile, S. (eds) (1993) *Place and the Politics of Identity*, Routledge, London and New York. For gay histories informed by such theories, see for example: Maynard, S. (1994) 'Through a Hole in a Lavatory Wall: Homosexual Subcultures, Police Surveillance and the Dialectics of Discovery: Toronto 1890–1930', *Journal of the History of Sexuality*, 5(2), pp. 207–42; Chauncey, G. (1995) *Gay New York: The Making of the Gay Male World, 1890–1940*, Flamingo, London; Chauncey, G. (1991) 'Policed: Gay Men's Strategies of Everyday Resistance', in Taylor, W. (ed.), *Inventing Times Square: Commerce and Culture at the Crossroads of the World*, Russell Sage Foundation, New York; Sibalis, M.D. (1999) 'Paris', in Higgs, D. (ed.), *Queer Sites: Gay Urban Histories since 1600*, Routledge, London and New York.

5. Lane, T. (1986) *Grey Dawn Breaking: British Merchant Seafarers in the Late Twentieth Century*, Manchester University Press, Manchester.

6. Nineteenth-century versions of this are described by Burton, V. (2001) 'Boundaries and Identities in the Nineteenth Century Port: Sailortown Narratives and Urban Space', in Gunn and Morris, *Identities in Space*, p. 140.

7. *San Diego Sailor* (1969) Black Knight Classics, Guild Press, Washington DC (no credited author).

8. Martin, A. (1987) *Seafood Platter*, His 69 Surrey Books, Star Distributors, New York.

9. Kirk, K. and Heath, E. (1984) *Men in Frocks*, Gay Men's Press, London, p. 31.

10. Robinson, J. (1988) *Jack and Jamie Go To War*, Gay Men's Press, London, p. 177.

11. For a useful discussion of the meanings of the cottage (public lavatory used a gay meeting place), see Houlbrook, 'For Whose Convenience?'.

12. Jarman, D. (1993) *At Your Own Risk*, Vintage, London, p. 52.

13. This lavatory was the Rialto at the bottom of Princes Drive. It was a popular place of assignation for gay men, including seafarers and the rare local black gay man.

14. Bérubé, A. (1991) *Coming Out under Fire: The History of Gay Men and Women in World War Two*, Penguin, London, p. 109.

15. Robinson, *Jack and Jamie Go To War*, p. 82.

16. Jan Jordan has written a sympathetic study based on heterosexual women's versions of these relationships. See Jordan, J. (1993) *Ship Girls: The Invisible Women of the Sea*, unpublished paper given to the Women and The Sea conference, Wellington Maritime Museum, New Zealand, December 1993.

17. Robinson, *Jack and Jamie Go To War*, p. 153.

18. For example, several seafarers said that it was unusual for heterosexual seamen to care whether or not they got a foreign woman pregnant or passed on a disease to her. The idea was that if she put herself in that line of business, she should know she had to take anything that was coming.

19. 'Peg boys' were one of the eastern myths that no one has substantiated for us: young, male sex industry workers who were displayed sitting with wooden pegs of various gauges up their rectum, to indicate to customers what size of penis they could take. As Alan points out, this was not really a useful guide as the sphincter has very expandable muscles.

20. Robinson, *Jack and Jamie Go To War*, p. 183.

21. Maggie May is the subject of a folk song: a 'dirty, robbin', no-good' Liverpool woman who robs a 'Homeward bounder' while he's sleeping after sex. Many classic seafarers' yarns include stories of sex industry workers who help them out with money and comfort after they've been rolled in a foreign port.

22. Donaldson, S. (1989) 'Seafaring' (encyclopaedia entry), in Dynes, W.R. (ed.), *Encyclopaedia of Homosexuality*, Garland, Garden City, NY, pp. 1172-5.

23. See: http://huzbears.websitenow.com/gayhistory/ts.html. See also Bérubé, *Coming Out under Fire*, p. 116. He talks about the areas also used by gay soldiers and seafarers in Washington, Boston, New Orleans and San Diego.

24. Ibid., p. 109.

25. Robinson, *Jack and Jamie Go To War*, p. 115.

26. Derek Ogg, quoted in Jivani, A. (1997) *It's Not Unusual: A History of Lesbian and Gay Britain in the Twentieth Century*, Michael O'Mara Books, London, pp. 173-4.

27. Jivani, *It's Not Unusual*, p. 174.

28. Lisa Power (1995) *No Bath but Plenty of Bubbles: An Oral History of the Gay Liberation Front, 1970-73*, Cassell, London, p. 100, quoting what she says appears to be the text of a leaflet of the time.

29. Tosh, J. and Roper, M. (eds) (1991) *Manful Assertions: Masculinities in Britain since 1800*, Routledge, London and New York, p. 6.

30. Seidler, V. (1989) *Rediscovering Masculinity: Reason Language and Sexuality*, Routledge, London, p. 21.

31. Power, *No Bath but Plenty of Bubbles*, p. 221, 222 and others.

32. Spencer, C. (1995) *Homosexuality: A History*, Fourth Estate, London, p. 373.

33. Hooven, F.V. (1995) *Beefcake: The Muscle Magazines of America 1950-1970*, Taschen, Germany, p. 60.

34. Norman, T. (1994) *American Erotic Paperbacks: A Bibliography*, by the author, Burbank, CA.

35. Stryker, S. (2001) *Queer Pulp: Perverted Passions from the Golden Age of the Paperback*, Chronicle Books, San Francisco, CA.

36. McIntosh, M. (1996) 'The Homosexual Role', in Seidman, S. (ed.), *Queer Theory/Sociology*, Blackwell, Oxford, p. 37.

Chapter 7

Part of a Team

How did gay seafarers get on with colleagues and passengers on their ships? The answer is not straightforward. Not only did situations change with different periods of history on different ships, but the people who gave us evidence viewed it differently, depending on their frame of mind when they told particular stories. Also, we cannot make this a simple summary based on the binary idea of gay/straight people because sexual identities could be so fluid. People could be gay for one trip or they could be gay at sea generally, but straight each time they went ashore, as Chapter 4 shows. They could be queens, butches, experimenters and swingers; out, sometimes out, or quite covert. On ships, you had to take people as they came, so to speak, on that particular voyage. This chapter examines social relations on ships, which help to explain the structures that could encourage or inhibit different kinds of homosexual behaviour. Having established that context, we then look at gay men's relations with straight crew. Finally, we explore how gay seafarers related to passengers.

Social relations on ships

Let's think about ships as social organisations, not vehicles that move people. This allows us see that what gay seafarers could do was partly determined by the setting in which they operated. They did not always have freedom of choice.

Social organisations have routines and codes of behaviour that can determine what members of that organisation can and can't do (or at least be *seen* to do). Organisations are set up for different reasons, to do different things; they function in different ways, and that affects how different people within them operate. Three categories have been identified by Michael Argyle, who studies social organisations. They are coercive, util-

Seafarers were part of a team – on and off duty. Picture courtesy of private donor.

itarian and moral organisations, as we discuss below. Each type helps explain what was and was not possible for gay men on ships.

First, there are coercive organisations, such as prisons or hospitals, where people do what they are told because they are unable to leave. Sailing ships had been a bit like this – even the passengers were told when to go to bed – and sometimes twentieth-century crews experienced ships as being coercive because they had so few rights. They signed a contract for a whole voyage, which bound them to a job in the way most workers ashore are not; to leave was an illegal offence. The captain could legally clap an offender in irons. To some extent control was justified because seafarers, like air crew, are safety professionals who are responsible for safeguarding lives. Discipline is necessary. But how far should it go? And how does this affect the people on board, such as gay people, who don't see why they should do what is 'normal' – especially when they are off-duty?

Ships have been likened to the prisons, mental hospitals, boarding schools, monasteries, barracks and concentration camps that sociologist Erving Goffman defined as 'total institutions'. In such total institutions blocks of people, isolated from outside life, are bureaucratically processed. The routines for inmates – administered by guards, warders, nurses – is that they sleep, work and play within the right confines of this institution; it controls all they do. Is this true of ships too? Are passengers inmates and seafarers guards? It's controversial; some maritime historians argue that seafarers have more autonomy than that,[1] and anyway, passengers are paying guests so they have to be given at least the *illusion* of power.

Whether or not we agree that ships are total institutions, we can certainly take on board Goffman's ideas that 'guards' in such a situation are confined like the inmates. And such confinement on ships can mean that 'guards' have their sexual behaviour severely limited – even when they are off-duty. (The situation, pre-1980s, was even more odd because homosexuality itself was grounds for incarceration. So there is the ironic situation that on ship seafarers were the 'prison guards' while ashore they may have been the prisoners.)

It is useful to think that postwar, gay-friendly passenger vessels had *some* of the structural characteristics of total institutions. But they were unlike other custodial institutions because the 'guards' were so good at getting round rules; the higher officers (unlike asylum superintendents or head monks) customarily turned blind eyes, and the inmates were to some extent playmates and bosses, not prisoners or patients. In the real ships we are talking about, boundaries were blurred, functions overlapped and ambiguities were dealt with by the tiniest of niceties. There was a resistant subculture. However, the underlying whiff of strictness meant that many gay seafarers, particularly officers, felt very much under surveillance and were obliged to be obedient to the organisation's culture.

Perhaps Argyle's second category of organisations is more appropriate: the utilitarian social organisation, where rewards are worked for and thus earned. So people (seafarers in our case) were colleagues in the routine business of producing batches of safely and happily transported passengers. In processing these 'units' the workers were organised into doing different tasks: there were divisions of labour similar to those in the Ritz or Fortnum and Mason. The difference was that safety on a ship is paramount; there is a shared sense of danger that is not present in an hotel or a shop on dry land generally. Heavy control can be justified. By implication, social relations in a utilitarian organisation could involve a conflict between company needs (a satisfactorily finished product, that is a passenger who would recommend the shipping line to other potential customers) and the seafarers' *own* ways of working around the job and with colleagues. In relation to gay seafarers, one question that arises is how could homosexuality be accommodated or even utilised in this processing of passengers? It is here that we understand that *camp* employees were utilised – even valued – as desirable entertainment for the passengers. And the many *other* gay men, who were committed to a higher standard of personal service than heterosexual women and men were thought to offer, were prized employees because they improved passenger satisfaction.

Labour shortages, and the fact that so many of the British working-class people who were prepared to do stewarding work were troublesome – drinking, fighting and not turning up for duty – meant that a queen was popular. They were so industrious and good at being housewifely that they would be allocated the main suites of rooms, secured by the most prestigious, wealthy passengers, says a former personnel officer for a shipping line, speaking in a personal capacity. 'We knew the suites would be immaculately serviced.'

However, on many of the larger passenger ships seafarers were not just working for the company's rewards; some were there just for that extra gain – the trip. Others were working on their own account, for tips from a score of fleeting mistresses and masters. A number saw the job altruistically, or as their vocation. So this ties in with Argyle's third category: moral organisations such as the hospital, university and church.[2] Members of these sorts of organisation are committed to its values and goals: in this case, the ship was a form of public transport that was viewed, among other things, as the floating arm of the empire. And everyone was committed to the ship's safe arrival in foreign ports. There was a sense of rallying together, as a 'family', against the common threats – the sea and troubling foreign-ness. Some officers were concerned for the greater good of the ship's population – if only partially. Therefore they had a lot invested in securing the best possible working relations between all members of staff. As the ship-owners formally stated: 'It is one of the Owners' main aims to produce conditions and climates in which crews will be contented, live in harmony and be prepared to give of their best. This, at its lowest, is essential for the efficient operation of a ship.'[3]

The senior members of these organisations have very different types of power in each of the three categories described above. Respectively, these are punishment, rewards and appeal to shared goals. On ships, therefore, gay seafarers' relations with colleagues might include developing strategies to avoid punishment, co-operating to create an atmosphere on board so that passengers disembarked as satisfied customers; and working – or at least *seeming* to work – with others to ensure the best possible trip for all. Within that organisational structure there were a number of key questions for crew members of stigmatised minority groups such as gay people: How can I safely be me? To whom can I be 'out' without risking too much?

And for historians there are equally key questions. What did the structure allow, dictate or create? What kinds of gay behaviour (for example, camp performances) emerged *because* of the particular social set-up? How might that have been different in a structure where there was less focus on a particular kind of masculinity, which was 'proved' by being protective towards more passive and 'feminine' colleagues or by successful, penetrative sexual encounters? Given that identities are at least partially constructed or reinforced by a complex network of social relations, what kinds of social relations on ships might have created different kinds of gay behaviour? For example, what social factors determined that sea queens were welcome on those off-shore resorts that were passenger ships? And how did social relations ashore and at sea benefit from some ships being places where being gay was unexceptional (because if there was no social benefit it would not have been so permitted)?

Order and tradition

Ships are, of course, floating towns with all of the associated hierarchies and tensions, orders and disorders that occur within them. 'See, we all knew the codes,' explains Chris. 'You accepted your allocated place because it was a good life that you didn't want to up-end.' And until the mid-1960s seafarers accepted those boundaries despite their restlessness about all sorts of constraints, including status divisions and protocol, he points out.

The carefully calibrated social order was challenged in two ways. First, politically-aware trade unionists protested at multiple injustices and exploitations, to the extent that there was a major strike in 1966 and ship owners kept a careful – but unsuccessful – list of banned employees.[4] Secondly, the official regime was also more anarchistically ignored, disrupted and denied on ships through the systematic crime that went on, particularly illegal gambling syndicates and theft by people in the catering department.[5] Even ditties challenged the companies' official face, converting the PR slogan on the old *Oriana* ('42,000 tons of Oceanic Splendour') of 'Every meal a banquet, every steward a film star' into 'Every meal a work-up, every steward a queer'.

So a key aspect of social relations on the ships was the tension between those who supported and wished to control the established order and those opposed to that order, and all those who fell somewhere in between at different points. Some of those officers employed to maintain order (for example, by suppressing too much openly camp activity) were gay themselves. Some, particularly camp gay men, would have liked to establish their *own* sort of order (for example, a minority would have liked to exclude women from ships, even as passengers). And some of the ship's complement pretended, or even *believed* themselves to be orderly but actually behaved quite transgressively when the opportunity arose. So there were those who conformed, and those who appeared to conform.

Fortunately, the shipboard population seemed to be capable of coping with these differences.

A related tension was between those people who were serious about the sea and those who were simply using the experience for their own ends – whether that was enjoying daily gay company, making money on the side or seeing the world. Catering staff were seen historically as 'not proper seamen', and not masculine.[6] This feeling even extended towards Chief Stewards, as seafaring historian Frank Bullen argued:

Every seaman, no matter how humble, feels towards them ... a certain disdainful sense of superiority. He can never quite get rid of the feeling that they are menials ... there is amongst sailors a marked repugnance ... to being expected to do body service to other people, except in an emergency or as an act of charity.[7]

Stewarding staff were often particularly opposed by the die-hards who were unhappy about women and passengers being on ships at all; about ships being fancily-decorated chocolate boxes, not functional vehicles; and about the general disruption of the 'masculine' craft of 'mastering' the sea.

The hospitality industry ashore and at sea attracts people who want casual work and tend to be opportunistic, according to retention studies.[8] Career durations are usually just two to three years. So the shipboard department that happened to have the largest numbers of gay people in it – catering – was that which 'serious' career seafarers disliked anyway, particularly in the interwar and immediate postwar years. It contained people who, gay or not, were not traditional and committed seafaring men but members of that derided group: shore-siders out on an exploitative spree, trivial and feminised landlubbers who were, in their view, without much of a clue about the things that matter in life.

Traditionally, then, there was a divide between hotel-side workers and ship-side workers, perhaps unconsciously focusing on the definition of who was a core worker and who was a peripheral one. And this was made all the more tense because the masculinist die-hards saw catering staff as an innovation, doing feminised work and operating from an entrepreneurial rather than team-oriented mindset. This denigration and exceptionalisation of catering staff waned as traditionally-minded white deck crew became fewer in the 1970s, 1980s and 1990s but the historical legacy lingered.[9]

Ships, in all their diversity, were, as Chapter 2 indicated, social situations where people from many backgrounds were flung together for short durations. A vessel contained people from different cultures and different classes, with different goals (from making a bit of extra money on the side to a long-term career) and different affinities with maritime business; unity would not necessarily be expected. A voyage almost inevitably *had* to include trouble. One ex-purser says, 'I remember one three-week Caribbean cruise in the late 1970s, where in that short space of time a gay seaman cut his wrists because his lover had left him, a bell-boy (age 16) was found in bed with a 15-year-old girl passenger, and two

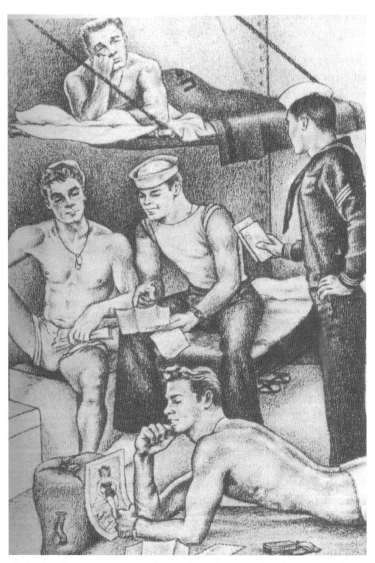

People had to learn to get on well, not least because they became each other's replacement family while at sea. 'Mail Call' by Bill MacLane, *Physique Pictorial*, Summer 1955. Courtesy of Wayne Stanley, Athletic Model Guild.

lesbian telephonists attacked each other with empty gin bottles. All human life was there.' Maritime occupations, particularly casual ones, are noted for attracting 'misfits' and people who want to get away from 'normal' life. And perhaps the very *lack* of cohesion worked in gay sea-farers' favour. Diversity was *expected*.

Even within the gay community there were tensions, particularly about campery. Geoff, being a gentle person, found it upsetting to see queens 'being horribly bitchy. . . . [I handled it by just] ignoring it. . . . It's a shame when you've got to work together. But I think a lot of it was jealousy.' Certainly there was sexual rivalry because sex between gay and straight men was so common. Similarly, Rick Norwood recalls the Chief Tourist Steward on one of his ships: 'He dressed totally "straight" and hated all the "top side" (first-class) stewards who were made up with lipstick, etc.' Jack Robinson, though he had gay sex, shared similar feelings about his camper colleagues, particularly when he first encountered them. Some of his wartime convoy were picked off by the enemy in the night. 'It was quite disturbing at times but not as frightening as what went on in the glory hole. It shocked me! Guys called each other names and used words I'd never heard in my life. What was a queer? How could they use such words, calling each other fruits and bitches, paint their vacant faces, dye their flowing locks and mince around with hand on hip? Disgusted, I bowed my head in shame, kept well clear of the frightening creatures.'[10]

So, a ship's company was not a homogenous and cohesive group. But what helped it be one that worked, for both gay and straight people, was the shared need for the ship to function as a vehicle and hotel. People had to learn to get on well, whatever their sexual orientation, race, gender and class. And they did, by and large, through dozens of nimble adjustments, acts of reciprocity and adherences to unspoken protocols. Many had a whale of a time. It was very possible for people on the ship to be able to say 'He's queer, but he's all right.'

Getting on together

What factors enabled this sense of solidarity? First, there was the excep-tionality of sea life, away from land; as the wry slogan has it, 'nothing is queer once you've left that pier'. Not only did the morals of land no longer apply, but also the physical need for mutual support was there: a ship is a relatively fragile container on dangerous waters, and all workers are dependent on each other for survival.[11] It was a familial situation, and the atmosphere of mutual support, even fraternal tenderness, cannot be overestimated. For men sailing just after the war, there was a still a culture

A holiday atmosphere reigned onboard. Picture courtesy of private donor.

of camaraderie: 'You didn't moan and you made the most of being alive,' as cabin steward Martin says, 'There are no pockets in shrouds.'

Secondly, there was the holiday atmosphere on many ships, especially passenger ships. By the 1980s cruise ship writer, Gary Bannerman, could say, 'Residents of passenger vessels are rather liberated individuals. ... There is an air of detachment from the world, which reduces levels of inhibition. Nude beach parties in tropical zones are always on the agenda.'[12] Most people could be relaxed and tolerant about what happened, unlike the Royal Navy where national defence was a serious concern and there was a culture of rectitude not frivolity.

Thirdly, good working relations helped. The feat of processing thousands of people over thousands of miles – and in a very confined space – required fast, efficient teamwork. As Martin says: 'You couldn't refuse to do a job because it would split your fingernails.' You did it. The teamwork was aided by reasonable amicability, or at least *controlled* hostility. A container of human beings far from external regulatory devices such as law courts cannot afford trouble, let alone mutiny: all problems must be settled within it. Visible and expressed homophobia would not be helpful. The point was to get the ship to the other shore safely and profitably, and to please the paying passengers, whose good word and return custom were economically necessary. Also, it was just something that had to be got on with because of the recruitment practices. Bannerman writes: 'Homosexuality is not so much a problem as it is a fact of life in the cruise industry. Some ships rigidly try to control this but when large numbers of service staff are hired sight unseen, the situation is unavoidable.'[13]

So a relatively co-operative cultural climate existed, and was aided by individuals' unwillingness to rock the boat too much. There was tolerance of colleagues' differences, from the level of foibles, to major aspects of one's identity such as homosexuality. Ex-AB (Able Bodied Seaman) Don Trueman claims: 'British seamen then were the most tolerant people in the world.' Although that tolerance did not always stretch to people of other nationalities,[14] it worked for white gay men. And people who'd been on a ship for any length of time knew the social codes about what was acceptable. They stuck to the implicit social rules that governed shipboard order. Most knew about situational propriety. For example, Martin was careful about how much make-up he wore when on duty. Humour also oiled the wheels, particularly on those ships inhabited by witty queens and masters of repartee, an art in which some Liverpudlians were proud to excel. People also learned to cope with many difficulties on ships by seeing them as temporary. They could tell themselves 'Oh, well, it's only for this trip.'

Perhaps also, the high ratio of gay to straight men on some ships made it possible. After all, Argyle found that if a minority is persistent and displays enough conviction, then even if the group is only two in number it can change norms, cast doubts on group views, and offer new views,[15] such as that queerness is not so reprehensible. And, as Dave said, on some of his ships the *straight* white catering crew were in the minority in the 1960s.

This critical mass meant that a new climate in relation to homosexuality could exist. And perhaps there were management fears of expensive disruption if they were too harsh, especially in a period when the militant National Seaman's Reform Movement was developing. After all, one of the two unofficial strikes in the 1960s was triggered when the captain of Cunard's *Carinthia* logged four members of the catering staff for playing guitars too loudly early in the morning and disturbing passengers. As one of the strikers said, the organised resistance 'was like a breath of bloody spring to us ... because we were able to all beef at once instead of going to the Master as individuals and ending up in the log book being fined. Years and years of pent-up feelings were being expressed.'[16]

Gay relations with other workers

What were gay people to their (nominally) straight colleagues, and what were straight colleagues to them? The answer varies with the ship, the period and the individual.

Knowing

One important factor in determining how relations worked was knowledge. Who knows who's gay? Not every worker knew that homosexuality even existed. And not every gay seafarer was out, let alone camp. Who knew depended partly on whom they encountered, and what they knew to look for, as well as the information that individual gay seafarers offered to others about their orientation.

The lack of knowledge about whether individuals were gay or straight was assisted by a contemporary lack of knowledge of homosexuality. As Alan, who worked as a radio officer, insists about his life in the early 1960s, 'I lived a restricted circle, nobody to my knowledge ever said [anything about the chief steward although] it was a bit obvious to those that realised, but ... I was in this age of ignorance.' And if you were gay 'you didn't make a fuss of it'. Rather than a sense that you should be out and proud, there was the idea that it paid to mind your own business, because then maybe others would mind theirs. Putting your head above the parapet unnecessarily was not done – except by some screaming queens.

The sexual orientations of many gay seafarers were often not known to straight colleagues. Alan thinks that the straight people on his ships in the 1960s didn't suspect anything at all about those who were in the closet. Those who chose to be camp, like the chief steward he knew, were understood to have something different about them: 'Everybody knew that, I think he was just accepted, he was just outrageous. ... I suppose people in the know must have realised what he was.'

Others, of lower rank, or those who were more streetwise or chatty, remember it as a more gossipy and aware situation, especially as the 1960s progressed. Bill, an engineering officer in 1970s, 'kept it to [himself] but there was always the innuendo you know ... chemistry, whatever. People suss you out, you're living in a small, confined community, I'm more dominant than Church of England [an acronym for 'Camp or Effeminate'], I'm quite butch. I mince a bit apparently. So I ... didn't get away with it.'

Information about sexuality travelled indirectly too. It was possible to be known by reputation rather than in person. Gossip could be as influential as actual social transactions, and colleagues' views mattered. Gay people were also 'outed' to some degree by the shipping company's intelligence network. A former purser confirms this: 'In the 1960s the "Purser's Memorandum" was the regular statement to the company that made reports on crew – usually when there was something adverse to say. If it was the case that [there was] a clique of gays – and there were cliques – there would be the code – SQ, suspected queen, by their name. The clique would then be purged. That certainly happened once on the old *Oriana* but shortly afterwards the whole clique had been taken on by the Canadian Pacific *Empress of Canada* in harbour with the *Oriana*. They had just moved'. Seafarers could move easily between companies because they were employed by the Merchant Navy 'Pool', rather than as employees of a specific company.

Bill was also aware of the reports on new recruits, but he believed that in some cases, rather than purging cliques, suspected gay men were actually placed together. He and his friend Thomas were both gay, and covert about it. 'I worked for a large company, we had about 80 ships, and the chances of sailing with the same person twice or three times was pretty remote. I sailed with Thomas three times. I think they put us together.' Perhaps putting gay men together was seen as a way of increasing their morale, or maybe it was hoped that if they got into a relationship, then they wouldn't be the risk of them having sex with 'straight' crew members.

A ship was not as polarised a situation as land, where Carol Warren distinguishes between the relationships that gay men had with other gay people and those they had with heterosexuals. Relationships between gay people were 'fairly simple in outline', she believed, since homosexuality, the core of their lives, 'is known and understood in a way that makes for instant familiarity of at least a superficial sort, which is expressed in ... physical warmth'. By contrast, relations outside the gay community are 'far more complex, since they involve the management of stigma and the concealment of the essential self even under conditions of friendly or familial intimacy'.[17] In fact, this drastically oversimplifies the situation. There are many relationships between gay men that are not characterised by even superficial familiarity, let alone physical warmth. Similarly, straight relationships don't have to be so complex. A gay-friendly ship was a close cluster of people, where increasingly many knew about homosexuality, so there was both simplicity *and* complexity, and often an absence of that positive aspect of secrecy: the frisson of superiority, the thrill of the exclusive forbidden fruit. While knowledge of homosexuality helped to determine social relations, the places where encounters between different types of crew occurred were also an important factor.

Where encounters happen

Gay and straight colleagues' encounters were dictated partly by the type of ship and partly by the social spaces in which they were supposed to mix. Not every shipping line enabled ships to be non-homophobic spaces, as P&O did. Gay men could be relatively out on P&O ships, unlike the ships that were run by its competitors, because of a race-related staffing policy. Dave explains that in the 1950s: 'P&O's ... competitors were the Orient line. All the boats starting with an O [like *Oriana* and *Orestes*]. They were 100 per cent white crews with the big butch deck hands and there were a lot of villains and all the football mobs. All I heard about on those ships was a lot of trouble ... things were much quieter [on P&O]. There was certainly no homophobia.' Guys in high-heeled shoes were tolerated because straight white seafarers 'were in the minority more or less. The deck crew, all the seamen, the painting, was all done by Indians. So the only ones [who were white] were the writers, the secretarial staff and the catering. ... All the camp things mincing around doing the cabins ... so it really was, there wasn't any homophobia,' as Dave sees it. Anyway, so many straight men were trade (available for gay sex) that the high percentage of male manual workers aboard was no indicator of likely homophobia.

In addition, because the ship was a honeycomb of compartments, people might have only known those with whom they worked directly, or people quartered nearby. As Rick Norwood notes, 'The gays never presented a problem with us carpenters in every day work on board, as we did not encounter them about our business.' It was very possible that seafarers wouldn't know many people in this 'town', let alone be privy to information about their sexual identities.

Maybe part of the reason that gay sexuality could be so tolerated was that it was largely confined to those doing 'women's work' and to the lower part of the ship. If gay men took on a feminine occupational role, then they could be constructed as 'not really counting as men'. They were one of an already despised category so their further 'fall' into 'feminine' positions sexually could just be seen as an extension, or even proof, of their lowly status.[18] And the nether space of the lower decks might well be associated with dirt and darkness, the unsavoury and the revolting. Certainly those with puritan morals construed the public lavatories where cottaging took place (often down under streets until at least the late 1960s) as such: those 'miserable little back holes of Calcutta ... just the sort of places for those fellows', as magistrate Paul Bennett saw it.[19] It was part of the enduring polarisation between the sanitary and the bestial that writer on dangerous sexualities, Frank Mort, describes.[20] Gay sexuality was okay if it was not in your face and high on the ship's bridge. The carnivalesque, as Chapter 5 shows, had to be confined to particular backstage opportunities.

Bill emphasises this spatial distinction: stewards were a more open 'kind of stereotyped gay ... it was all below deck. The people above, upstairs ... were all in brackets "straight". ... A lot of ... stewards, or the pantry

Below deck, the *Orcades*, late 1950s – all girls together. Picture courtesy of private donor.

boys ... were openly gay and they could get away with it. Because that was their job, their occupation ... it's just like ... today. A lot of people believe and perceive that anybody in the hairdressing fraternity's a puff [gay], or any nurse, anyone in catering. ... People then think, if you're a steward, or a nurse, then you're homosexual.' The very fact of quartering out gay men together reduced the friction that was part of living in close quarters. As purser-steward Lewis summed up the situation, 'Until one has worked ashore *and* afloat, it is almost impossible to realise the difference between the two lives. Ashore ... an unpopular workmate is forgotten when the clock is punched. Afloat, the nerve-wracking moaner may be at one's elbow at table and in the bunk above at night. ... For the sailor there is no escape.'[21]

Social class divisions

Workplace gulfs were mixed up with social gulfs. Alan remembers it from his point of view on the upper decks in the late 1950s and early 1960s: 'It was a very hierarchical society, you didn't mix with the other people really. There were separate accommodation areas for officers, petty officers and crew members. It would have been virtually impossible for anyone to visit any other accommodation, except on duty. No possibility of cross rank intimacy ... in those days you didn't mix with officers above or below in a sense. You tended to stick to your own ... so you didn't have a very wide range of friends or acquaintances. ... Plus the fact that you were working a three-shift day, which meant that even among your own accepted group, some would be sleeping it off and some would be working. In a sense it could be quite lonely.' And working so hard, on different shifts or watches meant there wasn't much opportunity for socialising in that situation anyway.

Not only did people not meet; they didn't come into close contact with their superiors. Even in the 1980s, when the British Empire had long waned in practice, if not in people's attitudes, Ian found that 'there was a very big officer and crew thing, and that was quite important. It's very colonial, really. The officers didn't mix with the crew and vice versa. ... We kept away from them more because there's always the fear that they're the ones to watch out for. If we were in the wrong place at the wrong time [there would be] all sorts of trouble.' As an officer, Bill could see the logic of this: 'The old familiarity breeds contempt, if you're sitting in the bar and you're socialising and everyone's pally-wally, then your superiors can't get you to do the job, stick to their boundaries. The officers' wives kept their boundaries as well, of course. If they went astray and got shagged, they were [sent] off the ship as well. The third mate's wife, she was fucking about, and she disappeared quite quickly.' Middle-class notions of the ship as ruled by self-controlled men may well have depended on defining themselves in opposition to the social other: people who lowered themselves by having extra-mural sex.

Chris pointed out that this became part of the way of thinking that 'the P&O were the *crème de la crème*. We were programmed. It was in our culture to behave and think like that. You were before the mast. You were a ship steward, you were a stoker, you were a bedroom steward, you worked in the offices, you probably spoke six languages. But because you were before the mast you were regarded as inferior.' And if an officer wanted to have sex with a steward then it would only be done 'very discreetly ... it wasn't really regarded as "done". "We don't want the engineers mixing with the crew." '

Race further exacerbated these class distinctions. Alan points out that there was no way that he was in a position to have gay sex. 'I was only on minor passenger ships so I wouldn't have come into contact with gay stewards. And the passenger ships I was on were actually Indian crewed, and almost all the passengers were Asian so that made a difference as well. ... White officers and Indian crew ... really were not allowed contact except strictly, and very formally, for duty purposes. We had to learn how

The British and non-British crews sometimes mixed well, as this picture of New Year's celebrations shows. Picture courtesy of Bill.

to speak their language ... they weren't allowed to speak to us in English ... it was really colonial.'

Bill notices: 'I sailed with different crews, some who were Hong Kong, Chinese or Barbadian. And the British crews were the worst. They didn't like the class distinction down below and upstairs.' The non-British crew ... "knew their place". ... I think the Barbadians, the black guys, they were into it [likely to have gay sex]. ... When I was on the deck, I had my white shorts on, one of them in particular was sort of eyeing up my packet, and coming up to see us for any excuse, wanting sex basically. But if you did that and it got about, you'd be [kicked] off the ship the following day.'

However, one of the reasons why peace was maintained on ships was that officers did not usually challenge problems on the spot. A former human resources officer remembers that, generally, it was the personnel office on shore that did the disciplining. 'The captain and purser would often ask them to intervene, rather than risk bad feeling on board ship.' There was a kind of shyness about making trouble that worked in the gay guys' favour, while far out at sea. Then when the ship came into port the 'miscreant' was asked into the personnel office and told 'clean up your act', or 'wind your neck in' or 'you've become a source of concern'. Two examples of this are very mild. 'In one case, on a *Princess* cruise vessel, an off-duty guy was walking round crew quarters in a blouse-type shirt. In another case, a very flamboyant head waiter's hair was out of control. The Purser complained and it was the shore staff who had to ask him to get his hair cut.'

How gay men were seen by heterosexuals

Judging from reports by both gay and straight people, gay seafarers were seen by straight colleagues in the following five ways: as mates and members of the team; sometimes as sexual partners (as Chapter 4 shows); as an entertaining and often admirable spectacle; as people to be scared of or despise; and as an education.

Every seafarer explains the fundamental point that may not be apparent to landlubbers: that in a social situation like a ship where mates mattered and teamwork was crucial, gay seafarers were accepted if they were prepared to pull their weight and be amicable. Being a good sort of colleague could lessen homophobia, even to the extent of shipmates fighting to defend the gay guy in a foreign bar brawl: 'He might be queer but he's *our* queer.' This was extended by the sense some seafarers had of joining an historic, even romantic, fraternity of men who preferred the company of men, the 'sea-brothers' that Bert Bender, a writer on American sea fic-

tion, found in *Moby Dick* and *Billy Budd*, and in the sea-related novels of
Richard Dana, Herman Melville, Jack London and Ernest Hemingway.
Chris gives an example of straight acceptance of homosexuality: a very
drunken shipmate was bundled protectively off to his bunk one night by
straight colleagues. He was so confused and resistant that they tried to
lure him there by saying 'Come on, there's a big, hairy-arsed sailor waiting there for you'. That is, people's sexual preferences could be known,
acknowledged and tolerated, as family members tolerate each other's
foibles.

And it was for the sake of tranquillity in the community that officers
did what they could to maintain happy relations between colleagues,
whatever their sexual orientation. Even a decade before the 1967 Sexual
Offences Act there were deliberate attempts at harmony. Chris remembers: 'Now this is an extraordinary one. When I was on the *Canberra*, in
particular, there used to be two-berth cabins for all the crew. It was quite
a modern ship and the captain, bless him, and the ship's officers [were
supportive]. You used to get "John's fallen out with Paul." "Oh, he
hasn't? Oh, dear, dear, what's happened?" [they'd say.] And all the cabins
were done up rather. "Oh dear, Paul wants now to be in with Simon. Oh
well, we must arrange that." There was a completely different culture,
contrary to what the forces and what the politicians and ... police would
like to think. The ship's senior officers were terribly good.'

Some heterosexual seafarers saw gay colleagues as potential partners.
Some of our gay informants have talked – occasionally with sadness and
bitterness – about straight colleagues who had sex with them but then
went home to their wives. Although we have found no straight men who
will tell stories of this today, there is plenty of evidence from gay men that
straight men used them. Robert found that there were straight men who
were prepared to have contingent gay sex because they thought, 'There's
nothing around here, I'll take the next best thing.' And the next best thing
to a woman was a gay man. Fears of sexually transmitted diseases (STDs)
may have worked in gay men's favour too. In that climate of ignorance
about means of transmission some straight men believed disease could
only be caught from women, not men.

Sometimes straight men made crude assumptions that to be gay was to
be promiscuously available. Some mistook genuinely fraternal friendships
for something more sexual, as Ian described in his backgammon story in
Chapter 4.

Sex was one form of currency on ships, and those with power could
abuse it. Just as stewardesses on ships could be offered career enhancement in exchange for sex,[22] so could gay men. Ian was approached in this
way. He was offered sex: 'not to give me money, to give me promotion

... well, we didn't have sex. But I did get promoted – [we] came to an agreement.'

Seafarers often describe passenger ships, like hotels, as having a shaft-or-be-shafted ethos, particularly around tips and fiddles. In that climate, sometimes the more masculine, heterosexual, manual seafarers took sexual advantage too.

As well as being potential sex partners, some gay men were seen by straight colleagues as an interesting spectacle. Working for P&O in the 1950s, Dave noticed that 'a lot of the straights enjoyed it. They enjoyed the campery.' Camp queens could be such sparkling company and such entertaining *bon viveurs* that straight people were happy to go partying with them in foreign ports. The Queen of the Pacific 'was so popular that even officers would go ashore to bars with him and a gang of Liverpool ABs', remembers Don Trueman. These ABs weren't used to officers being nice to them as they had a reputation for being fighters, so this was a tribute to the queens. As Bill found too, 'the captain and the officers didn't bother the gay men at all'. In fact 'they seemed to quite enjoy the laughs and stuff, when we did mix with them, which was very rare. They seemed all OK about it, no problems.' Part of the reason for this is that once a group is labelled 'deviant' it makes social control easier; they are segregated and 'contained within a relatively narrow group. The creation of the specialized, despised and punished role of homosexual keeps the bulk of society pure in rather the same way that the similar treatment of some kinds of criminal helps keeps the rest of society law-abiding,' argues Mary Macintosh.[23] So officers could perhaps most easily go ashore with *queens*, because they were so marked out as different, whereas going ashore with someone who was *covertly* gay could feel like running the risk of contamination, at least in other people's eyes.

Perhaps those gay men who were most respected by straight men were those who combined butch masculinity with their camp performance. Queens who were also tough might cause straight men to suspend or moderate any tendency to despise them as 'un-men'. Rick Norwood was admiring: 'There was a queer steward with dyed blonde hair (this was in 1970) who was a real tough hard bastard. ... You did not fuck with him!'

Straight colleagues could also see gay men as people to be scared of, people who had to be controlled because they were so different and because some of them appeared to cause disorder to the ship. They wanted to stop gay men from going too far, to call them to order and maintain the implicit rules of situational propriety. Some of the most overt cruelty was the kind of ragging that 'misfits' get. Significantly, it involved 'cleansing'. A Cunard waiter from the 1940s and 1950s remembers that when he was a bellboy, a 'kid ... on the *Queen Elizabeth*, one of the things we used to do if any of these "poofs" were on board, we used to round them up ... we dragged one up on the pig deck ... and we tied him up to the gates on the pig deck and squirted one of them down with hoses.'[24] However, our informants had never heard of such a situation and they stress that the bellboys would have been punished if they had been so out of line. Other responses were more sophisticated. Martin recalls one of the queens, 'Carol Baker'. She 'went up to the Captain on Christmas Day and said "Captain, I don't know what to wear for dinner." And he said, "What do you mean?" "Do you think I should wear a cock-tail dress or a nice Lurex trouser suit?" So the Captain sent her to a psychiatrist.' This sounds like an urban legend but it does indicate that there was a glass ceiling as to what was acceptable. Sometimes straight people were unable to tolerate some behaviour, as in Geoff's story in Chapter 4 about a gay wedding. The 'happy couple' had broken one of the classic rules of many institutions, which is not 'don't do wrong', but 'don't get *caught* doing wrong'. Perhaps they simply refused to accept an alien definition of wrong-ness, or just went a bit too public for the circumstances.

By the 1980s, according to writer on P&O cruises Garry Bannerman, the straight management view on gay men on ships was that 'the only disturbing aspect is that the more effeminate homosexuals may be extremely bitchy, jealous of their mates and demanding ... [but gay activity] really is of little consequence ... the sight ... doesn't shock too many employees'.[25] In fact, gay men could be a relief. A female purser sailing with Union Castle to South Africa in the 1970s said 'Quite honestly, if you're having quite a lot of ladies sailing by themselves it's much less hassle if you're supervising staff that aren't interested in women.'[26]

The only exception was if a gay man was too predatory and tried to turn fraternity into sexual intimacy. This generally does not seem to have been allowed to get in the way of comradeship, particularly if 'no' was taken as a firm answer. As Rick, then a 26-year-old heterosexual carpenter explains, 'The ship's surgeon was totally gay. When I had to fit a door closure on his surgery door he tried to procure me for evenings of fun until I threatened to punch his face in. Then he became a perfect gent and was, in his capacity as a surgeon, always totally professional. I think the threat of violence made things worse for me! It ignited rather than defused the situation.' A straight Cunard waiter says of his time on the *Andes* 'I've never known a ship with so many poofs ... but she was a good ship to be on ... some of them used to try and get friendly if you gave them half an encouragement but they didn't trouble you if you weren't that way inclined.'[27]

Sometimes straight colleagues were confused by some gay men's non-static sexual identity, particularly if they were straight during one trip and camp on the next voyage. Rick explains: 'On Union Castle trips to South Africa we had a situation with a rough tough deckhand who suddenly appeared on a trip as a steward and gay as you like! Every trip us 'chippies' had to lay a temporary dance floor over the carpet for a banquet and dance and get up damn early in the morning to dismantle it. Whilst laying said floor I dropped the tin of screws. To this the newly gay ex-deckhand remarked "Oh, you've dropped your bracelet dear." To which I replied "When are you going to fucking change back again!" I think he made some churlish remark along the lines "when you change over to us dear!"'

Part of the explanation behind such fluidity was simply that, in some situations gay seafarers felt they had to pretend to be straight, for safety. Chris, a steward, storekeeper and writer in the early 1960s, says, 'there were times when you veered. I'd pretend to be straight or not know anything. I'd go very neutral, straight, if you could ... then after a time, you started. There were some who didn't care a damn and who were outrageous. But ... you were discreet where it was appropriate. And then there were other times when you didn't care. For example, in the crew quarters, I found myself half the time not caring a damn.'

Another explanation for the changeable identity was that men were struggling against their homosexuality in this hostile period. Rick recalls one such instance in the 1970s: 'I used to drink in the Pig and Whistle [crew bar] ... where I met a great chap who was to all intents and purposes straight and "normal" – the Chief Tourist Class Steward. After a few drinks one night it became quite apparent he was ... homosexual, although he was engaged to a woman and about to marry. He tried to get me back to his cabin and offered me all kinds of silly things. Again I threatened him with the choice of a slap or continue as a drinking pal, and that's how it was. His attitude when I asked him about marriage to his partner was "I have fought this all my life. I want to be straight, I love children. And my parents would be totally devastated if they found out my sexual preferences."'

It gave Rick pause for thought. And most straight people say that encountering gay people close up, every day, was educative. It is noticeable that the most homophobic seafarers tended to be the ones who had had the least contact with gay men, just as the most racist citizens are usually those who live *near*, but not *in*, areas with high ethnic populations.

Perhaps straight men were more shocked by this new view of humanity than were women. After all, women had no masculinity to feel protective about. To straight women on ships, gay colleagues could often be rivals or sisters. On a voyage gay men could be enjoyed because they weren't going to make unwelcome advances. Bill, a gay officer, found that some women in the ship's complement could be bitchy: 'They can be a bit jealous if they think you're moving in on some of the people that they fancy. But in general, there was a bit of a class.'

Straight people found they had perhaps more in common with gay people than might be expected, but generally they seemed to feel less affinity with gay people than gay people felt with them. This was not least because so many straight people had not been gay, whereas many gay men had once led, or tried to lead, a straight life. Some could feel jealous. Chris remembers straight stewards grouching about 'they've got all the best jobs', but the point was that gay guys felt they had to give extra to the job in order to stay ahead. If they did get the best jobs, it was because they worked extra hard.

How gay men saw heterosexuals

In comparison to these straight views of gay seafarers, straight colleagues were seen by gay men in at least one of five ways: as colleagues who had to be worked *around*, if not worked with; as an audience; as people to keep your secret from; as potential lovers; and as men who might dislike you as a symbol because of their own unease with their sexual orientation.

For some gay men there was a slight sense of distance, as if they belonged to another world, often one long ago left behind and much more secure but also more rule-bound. Dave, as a waiter in the early 1960s, felt that he got on 'reasonably well' with the straight 50 per cent of his colleagues. 'There was never any fighting or anything like that. I didn't come across any. They accepted it.' Ian, in the more permissive 1980s, felt comfortable enough about heterosexuals to share rooms with them. 'I only [once] shared a cabin ... with another gay man but mostly it was with straight friends that I shared. That's what was so nice actually, because if they wanted the cabin one evening because they'd got a girl passenger or whatever, they'd say to me, "Don't come back until such and such a time" and then vice versa. It was all very relaxed.' Some of our informants enjoyed having heterosexual friendships that drew on their skills as confidantes. They were proud of being better at talking about emotions than the straight men to whom they might act as agony aunt, and enjoyed being the Evelyn Home of the High Seas for problems of the heart.[28] Queens could also help the social cement that kept people sane in those 'prisons without bars': reading teacups and cards, organising raffles, mending for others, says Martin. They made a point of having hobbies, to allay the depression that many men could feel so far from home, dressmaking and doing interior design, just as early sailors painted ditty boxes, carved scrimshaw, knitted and knotted.[29]

A party on deck, stewards and female workers dancing. Picture courtesy of
private donor (anonymous).

Gay men's feelings towards women crew varied: some were hostile to
them as competitors, some were lukewarm, others appreciative of sister-
hood. In any case, contact was formally restricted and there were only a
few women on board in the decades after the war. When the 1951 census
counted stewarding workers it found only 730 women but 16,211 men.
On a large passenger ship there could be three to 20 women out of a crew
of 500.[30] Robert noted the changed trend after he left in 1968. 'Women
crew members came along a bit later. . . . You started to get female pursers, and then a few more entertainment officers, things like that. . . . At the
time I was in the Merchant Navy, there were some female cabin crew,
stewardesses, none of whom, I really knew or mixed with. I certainly
wouldn't know if any of them were gay or lesbian, mainly because they
tended to keep themselves to themselves. One or two of the officers . . . the
nursing sister, were gay. And the ships' hairdressers, there were a few of
those. On the cargo ships, of course, there were no females at all.'

Chris mixed with both female officers and ratings in the early 1960s.
'There used to be the stewardesses and the ship's nurses, I used to get on
all right with them. There was never any problem. They knew we were
gay and we left it at that. We got to know them very well.' Some enjoyed
camaraderie with women. In the 1980s Ian found 'they were great. That's
who we used to borrow most of our costumes from. [They didn't mind.]

Many friendships with female colleagues, like this attendant in a ship's shop, were jovial and comfortable. Picture courtesy of Ian.

We'd go round, knock on their doors and see what we could beg for the next show, what glittery numbers they had hidden in their closets. They were very accommodating.'

Their friendship could be quite frank and familial, with women having a caring role. Dave characterised 'the old stewardesses who would look after cabins were spinster ladies who were terrified of men . . . . They'd fold their knickers away and stuff. . . . They'd look after baby-sittings, children, for bottles, that type of thing. [I got on] fine. They were old battleaxes. They were lovely old things really. There were no tarts.' And yet he also saw them as useful mates when gay guys wanted companions for 'feminine' activities. 'They'd been at sea for years, the ones I met. They knew all the shopping to do; they'd bring back certain teas from Ceylon. They were always invited to the parties because they were real fag-hags.'

Table 7.1 Ages of female and male stewarding workers, 1951

Age	Women	Men	Total
15–19	19	2,737	2,756
20–24	44	2,511	2,555
25–34	169	3,394	3,563
35–44	181	2,974	3,155
45–54	170	2,480	2,650
55–64	98	1,169	1,267
65–74	46	214	260
75+	3	11	14
Total	730	15,490	16,220

Source: Census of England and Wales, summary tables, HMSO, London, 1951.

But many sea queens were disappointed by the influx of women in the early 1970s. That unhappiness had already existed for decades among many male seafarers, whatever their orientation. They felt a (slightly wavering) misogynist and ageist hostility towards women workers who, pre-1970s, tended to be in their late thirties and early forties, whereas the bulk of male stewarding workers tended to be in their late twenties, as Table 7.1 shows.

Some of the camp men could also be both sexual and professional rivals, as Martin shows. He liked it best when the ship was free of women. 'It was just men, which was lovely, dear. As I'm saying, they should be for children then stitched up, dear. We always say, I mean they're called fag hags now, some people say a "bona palone" [a Polari phrase meaning *nice woman*], and this old sea queen says, "Listen girl, there's no such thing as a bona palone, there's only one bona palone and that's your mother."[31] And I'd say, "Yes, that's true, dear."' Martin took pride in professional skills and didn't want his significance usurped. 'The captains liked queens, because they knew they were well-looked after, because we used to do the cabins up lovely. After a while the captain's wife was on board, and we'd make sure she had a nice bunch of flowers, the little femme touch.'

Unlike their dealings with these 'fruit flies' and 'faggotinas', gay men had sometimes to face homophobic men who felt threatened and affronted by gays, and expressed this in disapproving silence or jibes. However, the hostility varied greatly.

Rick Norwood remembers one chief carpenter he worked for who 'hated gays so much he would go out of his way to get them thrown off the ship'. But mainly abuse was verbal and moderate, if only because of the live-and-let-live climate on ships. For example, Bill noticed that on his ships in the 1970s 'there was a few [who'd say] ... "root toot toot, the Fourth's a fruit" and things like that'.

Dave saw homophobes on P&O in the 1950s as people who'd simply take themselves out of the situation: collision was avoided. 'They kept very quiet, they did one voyage and then got off. They had other ships to go to. It wasn't them. They only had to put up with it for a maximum of ten weeks or a couple of months and they'd be off to another ship, and that was quite in order. You got off one ship and signed on another one. That was your right. You weren't marked down for that. A lot of people did. They changed ships all the time.'

By the 1980s on P&O ships, gay men saw straight colleagues as having less power. Homophobia 'was never an issue. Gays ruled and that was it. I don't think they'd dare upset a queen. . . . Particularly on the *Sea Princess*, gay definitely reigned: a very camp ship to work on,' Ian comments.

What other meanings did straight colleagues have for gay crew? Often, they were people to protect your identity from. This was particularly true of officers on some of the less tolerant ships, but stories repeatedly indicate that homosexuality was often an open secret. Straight colleagues deduced orientation from gossip and dozens of clues from body language. Many gay men found out only years later that there had been no necessity for subterfuge and that silent support had existed for some time. Gay Royal Naval officer Duncan Lustig-Prean, who recently won a major European Court victory against homophobia, records that when he told his men why he was being sacked they replied 'That's old news, boss, we've known for years. . . . Some of them cried. They didn't want to lose me. My gayness did not matter to them. I was shaken and touched.'[32] Chris recalls being similarly touched one night in Singapore. He was chased back to his ship by an angry would-be lover. His colleagues rallied round, saying 'Don't worry, we'll protect you.' And they did. Chris wonders if maybe this is not just because of the warmth and familial atmosphere but some men's desires to have 'a little woman' to protect. In the absence of a wife, one way to assert your masculinity is to 'make someone into a protectable figure'.

As well as being sustaining colleagues, straight men could be seen as potential lovers, in surprisingly plentiful supply. As Chris points out in Chapter 4, gay seafarers did have quite a lot of sex with men who were straight. Alcohol allowed straight men to suspend heterosexuality temporarily. Geoff remembers: 'Oh yes, yes, you'd get them in the right circumstances they would [have sex], a few drinks, and so on. I've had straight men myself. It was a one-off. If somebody came to your cabin, you knew what they'd come for, and that was that. But [it] didn't seem to bother anybody. I suppose really we were very relaxed about the whole thing.'

The non-white crew were sometimes surprisingly available for sex despite several factors: many observed religions that opposed sex outside of marriage (but believed homosexuality didn't count); there were tensions because, as Ian says, Asian people 'were paid on different pay scales, and some of them were doing the same job as us'; inter-racial sex could mean the non-European party was treated with less respect; plus the encounter had to be covert if the white man in those more racist times was not to lose face.

Ian remembers P&O ships that were 50 per cent Goanese, with Chinese laundry staff: 'It was quite a mixture of nationalities. We all had our separate areas as well, places to eat, and sleeping areas, and socialising areas.' This lessened the inter-racial sex because 'mostly, you stayed with the same. Some of the Goanese did have sex with the Europeans. I don't know if they were gay or not. But they ... they were on [ships] for nine-month contracts: a long time. I think at times they just got desperate, and succumbed to various demands by the time we got to the eighth month. [Whereas] we were just three months on, six weeks off.'

Honest sexual usage by straight male partners seems to have been acceptable.[33] But hypocrisy was not. Chris describes an example of how this worked in the early 1960s on P&O: 'I did know of a case of the assistant laundryman. The head laundryman was a chap. He was known as Bambi [because] he was very pretty [with] big eyes and dark hair. And he was straight. The assistant laundryman was a snide; he kept taking the piss out of people who were gay. Then one day he had too much to drink, and he made an advance on Bambi. The head laundryman didn't mind gays and told everybody, so we were in hysterics.'

Straight colleagues had additional meanings for gay seafarers. They could be the audience at which to flaunt your sexuality, as Chapter 5 shows, be that at formal spectaculars or in everyday routines. Martin remembers: 'Sometimes the captain would even call you "girl" ... or they'll say, "Have you seen Alice?" although it was a man.' It was part of the campery on P&O in the 1980s that the captain was 'she', according to Ian. It was done in 'a camp way'. They used 'she' instead of 'he' a lot, even if a person was straight. 'We used to say, "get her." ' He remembers how close to the bone they would get. For example, when performing a skit of *The Wizard of Oz*, 'they renamed her [the captain's] dog Dildo [in the movie it was Toto], and then we had to ask the captain "Have you seen my dildo?" Things like that ... it was fun.'

So gay and straight colleagues had complex and varying relationships. Their meanings to each other were affected by being together, sometimes for several trips, and by being united in one thing: they were not the paying passengers but part of the team that served (and sometimes exploited) the guests.

Relations with passengers

Passengers were not always encountered by seafarers. Cargo ships did not hold passengers, other than officers' wives. And on cruise ships only some of the hotel-side workers met passengers, and then just those in their class and in situations that became increasingly less restrictive as times changed and limited fraternisation was permitted. So how did gay seafarers get on with passengers?

To passengers, gay seafarers seemed to have three main meanings: they were theatre, exceptionally good servitors and educators. Frank's view was that 'the passengers loved it. They loved to come down to the crew concerts. I think Cary Grant came down, whoever's travelling came down to the crew, and they used to put on a big show for the crew, and for the passengers.'

The most camp seafarers were refreshing theatre: a humorous and enjoyable spectacle, particularly enjoyed by older women. After all, hospitality workers are often viewed by tourists as a picturesque part of the scenery. Because a voyage was such a bracketed-off, make-believe space, queens could be seen as exotic and entertaining objects.

Less camp but still 'feminine' gay servitors were appreciated for their excellent manners and willing service, for which the company had employed them. They were doing what was only later recognised as emotional labour.[34] This could often be performed for tips. Dave remembers

Gay staff were often very popular with passengers. Picture courtesy of Ian.

that 'when I was the head waiter, Diamond Lil was one of my waiters, tall elegant thing, very good looking, knew her stuff. A lot of the passengers, who were regular passengers, they weren't going by air in those days; you had to be very rich. When I was the head waiter they would come to me to book their table and I'd say "I've got table twelve for you." "Who's the waiter? Is it one of your gay boys? I hope it is," they'd say. "Because we always have someone who's gay. We had Big Freda on the last one." So the passengers used to ask [for them]. They were in big demand, because they were so good at looking after them.'

High levels of service could also be used as a statement of superiority over straight men and women: only a camp man could be both efficient and give a passenger cabin the 'woman's touch' that Martin's captain appreciated, as shown in his story about rivalry in Chapter 8.

Out gay men were also informal educators: passengers could disembark with very new knowledge of what gay sexuality was and with a different understanding of their own sexual identities.

Passengers' meanings for gay seafarers

The gay seafarers who worked on the hotel-side of the ship related to passengers in three major ways: they were an appreciative audience for camp informal shows, as Chapter 5 describes; a resource to be borrowed from, emulated, and even bedded; and finally they were even more of a bane than they were to straight hospitality workers because of their power to complain.

Many of the more camp men enjoyed being 'on stage' to passengers. This applied both to the formal shows, but also informally, particularly with bedroom stewards in cabins and waiters in the dining room – places where impressions could be managed.

For many hospitality workers, passengers were a telling example of how a wealthier life could be lived. By their clothes, manners and behaviour they were models who could be copied and signposts who indicated that more leisured ways of life existed. They had a position that their servitors might like to acquire, and the next best thing for socially ambitious staff was to reproduce and adapt some of the more visible symbols of that affluence. One way of doing this was, as we saw in Chapter 5, to borrow clothes – with or without permission.

Passengers were also possible sexual partners. However, this was hindered by the company rules. In the 1960s 'passengers and crew weren't allowed to meet so you kept to yourselves' says Dave. Seafarers did not have sex with the passengers 'because it was against the company rules and you could be sacked. The only way you could get there would be to get out of your uniform and wear civilian clothes. You'd have to sneak around the corridors. So it was a risky business.'

However, some managed it. Geoff recalls a trip in the 1960s. 'We were going to ... Hong Kong, and ... on board this ship ... was ... [a Hong Kong media boss] and his wife. Arthur and I ... were working through that particular afternoon. I was on duty and Arthur was doing something else in the back of the office. And I went round, and he'd disappeared. Anyway he came back and I said, "Where've you been?" I said, "You've look as if you've eaten a bowl of cream or something." And he'd been into this man's cabin. The wife had gone out, somewhere on deck. ... And they [Arthur and media man] had sex. And I thought, how very bold ... I mean the wife could have come back at any moment and found them.' Dodging to get (heterosexual) sex was a popular shipboard game anyway. As Bannerman says, 'Passenger corridors can be quite amusing in the early hours of the morning, especially if there is a large contingent of Italians (masters of the sport) on the staff.'[35]

Even as late as the 1980s, says Ian, 'There were strong guidelines. We weren't allowed in passenger areas, unless we were on duty. And if we were on duty, we had to wear full uniform ... but it still happened. You could go to a passenger's cabin. It was done, but hidden I suppose. ... And vice versa, the passengers weren't allowed in the crew areas. But they were. It was just a rule that was there. But as long as you weren't outrageously overdone and too bold, then it was OK. It was acceptable, as long as you were careful.' Particularly in the last decades of the twentieth century when the demarcation lines on passenger ships were much less upheld, Ian reports having sex 'with the passengers, and ashore. ... Most passengers that came on there, if they weren't with somebody, they were looking for someone. It was quite easy really, to work out who was available and who wasn't. Though I think it was probably a mutual thing really, with the passengers who you fancied. I was working in the bar, and that was an easy place to chat anyone up. Also ... most cruises were only ten or fourteen days [long]. Time was limited and everyone was bolder than they would be at home, because you knew in two weeks time you were never going to see them again. So they made the most of it ... an awful lot of that went on.'

But to many hospitality workers in general, guests are a bane. Their spending power, preparedness to tip and potential to complain is crucial. Equally, their appreciation of services is treasured; passengers are assessed by the quality of their thanks as well as the quantity of bank notes pressed into a palm or left discreetly in an envelope in the cabin. To care workers generally, the guest/patient is a unit to be managed and regulated so that they cause the minimum amount of trouble possible and do not disrupt the order.[36] And to seafarers of any status the passenger is the stranger on *their* territory, whether they were greenhorns or such frequent travellers that they were almost family.

So what did this mean for *gay* seafarers? Homophobic guests might have to be won over so that they didn't use their power to complain, which in the worst instance could bring dismissal. Ideally they'd be brought to a point where they would tip generously. The more adroit seafarers managed their passengers through wit and thoughtful observation. Chris recalls the days when greeting cards were still a novelty and 'the practised ones would come on board with half a dozen birthday cards. And they'd come to me and want to look at the passenger list, to see their dates of birth. ... I'd give them the names, if anybody got any birthdays. The [passengers would] come down to breakfast and of course on their table would be a birthday card. ... You would imagine that went down extremely well with the passengers. And of course it resulted in a few bob ... it was geared, towards tips.'

Passengers who did not behave were subtly punished. Some of the more bitchy queens were particularly good at vengeance. Martin describes how one older woman passenger 'nearly freaked out' about the fact that her stewards were gay. So one of her stewards, Petunia, decided '"She always complains, I'll fix her up," [and] put some speed in her tea. In the tea-pot. And of course she was flying high all day. [Petunia later] says "I'll bring her back down, dear," she crushed some sleeping tablets. Oh she was evil! And there was another called Patsy. She was vile. This passenger didn't give her a good gratuity. She said, "I'll fix her up." Because she was a bedroom steward, so she managed to pick the lock, because we put the luggage out before for a disembarkation in Southampton. So she managed to open the case, and ... got a pair of scissors, and she cut all the nice evening dresses. Laid 'em all back and locked the case back up. So when she [the passenger] got home, to hang them up, she had a miniskirt. She [Patsy] was evil, oh vile! Oh but some of them were bold. Really bad to people.'

Where there's a will there's a way

Gay seafarers could be operating in tricky situations. Their well-being and ability to manoeuvre socially with colleagues and passengers could be based upon them denying a very important aspect of their identity: their sexual orientation. The trickiness varied with different ships. Passenger vessels with a high percentage of gay crew made life much easier. So did more permissive attitudes as time went on.

What seems extraordinary is how much shipboard populations could accept men being camp in the 1930s, 1940s and 1950s. This was decades before the law changed and even longer before homosexuality was constructed as something that wasn't to be ashamed of. Colleagues coped, as long as you were a good team player; officers turned blind eyes, because some sexual release was good for morale; and passengers positively revelled in the more seemly and performative aspects of it. The cruise industry recognised the importance of congenial staff. As hotel business analyst, Laurie J. Mullins, points out, 'benefits derived from [hotel] services are associated with feelings and emotions. The quality of service in an hotel is usually identified with its general culture and ambience, the disposition and attitudes of staff, and the nature of the other customers.'[37] Writer on cruise industry economics, Bob Dickinson, echoes this: 'we have observed that some captains, because of their social and sexual prowess, have contributed meaningfully to the revenue occupancy of a vessel.'[38] A happy ship was a profitable one. And genial, accepted, gay catering staff could contribute substantially to that happiness and enrich the ship.

Stories of how gay and straight people got on at sea suggest that straight people can be more much tolerant than might be expected, particularly in situations where they can exceptionalise unusual behaviour, such as during time out and time away. And it also suggests that people with power, such as shipping line employers, can suspend the usual moral qualms when it is in their interests to do so, particularly in the 1970s, which historians of the National Union of Seamen characterise as a decade in which seafarers were wooed as a scarce resource.[39]

Homosexuality in the Merchant Navy appears to have often been well-handled from above and below, to the benefit of both parties. But it was something that was *managed*, and not allowed to simply *be*, in ways that heterosexuality was not. 'Gay' was still constructed as a *problematic* identity and the price for some gay men may have been that they felt constrained to act with far more tact and care than any residential worker would ideally like. There was stress, and the laughter that was used to manage unease can also undermine the gravity of difference between gay and straight. Jokes can be inclusive and implicitly permit people to be diverse. But laughter may also, as theorist Henri Bergson argues, 'depend ... on the emotional separation of that group from that object of their laughter'. It requires a kind of 'momentary anaesthesia of the heart', and is not necessarily done with affection or sympathy,[40] but as a way of expressing corrosive latent homophobia.

But there was the pleasure of inclusion. Acceptance by scores, if not hundreds, of colleagues could be bliss for someone used to ostracism. Chris explains: 'It was like a weight being lifted off you – to find that no one really cared [about your sexual orientation].' Added to that, there was the joy of being surrounded by like-minded people at work and having so many potential lovers available. While the community of some gay-friendly ships may have been, in Benedict Anderson's terms, 'imagined',[41] not least because it had cut-throat elements, there could be an affinity and camaraderie that could be balm compared to those distressed by homophobia in their western home countries.

Notes

1. Goffman, E. (1968) *Asylum*, Penguin, Harmondsworth; Gerstenberger, H. (1996) 'Men Apart: The Concept of "Total Institution" and the Analysis of Seafaring', *International Journal of Maritime History*, VIII (1), June, pp. 173–82; Aubert V. and Orner, O. (1958/1959) 'On the Social Structure of the Ship', *Acta Sociologica*, Vol. 3, Reykjavik, Iceland, pp. 200–19, and (1962) *The Ship as Social System*, Institute for Social Research, Oslo.

2. Argyle, M. (1994) *The Sociology of Interpersonal Behaviour*, Penguin, London, p. 179.

3. Statement prepared by the Shipping Federation and the Employers Association of the Port of Liverpool, 17 September 1966 as part of the evidence to the Pearson Inquiry, NUS's own copy, Warwick Modern Record Centre, MSS 175A/Box 16/file SI 22–62.

4. See Marsh, A. and Ryan, V. (1989) *The Seamen: A History of the National Union of Seamen*, Malthouse Press, Oxford, for information on this, particularly Chapters 9, 10 and the postscript.

5. The hospitality industry ashore and at sea seems to have a problem with staff taking goods for resale. See, for example, Mars, Gerald (1992) 'Hotel Pilferage: A Case Study in Occupational Threat', in Littler, C.J. (ed.), *The Experience of Work*, Open University/Ashgate, Aldershot, pp. 262–70, and Mars, G. and Nicod, M. (1984) *The World of Waiters*, Allen and Unwin, London. The Oral History Unit at Southampton City Heritage has been told many stories of systematic rackets, but these are almost entirely off the record.

6. The construction of masculinity in a ship's culture may be inferred to some extent from Barret, F.J. (1996) 'The Organizational Construction of Hegemonic Masculinity: The Case of the US Navy', *Gender, Work and Organization*, 3, (3), July, pp. 129–41.

7. Bullen, F.T. (1900/1979) *Men of the Merchant Service*, Earl M. Coleman Enterprises, New York, p. 180.

8. See, for example, Iverson, R.D. and Deery, M. (1996–97) 'Turnover Culture in the Hospitality Industry, *Human Resource Management Journal*, 7(4), pp. 71–82.

9. For example, the 1946 AGM of the NUS heard an argument about postwar

staffing shortages and skill dilution, particularly in relation to the *Queen Elizabeth*'s lack of 300 first-class ratings. The debate was whether it was better to allow in men who had at least been to sea before, though not since 1939, or to employ that apocryphal category 'salt water imposters' or 'all kinds of men out of hotels ... some might have been in concentration camps because they belonged to fascist countries'. Argument by Bother Yates of the Central Reserve Pool Executive, 1946 AGM minutes, p. 126, Warwick Modern Record Centre, MSS 175A/1/Box 2.

10. Robinson, J. (1988) *Jack and Jamie Go To War*, Gay Men's Press, London, p. 99.

11. This may be one reason for the hostility to stewards from deck crew: that a steward did not have the manual skills and was thought not to have the sense of collective social consciousness to be of use in a sinking ship. In fact, stewards have shown themselves to be heroic during sinkings.

12. Bannerman, G. (1982) *Cruise Ships: The Inside Story*, Collins, Toronto, p. 109.

13. Ibid., p. 110.

14. See work on racism such as Tabili, Laura (1995/96) 'Labour Migration, Racial Formation and Class Indentity. Some Reflections on the British Case', *North West Labour History*, 20, pp. 16–35; Tabili, L. (1996) ' "A Maritime Race": Masculinity and the Racial Division of Labor in British Merchant Ships 1900–1939', in Creighton, Margaret S. and Norling, Lisa (eds), *Iron Men, Wooden Women: Gender and Seafaring in the Atlantic World 1700–1920*, Johns Hopkins University Press, Baltimore, MD, and London, pp. 169–88.

15. Argyle, *Sociology*, pp. 170–1.

16. Marsh and Ryan, *Seamen*, p. 167.

17. Warren, C.A.B. (1974) *Identity and Community in the Gay World*, John Wiley and Sons, New York, p. 70.

18. Bérubé points out the irony of this in the Second World War military. 'Ironically, the informal process of segregating gay men and women into "gay" duties – a process that included both assignment and self-selection – not only integrated them as homosexuals more deeply into the military organization but also helped them develop their own work cultures as gay soldiers and officers.' Bérubé, A. (1991) *Coming Out under Fire: The History of Gay Men and Women in World War Two*, Penguin, London, p. 55.

19. Houlbrook, M. (2001) 'For Whose Convenience? Gay Guides, Cognitive Maps and the Construction of Homosexual London', in Gunn, S. and Morris, R.J. (eds), *Identities in Space: Contested Terrains in the Western City since 1850*, Ashgate, Aldershot, Vermont, p. 167.

20. Mort, F. (1987) *Dangerous Sexualities: Medico-moral Politics in England since 1830*, Routledge and Kegan Paul, London.

21. Lewis, J. (1945) 'Education as Recreation', *The Seaman*, 3(7–8) July–August, p. 107, Warwick Modern Record Centre, MSS 175A/4/1/32.

22. I have heard repeated testimony about this from stewardesses on a range of ships. JS.

23. McIntosh, M. (1996) 'The Homosexual Role', in Seidman, S. (ed.), *Queer Theory/Sociology*, Blackwell, Oxford, p. 35.

24. Story-giver MO132/2, Oral History Unit, Southampton City Council, interviewer Sheila Jemima.

25. Bannerman, *Cruise Ships*, p. 110.

26. Story-giver MO101, Oral History Unit, Southampton City Council, interviewed by Sheila Jemima.

27. Story-giver MO132/2.

28. Evelyn Home was a long-running agony aunt on a British women's magazine of the period. She became an institution, her name synonymous with the occupation.

29. Earlier sailors' recreations are best summed up in Creighton, M.S. (1982) *Dogwatch and Liberty Days*, Peabody Museum of Salem, Salem, MA.

30. The tendency to confine women to domestic work is illuminated by the fact that in Australia as late as 1981 the only maritime union with female members was the Marine Stewards Union. Fitzpatrick, B. and Cahill, R.J. (1981) *The Seamen's Union of Australia 1872–1972*, Seamen's Union of Australia, Sydney, p. 298 fn.

31. 'Your mother' was a Polari phrase meaning 'myself', rather than referring to the speaker's actual mother.

32. Lustig-Prean, D. (1999) 'Last Night I Dreamt of the Sea Again', reprint from Gay Times, November, pasted in at: http://www.davidclemens.com/gaymilitary/duncan.htm.

33. Acceptance of bisexuality seemed much more ready than in the lesbian feminist communities of the 1990s studied by Amber Ault, who used what she saw as four techniques of 'neutralisation' of bisexual women: suppression (bisexuals don't exist), incorporation (bi now, gay later), marginalisation (on the fence and irrelevant), and de-legitimation (they're disloyal bed-hoppers). Ault, A. (1996) 'The Dilemma of Identity: Bi Women's Negotiations', in Seidman, *Queer Theory/Sociology*, p. 314. These techniques were not used by the gay seafarers we know.

34. See work on this under-recognised aspect of labour, including James, N. (1989) 'Emotional Labour: Skill and Work in the Social Regulation of Feelings', *Sociological Review*, 37(1) pp. 15–42.

35. Bannerman, *Cruise Ships*, p. 133.

36. Lee-Treweek, Geraldine (1997) 'Women, Resistance and Care: An Ethnographic Study of Nursing Auxiliary Work', *Employment and Society*, 11(1), March, pp. 47–63.

37. Mullins, L.J. (1993) 'The Hotel and the Open Systems Model of Organisational Analysis,' *The Services Industries Journal*, 13(1), January, p. 5.

38. Dickinson, B. (1997) *Selling the Sea: An Inside Look at the Cruise Industry*, John Wiley and Sons, New York, p. 75.

39. Marsh and Ryan, *Seamen*, p. 216.

40. Stoddart, H. (2000) *Rings of Desire: Circus History and Representation*, Manchester University Press, Manchester, p. 99, citing Bergson, H. (1991) *Laughter: An Essay on the Meaning of the Comic*, Macmillan, London.

41. Anderson, B. (1983) *Imagined Communities*, Verso, London.

Chapter 8

Swallowing the Anchor

The party's over

It might seem incomprehensible that anyone would want to leave such a party. But gay seafarers eventually did want to leave. And of course, this party was also a job, not a chosen form of leisure. In this chapter we begin by discussing a number of reasons why people decided to end their time at sea. We then go on to look at what happened to the men after they left, how they adjusted to life on land, and how their years in the Merchant Navy continued to affect them.

Reasons for leaving can be categorised as internal, involving a personal decision to quit, or they could be external, owing to circumstances that are imposed upon an individual and therefore beyond his control. For many seafarers, their reasons for leaving were a complex mix of several factors, although external factors appear to have played a larger role.

Time to settle down

For many men, one internal reason for leaving was simply the fact that they were growing older. Seafaring was generally viewed as 'a young man's career', and many seafarers left in their late twenties or early thirties to 'settle down'. Table 7.1 in Chapter 7 (p. 198) shows the workforce's age profile. Hospitality work also tended to be viewed as casual work and a rapid staff turnover was not thought to be unusual. Between four and six years of employment was considered normal, even long, for staff in service-related jobs. Officers, who had bought into the job through years of expensive training, tended to have long careers, however.

Dave, who left in 1964 after eight years, stressed that he needed a change. He'd bought a house that was being let by agents while he was away and decided that it was time to get a grip of the place. 'I was getting

Life onboard ship could be a party but, for everybody, it eventually had to end.
Picture courtesy of private donor.

older, and I didn't want to be a tired old poof living out of a suitcase at 50. It's no fun.' In general, as people age, factors like comfort, stability and security become more important to them. And in addition to that, as the men grew older, the demands that life at sea placed upon them weren't as easy to meet. 'You're up at six in the mornings, you have a kip [sleep] in the afternoons if you can, and then you finish work at half past nine or ten o'clock. It's from then on that you have any parties. And there were no days off when you were at sea.' Dave pointed out that the notoriously long hours could take their toll on some of the crew who'd been around longer than the others. In the past, working hours at sea had been less regulated, and so among the service-related staff there existed a culture where people took any opportunity for overtime pay that they could, at some expense to their health. Stewards, for example, were known for suffering from gastric problems because they often ate on the run. Years of this punishing work schedule could eventually take its toll. 'There were one or two older bedroom stewards, dear old things,' said Dave. 'They'd been slaving away, and they looked every year their ages!'

Age could also diminish pulling power. Jazz musician and former Royal Naval sailor George Melly makes the point several times in relation to older ratings. These were often Petty Officers who 'had been reduced to the ranks for some detected misdemeanor: habitual drunkenness, too open a penchant for young lads ... jolly fellows if ... a little pressing in their affections', who had become objects of slight amusement because of their years.[1] However, seniority could also be an asset, if you had the energy. Don Trueman makes the point that 'a lot of young men followed "The Queen of the Pacific" even though he was an old man, because he was so exciting and he would look after them, just like older hands in prison protect the more delicate newcomers from abuse, including rape'. This system was so established that it had its own name, Melly notes. 'The expression "winger" [a term common to the Merchant Navy too] means, at its most innocent, a young seaman who is taken under the wing of a rating or Petty Officer older and more experienced than himself to be shown the ropes. It can also, though far from inevitably, imply a homosexual relationship.'[2] However, for other seafarers, getting old meant they were no longer as alluring, sometimes resulting in bitterness or jealousy. The roles that they enjoyed playing – sexual adventurer, ingénue to be fought over, or gorgeous drag diva – would no longer be compatible with their circumstances.

For some, the same reasons for joining the Merchant Navy eventually became the reasons why they wanted to leave. Life at sea offered plenty of opportunities for sexual freedom, and in addition sailors didn't have to worry about the drudge of everyday life, paying bills and going to the same places every week. As seafarers, the world was purported to have become their oyster and every new voyage or port stop-over could result in a wealth of potential new friends or 'affaires'. Yet ironically, this freedom eventually became a kind of prison in itself. The sense of novelty and excitement was likely to subside after a few years and travel itself eventually became a thing of routine. 'We were going to the same places again and again, and it was wearing off,' said Ian, who left (also after eight years) in 1987. The holiday atmosphere that the men had created and enjoyed on the cruise liners was fine for those who were younger, but it could become increasingly incompatible with a more 'settled' lifestyle, particularly if a long-term relationship was desired. Ian elaborates: 'I was growing up really, and I wanted more. You could have an awful lot on the ship, but there were a lot of things you could never have. Towards the end, I really did want to leave.'

Ian's first serious relationship, in the mid-1980s, changed his attitude towards his life at sea. 'He was a passenger who got on at Miami and left at San Francisco where he lived. Our relationship lasted for the two weeks of the voyage. We were docked at San Francisco for two nights and I stayed at his house for that time. It was lovely. But afterwards we carried on around the world and he had got off. So we started writing to each other. At first we wrote a lot. You think you're going to see them

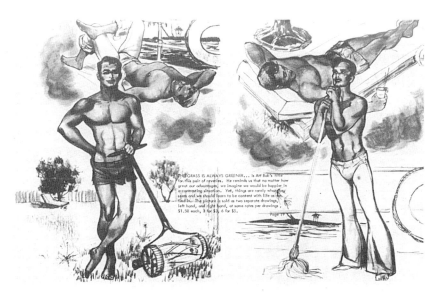

Home could look quite enticing when you were at sea, as this drawing by Art Bob shows. 'The Grass is Always Greener' was published in *Physique Pictorial*, Fall 1956. Picture courtesy of Wayne Stanley, Athletic Model Guild.

again. You start off with "I'll come and see you", but as time goes on, first you get a letter every month, then every two months, and you just know it's not going to happen. It was sad because he was the first person I fell for emotionally, and it was hard after that. I tended to avoid anyone who I thought was nice, or I liked, because I knew how it was going to end. I started looking forward to going home, to getting away from the ship.'

Frank cites the feeling of outgrowing his life at sea and wanting something different from life. 'You feel you can live in Paradise forever. Unless you've never been to Paradise. But there comes a stage where you feel that you've seen and done everything basically.' With the travel and the sexual and social opportunities, in terms of life experience, the average gay man was able to pack in a lot more at sea than he would have ever done by remaining on land. But experience can leave people feeling tired, jaded or ultimately bored.

So, in terms of internal reasons, a combination of growing older, with an increased desire for permanence, stability and long-term relationships, meant that many gay seafarers eventually exchanged a life of long working hours and intense partying on the ships for one which was potentially more sedate and secure. However, there were a number of external factors which also contributed to their 'retirement' from the sea. And in some cases, the decision was made for them.

The shake-up

A second key reason for leaving was that seafaring life changed forever for British seafarers. From the 1970s onwards, the employment policies of many of the shipping companies underwent drastic changes, partly as a result of a downturn in the passenger liner industry, before cruising took off. Membership of the National Union of Seamen (a reasonable indicator of the number of UK seafarers working) rose from 82,753 members in 1951 to 88,979 in 1961, but dropped to 50,000 in 1971, 34,938 in 1981, and only 24,405 by 1987.[3] The UK fleet was decimated in the 1980s with a radical and highly controversial shift to operating ships under Flags of Convenience. This meant that a variety of new labour practices could be adopted, particularly the sacking of all the (expensive) UK staff and the employment of people from South East Asian countries on punitive contracts. In effect, it was an extension of the racially exploitative behaviour described by historians of earlier periods, W. Jeffrey Bolster and Laura Tabili.[4] So for some British seafarers, there was no job to stay in, even if they wanted to do so.

P&O, one of the biggest players, had been committed to operating with 50 per cent British labour and 50 per cent Asian labour, whereas many of the other shipping companies had brought in more employees from less developed countries, such as India, and particularly from Goa. The reason for this was simple – Goan staff were paid less and were therefore more cost-effective than the British staff. So during the first half of the 1980s, P&O was one of the few companies left who took on British stewards, waiters and cooks.

However, this was to change. In 1986, British P&O staff were given 'golden handshakes', a financial incentive to leave. 'Everyone with a British passport was laid off,' says Ian, who worked for P&O. 'And we were replaced by Italian and Mexican crew. We could have stayed, but under a new contract and for a lot less money.' It therefore made more sense for people to find work elsewhere, especially as the industrial relations situation worsened. P&O European Ferries Dover were involved in a major battle over their use of non-union labour in 1988 – a major climatic change in an industry where the union had attempted to safe-guard jobs through negotiation for over half a century.[5] It was part of a general union-busting climate that affected miners and print workers too. However, some white British seafarers did stay on P&O passenger ships, particularly the *Canberra*, in spite of reduced pay packets, until the early 1990s.

Some of the seafarers speak about what happened with bitterness. Many union members see it as the worst of a long line of betrayals. The companies that had utilised their labour for years, or in some cases decades, chose a course of action that showed how little they valued their employees' work. Ian made the best of it: 'I was forced out, so my mind was made up for me, which was probably a good thing, because it kicked me back into life at home. And it gave me redundancy which was a great help, so I was lucky to get out the way I did.' Others were simply bereaved and in shock. Their way of life was gone.

Female competition

Tied in with the enforced redundancies was the third reason: women workers. The gradual employment of more female staff was another aspect of change that threatened the security of the traditional gay male service-related posts. Increased realisations by women of their unjust exclusion from many areas of the workforce brought major legal changes, such as the 1975 Sex Discrimination Act and Equal Pay Act. Until the 1950s, less than 1 per cent of most passenger ships' workforces were female and ships had traditionally been misogynist spaces. Old superstition was mixed with human resource management fears that men could be troublesome about sexual access to women and end up fighting over them.[6] Legal changes and increasingly permissive heterosexual moral standards, linked to the contraceptive pill after 1965, changed the social climate and paved the way for more women to be brought on to cruise liners as employees. However, typically, the jobs that they were given were stereotypically 'women's work', associated with household chores, low pay and low status. Women, like openly gay men, could be part of the ship's hierarchy, as long as they kept to their place. Unfortunately, the introduction of large numbers of female staff was not always viewed as a positive development by the gay men onboard, who were concerned that these women would steal their jobs and their men.

Martin disapproved of the introduction of female workers. During his last couple of years at sea a young woman was employed by the company. Prior to that, Martin had always acted as steward to the chief engineer's cabin. However, with the new female member of staff, Martin found that he was sharing parts of his job with her. The chief engineer kidded with him, saying he now had competition. Martin told him, 'Look chief, she can have three tits and two fannies as long as she does her job.' For the rest of the week, Martin continued his duties as usual. Then one night the chief engineer came down to the bar and said 'I knew you hadn't done the cabin this morning'. Martin replied 'No, I came back downstairs.' 'I knew it, there wasn't that woman's touch,' the chief engineer told him. The difference was that Martin had always done lots of little extra things for him, when making up his room, like turning his curtains back, whereas his rival didn't. Developing professional pride by defining the Other as less desirable has often been a way that ousted people counter changed arrangements over which they have little control.

But as well as being in competition for the same job, there was also competition for the same men. The presence of women went some way in reaffirming the heterosexual identities of the male crew, which had previously been more fluid. Frank, who left in the 1970s, also didn't enjoy the fact that there were so many women on the ship. 'I must admit, that was the end. The thing is, they brought cinema operators who were female, and they brought waitresses on, and that just killed it completely.' With the introduction of more female workers, the sexual dynamics between nominally 'straight' and gay seafarers was inevitably renegotiated, often with unfavourable consequences for the gay men. 'The girls were there, the door was always open. Even the Goanese were seen waiting to have sex with them. This was after I had left the ship but it was common knowledge to members of the crew,' says Frank.

Changed times

The fourth reason that propelled some seafarers to leave was that seafaring life began to lose many of its desirable qualities as tourism and transport became increasingly commodified. As well as the introduction of women and non-British staff, some of the men we interviewed noted that the atmosphere had simply changed. 'Great big, impersonal bloody vessels, mixed crew and single-berth cabins,' says Dave in horror, speaking of today's cruise liners. Single-berth cabins meant that the intimacy that was created from sharing with one or more shipmates was curtailed. The presence of non-British seafarers also limited the number of sexual opportunities available to gay men, as there wasn't a great deal of socialising between different races onboard. Other changes were also not viewed favourably by seafarers, for example, the reduction of stop-over times in ports. In the past seafarers could expect to get two or three days' leave to go and make the most of a new port. But later on, ships were in and out of a port in the same day. This curtailed the amount of time that could be spent exploring a foreign port.

While there are still plenty of gay workers on cruise liners, it's certainly the case that they aren't as numerous as they were in the 1950s, 1960s and 1970s. Another reason for this is the result of competition from airlines. Gay men who would have become stewards on cruise ships 40 years ago, can now find work as cabin crew with an airline company. In many ways, the role of airline steward is the successor to cabin steward or waiter in the Merchant Navy.[7] However, while some aspects of the work might be similar, there are others that are not. For example, today's flight attendants have more time off between journeys that are relatively brief, so tensions aren't as likely to build up. However, at the same time, the chance for developing intense comradeships with other staff or sexual relationships with nominally straight crew is also lessened.

And as well as competition from other modes of transport, many gay men simply don't have the same reasons for wanting to leave the country as they did. Staying on land was increasingly beginning to be a more viable option.

Liberation on land

As well as the 'pushes' that sent men back to land jobs, there was also the fifth reason for leaving: the 'pull' of changed conditions ashore. The decriminalisation of homosexuality in 1967 and the subsequent Gay

Liberation movement of the early 1970s had a marked effect on the way that many gay men on land viewed their sexual identities, even if it appears to have had less of an effect on the way that gay men experienced life at sea. On many ships in the 1960s and 1970s, particularly those without a large population of gay stewards, the situation could have been at worst homophobic and at best tolerant of homosexuality *as long as* it was only practised in the lower and feminised ranks, and performed with camp humour rather than with an overt sense of liberation. Indeed, as we noted in Chapter 6, the politics of Gay Liberation appeared not to be an issue for many seafarers, who had more traditional attitudes to homosexuality, rather than connecting it to radical politics.

However, for gay men who may have joined the Merchant Navy in earlier, more homophobic, decades, the alternative – a life on land – was slowly becoming more attractive. As Dave points out: 'Everything's so liberal here now anyway. You'd be more constricted at sea.' Attitudes towards homosexuality gradually became somewhat more tolerant from the late 1960s onwards, although they did take a nose-dive in the 1980s[8] as gay men were linked to AIDS and were portrayed negatively by the popular British press.[9] While legislation was often used to convict men for cruising for sex in parks or lay-bys, numerous commercial 'safe spaces'[10] had became available: bars, nightclubs and pubs, which were less likely to be subjected to the sorts of raids that the discreet private drinking clubs of the 1950s had been. The 1970s saw the launch of national gay and lesbian switchboard help-lines across the country as well as newspapers and magazines such as *Gay News*, *Jeffrey*, *Line-up*, *Lunch*, *Quorum*, *Man to Man*, *Play Guy* and *Q International*. Some of these aimed to raise the political consciousness of their readers; others provided erotic stimulation in the form of stories and photographs. Gay Liberation brought with it public demonstrations of pride, with annual organised marches. So on the whole, gay men found that it was easier to express their sexual identities and make contacts while on land, especially if they lived in urban areas.

As discussed at the end of Chapter 3, during the 1970s effeminate gay identities also began to be seen as outmoded and problematic by the new liberationists. This was despite camp gay men continuing to be stalwarts of mainstream British comedy, as typified by Larry Grayson and John Inman,[11] as well as drag artistes and female impersonators like Danny La Rue and later Dame Edna Everage (Barry Humphries). However, at the time, the roles these men played were viewed as pandering to negative stereotypes about gay men – flamboyant sissies who parodied women. The Gay Liberation Front *Manifesto* saw the butch and femme role-playing that some gay men and lesbians engaged in as an imposition of heterosexual gender roles, and ultimately oppressive: '... those gay men and women who are caught up in the femme role must realise, as straight women increasingly do, that any security this brings is more than offset by their loss of freedom'.[12] These gender roles had been typical of some gay seafarers, who had taken butch 'husbands' for the duration of a voyage, while performing a 'housewife' role.

Another problem with camp was that it simply wasn't viewed as sexy. In place of the simpering, bitchy camp stereotypes, gay men were reconceptualised in the 1970s as proud, butch and horny, to the point of being hyper-masculine. Although the politics of the British Gay Liberationists had aimed to tear down the camp/butch dichotomy, influences from American culture also had an effect on the social and political dynamics of the British gay scene.[13] By the 1970s, ideas surrounding the types of gay man who could find each other attractive had changed. The stud/queen binary of the 1960s and earlier[14] was replaced by the notion of 'real men' who were attracted to other 'real men'. The idea of two *camp* men having sex together was somewhat frowned up, even in the Merchant Navy. 'Bread and bread never mix, do they,' muses Frank. 'They never make a sandwich.'

Gay Liberation had an effect on the way that sexual identities were perceived. In the past, sexuality had been closely linked to gender performance, particularly among working-class men, so if you were effeminate, you were seen as homosexual, but if you were masculine, this wasn't necessarily the case. On the ships, this had meant that butch men could have sex with other men but wouldn't have been considered as gay. They might have been seen as 'making do' where no women were present or they could have been viewed as 'trade'. So before Gay Liberation, sexual identities were more unfocused and therefore potentially more fluid, simply because they hadn't been discussed that much anyway. However, after Gay Liberation, sexual identities were brought into a much sharper focus, with an emphasis on 'coming out' if you were gay. People were being encouraged to think more about their sexuality, and to make decisions that would have far-reaching repercussions on how they perceived themselves and the sorts of lifestyles they would go on to lead. For some butch sailors who had taken on camp male partners in the past, this conceptual shift from 'gay as camp' to 'gay as having sex with men' proved to be difficult to reconcile with how they viewed themselves. In their minds, in mainstream society's eyes, and within the higher ranks of the Merchant Navy, homosexuality was still stigmatised and viewed as weak and connected to effeminacy. And in any case, the increasing presence of female crew on the cruise ships meant that such men would no longer have to 'make do' anyway. In fact, if they continued to show a preference for other men in such circumstances, when their main excuse in the past (no women) had been removed, then they were bringing their true sexual identity into question even further.

So a number of external factors contributed to the inevitable end of many gay seafarers' jobs. Decriminalisation of homosexuality meant that acceptance and community could be increasingly found on land, while Gay Liberation had helped to create a dialogue about sexual identity that eschewed the butch/femme relationships which were common on the ships. In addition, the changed nature of the Merchant Navy, and the introduction of female staff had made the job less attractive, while the policy of employing cheaper non-UK staff effectively ousted many British gay seafarers out of their jobs, or meant that those who would have joined in the past did not.

Life after sea

So what was life like for the men who had spent years working on cruise ships, and how did they cope with the return to land? For some, adjustment was not easy at first. Seafarers generally find that old friends and relations are gone or have been outgrown. Fixity can seem boring for those used to roving, and shore life tended to offer less frivolity and a more narrow-minded approach to work. If seafaring was – as it could be for some – a protest against all that was implied by domestic masculinity, then being ashore meant having to handle expectations that you would fulfil that role.[15] Sometimes there simply weren't the basic necessities, such as jobs or affordable congenial housing; they faced the challenges of adjustment that people released from prison endure too. Ian returned home to the small town where he had grown up and, after the gay camaraderie of the cruise ships, felt an increasing sense of isolation. 'The hardest part was my first year when I came away from the sea, because I had no friends here, and I did find it very difficult. In just a small town, there's no gay scene, no gay people as far as I knew, and it was very difficult. I had to change totally, I just shrunk away, I hid until I found my feet again.'

For officers or men who had been discreet about their sexuality while at sea, returning to land did not particularly signify a large change in the way they viewed themselves. Alan, a radio officer who left after eight years in 1963, rejoined a society where homosexuality was still illegal and stigmatised. He did what many men of his generation did – he got married. His mother arranged a date for him with a young woman, and marriage seemed inevitable. He grew to love his wife and they had four children. 'I was outwardly happy. I had a home and a family. On the surface it looked to be ideal. But I wasn't inwardly happy.' After 14 years Alan admitted that it wasn't the life he wanted and he got a divorce. Now living with another man, he doesn't have any contact with his wife and children.

Bill, an engineer who left the Merchant Navy after six years in 1980, was only able to start a relationship with another seafarer after they had both left the sea. 'He was also an engineer, a good-looking guy and I had quite fancied him while we were at sea. The Third Mate's wife fancied him too, and there was a bit of hanky-panky between them. I think a lot of people thought that we were at it, which we weren't. But we were after I left. We both joined the same oil company and had a bit of a fling.' Bill went from one masculine environment into another, working for an off-shore oil company, where he continued to keep his sexuality hidden. 'I moved to a small town that was near the plant. It was dire, very hetero, very butch, a violent social scene. It was a very hard sort of town. You had to watch yourself.' Bill didn't come out until 1989, beginning with short trips to London and Tenerife, and eventually moving to a larger city where he began to explore its gay scene. For the officers and engineers who were closeted in the Merchant Navy, their 'coming out' on land was more gradual once they left.

Many gay seafarers settled in port towns or cities such as Liverpool, Aberdeen, Southampton or Portsmouth, which for some were their orig-inal hometowns. And while they took different jobs, the majority of men we interviewed stressed that they still had 'the travel bug'. 'I love to travel. It's in your blood,' said Geoff. And for others, leaving the Merchant Navy didn't necessarily mean that they had to return to the British Isles. Frank, who left in the mid-1970s after 23 years, had been impressed by what he had seen of America on his travels, and decided to live and work there for a while. Robert lived in Australia and San Francisco.

Some of them returned to passenger ships later in life, this time as pas-sengers themselves, experiencing the holiday atmosphere again, but with increased freedom and leisure time afforded by being paying guests. In addition, voyages were an ideal opportunity for them to meet up with old colleagues – there is a sense of reconstructing the past: a desire to relive the 'good old days' at sea, with the same people who were there with you the first time round. For these men, reminiscing about past adventures and trading memories with each other allows them to keep in touch with a secret, shared history, particularly as times have changed so rapidly.

The older seafarers are also able to compare the situation on cruise ships today with how they were when they worked at sea, and in almost all cases the feeling is that the atmosphere was better in the old days. 'It's different now,' says Frank, talking of today's stewards. 'They haven't got time to have fun and make friends with people.'

Many gay seafarers kept in touch with each other for decades after leaving the sea, via email, telephone and letter, and occasional visits to each other. They know who's died and indeed were careful in giving us some information because they knew their ex-colleagues lived in the same town and would be unhappy if exposed. In addition, they remained friends with the people they met in overseas ports, the people who had made them feel welcome and at ease years ago. As a result, some gay seafarers have formed networks of friends that stretch across the world. They know that almost wherever they travel, there will probably be a familiar face to greet them when they arrive, despite the decimations of AIDS.

Today some of our informants are retired and some are still struggling to find congenial jobs. One recently lost his job after being outed in a local paper. Just under half of our admittedly small sample are in enduring relationships. Some are in the closet, and feel nervous about continuing homophobia in the UK.

All of the men we interviewed spoke of their time in the Merchant Navy with fond memories, as people often do when speaking with hindsight of situations where camaraderie and unity against a common enemy were much stronger than today. Memories are particularly rosy for those who left in the 1960s and 1970s. For most it was a time of youthful pleasure, in a social period when Britain was not yet in recession and when state homophobia seemed as if it might be on the wane. 'It was a very nice period of time. It was excellent,' says Dave, recalling the 1960s. 'We had a pretty good fleet going, we had lots of ships. It made some good employment for a few months, maybe years. As you got on board we all had a feeling of relief. It was wonderful.' The NUS historians agree: 'The 1970s were years of optimism ... the UK proportion of world [shipping] tonnage, which had been falling for many years, stabilised at 11 per cent and the owners were struggling to retain crew by [some limited] improvement in conditions.'[16] The economic situation seems to be mirrored by the personal situation for gay men. As Frank sums it up: 'It was a very good grounding for me. I had a wonderful time. I loved every minute of it. People would deny it, but it actually happened. And God, it did happen!'

Notes

1. Melly, G. (1977) *Rum, Bum and Concertina*, Futura, London, p. 14.

2 . Ibid., p. 64.

3. Cited in Marsh A. and Ryan, V. (1989) *The Seamen: A History of the National Union of Seamen*, Malthouse Publishing, Oxford, p. 307. They draw on

statistics from the Board of Trade, Chief Registrar of Friendly Societies and Certification Office.

4. Bolster, W.J. (1996) ' "Every Inch a Man": Gender in the Lives of African American Seamen 1800–1860', in Creighton, M.S. and Norling, L. (eds), *Iron Men, Wooden Women: Gender and Seafaring in the Atlantic World 1700–1920*, Johns Hopkins University Press, Baltimore, MD, and London, pp. 138–68 and Tabili, L. (1996) ' "A Maritime Race": Masculinity and the Racial Division of Labour in British Merchant Ships 1900–1939', in Creighton and Norling, *Iron Men, Wooden Women*, pp. 169–88.

5. Marsh and Ryan, *Seamen*, pp. 228–47.

6. For a thorough bibliography about women on ships, see Stanley, J. (2002) 'And after the Cross-dressed Cabin Boys and Whaling Wives? Possible Futures for Women's Maritime Historiography', *Journal of Transport History*, 23(1) pp. 9–22.

7. This transition has been particularly noticed by Hochschild, A.R. (1983) *The Managed Heart*, University of California Press, Berkeley, CA who draws attention to the people-management focus of the job, particularly on the transport hospitality worker's essential smile and the emotional labour designed to combat travel anxiety.

8 . See Jowell, R., Brook, L., Prior, G. and Taylor, B. (1992) *British Social Attitudes, the 9th Report*, Ashgate, Aldershot, p. 124; Jowell, R. (1996) *British Social Attitudes, the 13th Report*, Ashgate, Aldershot, p. 39; Jowell, R., Curtice, J., Park, A. and Thomson, S. (1999) *British Social Attitudes, the 16th Report: Who Shares New Labour Values?*, Ashgate, Aldershot, p. 348; and Jowell, R., Park, A., Thomson, K., Jarvis, L., Bromley, C. and Stratford, N. (2000) *British Social Attitudes, the 17th Report: Focusing on Diversity*, Sage, London, p. 112.

9. See Sanderson, Terry (1995) *Mediawatch*, Gay Men's Press, London, p. 46.

10. Hindle, P. (1994). 'Gay Communities and Gay Space in the City', in Whittle, S. (ed.), *The Margins of the City: Gay Men's Urban Lives*, Ashgate, Aldershot, p. 11.

11. Although John Inman has always been coy about the sexuality of his character Mr Humphries in the British sitcom *Are You Being Served*, the part is certainly coded as gay. Notably, in one episode Mr Humphries emerges out of a huge parcel, dressed as a sailor.

12. Gay Liberation Front (1979) *Manifesto*, Russell Press, London, p. 9.

13. Jivani, A. (1997) *It's Not Unusual: A History of Lesbian and Gay Britain in the Twentieth Century*, Michael O'Mara Books, London, pp. 173–4.

14. Waugh, T. (1996) 'Cockteaser', in Doyle, J., Flatley, J. and Muñoz, J. (eds) *Pop Out: Queer Warhol*, Duke University Press, Durham, NC, pp. 51–77.

15. Such a refutation of not only a secure home life ashore but a heteronormative sexual identity was paralleled by some upper-class men in 1880-1914 who lived a homoerotic lifestyle in protest against their fathers. Tosh, J. (1991) 'Domesticity

and Manliness in the Victorian Middle Class: The Family of Edward White Benson', in Roper, M. and Tosh, J. (eds), *Manful Assertions: Masculinities in Britain since 1800*, Routledge, London, pp. 17 and 44–73.

16. Marsh and Ryan, *Seamen*, p. 206.

Chapter 9

Taking Stock of Gay Heaven

This book has described an extraordinary period in history, for both gay men and for gender relations in maritime situations. When gay men joined passenger ships in large numbers, they created a workforce that allowed them to enjoy a relative freedom and develop a sense of pride in their collective identity. The presence of gay men at sea was also enlightening for the rest of the floating population. For the straight crew and passengers, to travel on a gay-friendly ship was to experience a brief familiarisation training that often helped to counter prejudice. Passengers could get off a gay-friendly ship not only more tanned, lighter in wallet and heavier in weight from the luxurious living, but with knowledge not available to them on land: gay could mean celebration, pride and fun, not shame.

A gay-friendly ship was an alternative world with its own language and values, a culture where wages could enable gay seamen to buy the drinks they might need for Dutch courage in the ship's bar, to commission the frocks and make-up that would enhance their drag performances, and allow them to pay for entry to bath-houses in New York or gay brothels in Barcelona.

The camp atmosphere that was permitted or overlooked by the higher-ranking officers on the ships, implicitly shows how far gay sexuality could go, or how it could move, given the right space. What happened on ships offered an inkling of how different life on land could have been had that same sense of liminality existed.

However, gay activity could never have happened on the ships if the presence of camp and openly gay men had not led to the creation of a relaxed, happy environment. Gay staff flattered the passengers and were especially liked (and well-tipped) by the older females.[1] Heterosexual men saw their masculinity confirmed, in contradistinction to the camp men who were no threat to the pursuit of the female staff, and were sometimes willing to act as discreet sexual partners when no women were available. This highlights an extraordinary tolerance or bracketing off that can be achieved by people when they are away from their normal situations ashore. It could be said that shipboard society allowed more honest expressions of desire than those found on land, although it could also be argued that seafarers were simply met with a new set of sexual values and accepted modes of behaviour, based around a different sort of society, with its own forms of regulation.

So the confinement of the ships also produced something that Gay Liberationists would see as less positive: a polarity between masculinity and femininity (or effeminacy) and an obligation to perform somewhat narrow roles that copied or even exaggerated traditional male/female heterosexuality. One effect of that was that covert gay men were more likely to stay that way, rather than feel their own masculinity compromised. The experiences of individual gay men differed widely, depending on a number of factors: their ranking, the type of ship (for example, cargo or passenger), the atmosphere of particular ships, the voyage, the prevailing attitudes of those in charge, the proportion of gay men on board, their place in their lifecycle, and the time period.

Additionally, the presence of so many gay men on the ships could have presented a challenge to traditional social norms and gender hierarchies. But maybe it simply reinforced the *status quo*. Some openly gay seafarers rose to relatively high positions, such as headwaiter. One is a very senior manager today. Other iconic sea queens were so cherished by shipping company directors that they became legendary. Such stars include the famous steward who was not only allowed to climb onboard up the passenger gangway, not the crew one, he was even allowed to get on at Cherbourg not Southampton, and was seen flouncing up the gangway with his long floating white scarf and hatboxes. There's even an apocryphal tale that one steward, who'd made good through tips and deals, rolled up to the dock in his Rolls Royce at the same moment that his captain turned up on a push-bike. Or so the stories go.

Some sea queens became the stuff of enduring legend, deservedly. But because many gay men were in the job for the short term, the majority remained on the lower rungs of the shipping hierarchy, performing the service-related roles that were unsurprisingly later filled by female and non-British staff. On the less camp side, officers found that they would not usually be allowed to occupy a position of power that commanded respect *and* be open about their sexuality.

So homosexuality was permitted, as long as it knew its place. A gay man might be lauded for making a passenger feel at ease, entertaining his crew mates, cooking an excellent duck flambé, putting the finishing touches to a cabin, or even for his skills at oral sex, but when it came to his life in the rest of the ship, he had to know exactly where the limit was, and stick to it. It is self-regulation that makes these microcosms work, and these gay seafarers had to accept boundaries that were not of their choice. Therefore, the power that many gay men had on the ships was gained in other ways – it involved implicit knowledge about the workings of the ship, humour, irony, parody, forming social networks, gossiping about and playing tricks on people who were disliked, and knowing how and when to break the rules.

It seems likely that gay activity was more easily tolerated when it had a 'girly' guise. Compulsory heterosexuality was able to remain fundamentally intact – and retrievable once the ship tied up again at the pier – precisely because some gay men could be cast as acting like substitute women, not as adults claiming a free sexual orientation that deserved respect. This raises questions about the need of some men to express dominance by penetrating those who take the position of social inferiors.

Homosexuality was only made legal in the armed forces, including the Merchant Navy, on 27 September 1999 (as the result of a ruling by the European Court of Human Rights). Therefore, the fact that openly gay men *were* tolerated in large numbers, in such a patchily conservative, hierarchical environment before then, is noteworthy in itself. For many of these men, liberation meant three key things. First, they could have sex with whomever they wanted. Secondly, they won acceptance of who they were. Thirdly, they gained freedom from guilt, fear, arrest and threats of extortion. In that respect, the Merchant Navy was truly a 'gay heaven' for many seafarers. It provided them with a source of income, a home, a new family, supportive camaraderie and the most unforgettable time of their lives. If coming out is a political act then gay-friendly ships may well have been very political spaces.

This book has tried to show the kind of life gay men after the Second World War might have on land and, contrastingly, at sea. It has revealed the secret language that helped make the gay community so strong and colourful in the shipboard culture: the frocks and the relationships with gay and straight colleagues and passengers. It's a story of tolerances, blind eyes and careful steps around. And maybe it isn't possible to know just how careful and how carefree gay men could be, both on their ships and ashore in the foreign ports where some of them learned so much. Their freedom varied with the ships, voyages and ports, and it varied with their own perceptions. We have suggested ways that shipboard life embraced, resisted and benefited from gay men's presence. And finally we have shown what happens after the party is over, in a now changed period.

Other navies

Our findings only stretch as far as the Merchant Navy. Expressions of sexuality would have been different in military situations, as they are even today. Our informants were able to lead the lives they did because the defence of the realm was not involved. Passenger ships were seen by more traditional seafarers as 'not proper ships'; not pollutable because they were already 'contaminated' or emasculated by the feminising act of turning 'men's' ships into hotels for landlubbers. But men in the navies of many countries are still fighting fierce battles for their rights. Their situation today may serve as a way for us to understand the climate in the Merchant Navy 50 years ago too.

Randy Shilts, author on *Conduct Unbecoming*, (1994) points out that today 'Gay sailors dive with the Navy SEALS, tend the nuclear reactors on submarines, and teach at the Naval War College. One gay admiral commanded the fleet assigned to one of the highest-profile military operations of the past generation. The homosexual presence on aircraft carriers is so pervasive that social life on the huge ships for the past fifteen years has included gay newsletters and clandestine gay discos. ... Never before have gay people served so extensively ... and rarely has the military moved so aggressively against homosexuality.'[2] In the USA, discharges of gay service personnel increased from 617 in 1994 to 1,034 in

WHAT WE WANT TO KNOW IS ...   COULD YOU KILL A MAN?
OOOHH YES ...   EVENTUALLY

As this postcard shows, the stereotype about gay men in the armed forces is that they are frivolous liabilities. Picture courtesy of Bamforth and Co. Ian Wallace.

1999, despite the 'Don't Ask, Don't Tell, Don't Harass, Don't Pursue' policy.[3] A 1990 study by the Royal Netherlands Navy found that gay sailors can allegedly impair the living and working environment on ships. One gay lieutenant in the Italian Navy had to challenge the allegation that gay people were dysfunctional colleagues. And Germany does not allow gay service personnel to be promoted.[4]

While there are many small battles being fought, some have already been won. In 1992, 30-year-old US Petty Officer Keith Meinhold, a 12-year US Navy veteran, became the first man to return to military service after publicly declaring his homosexuality under the then mandatory discharge policy. A teacher of submarine-hunting techniques to sonar crews, he decided to speak out on ABC television's *World Tonight* and show the nation that 'all the assertions the Pentagon made against gays serving in the military are wrong' after hearing that the Naval Investigative Service was trying to find and discharge gay sailors based in Japan.[5] Also the Royal New Zealand Navy in 2001 won an equal opportunities award for inviting an openly gay man, Eugene Moore, to go to sea to raise awareness of sexual orientation. He found: 'You could tell that people were a bit leery. I mean a lot of crossed arms and no eye contact ... which really changed by the end of the voyage.' Australia and France were reportedly watching this development with interest.[6]

So while these changes are taking place in state's navies it is worth comparing the situation in these somewhat butch environments now with the situation in the UK Merchant Navy during the late twentieth century. From the evidence we might wonder if some seafaring men could be gay precisely because of a shameful lack of progressive thinking by others. As Chapter 7 shows, our informants made the point that it was easier to be gay on ships where there were great numbers of Asian, rather than white, seamen doing the rough-tough work of Able Seaman and Ordinary Seaman. There was no one to beat them up for being a faggot. So racial staffing policies by shipping lines may actually have meant white British seafaring men's homophobia did not have to trouble gay men on certain ships.

Gay cruises

In comparison, the position for gay men as passengers is entirely different. Today there is a way gay men can sail without working: as a paying passenger on a gay cruise ship.[7] Any kind of pound, including the pink pound, is welcome. And trips that are offered on the World Wide Web include activity holidays where you can live out pirate fantasies or cruises that sometimes exclude heterosexuals. Tour company

Swashbucklers offers macho-type sailing adventures in the Virgin Islands for men excited in boyhood by '*Long John Silver in ... Treasure Island, Errol Flynn in The Sea Hawk* and *Captain Blood, Mutiny on the Bounty* and *Captains Courageous* ... be a "salt of the seas" like the daring adventurers of the past'.[8] Cruise companies offer trips where same-sex kissing is normal but making love on the decks of mixed-sexuality ships is not, and cross-dressers are warned to leave their leather and wigs at home. Such pink-pound funded trips are staffed by gay-friendly hospitality workers. Indeed, the President of Ocean Voyager Cruise Consultants offers an etiquette guide which advises: 'Hands off the staff unless you like to flirt with big problems. [A] ship's staff member caught in a passenger cabin (unless they are cleaning it) is immediately fired. However, there are no rules against meeting them during a port visit.'[9]

Gay trips were something that began surprisingly early. Robert was in at the very start: 'From 1970 to 1972 I worked for P&O Lines of Australia in their Sydney office as a reservations supervisor. I think it was in 1970 that *Canberra* was due to arrive in Sydney on a voyage from England just before Christmas – about December 23 and would not be leaving on the return trip to the UK until about January 4 or 5. For financial reasons the company did not want to have the ship lying idle in Sydney harbour for almost two weeks. So at a meeting of supervisors there was some discussion as to what we could do with her for some of that time. A large number of those employed at the Sydney office were gay so it was not too surprising when Tom, one of the more flamboyant and outrageous queens at that meeting, suggested a gay cruise to nowhere. Just

Toto tours are one of the companies offering gay people the chance to see what kind of pirates they make. Picture courtesy of Toto tours.

sail her out into the Pacific over the New Year for a six-night voyage – no ports of call!

'Greeted at first with some hilarity, the idea actually caught on. Arrangements were put in hand and the cruise was advertised – albeit with some reservations on the part of many of those at P&O. But to everyone's surprise (particularly the sceptics), it sold out in record time. *Canberra*'s captain apparently was not overjoyed when given the news that his ship was to be home to a thousand or more queers for almost a week!

'I attended the embarkation and it was quite something to see gays of all persuasion turning up in their finery – especially some of the drag queens. It was truly a feast for the senses – and how I wished that I could be one of those sailing away on what was obviously going to be a riotously fun cruise. I also attended disembarkation when the ship returned to Sydney six days later. How very different her passengers looked then! I think the best description is "shagged out". However a good time had been by all – and I suspect all had been had by all too! At the post-voyage meeting even the captain and his senior officers, who had at first been horrified at the idea of a gay cruise, admitted that it had been no trouble at all. They even went so far as to say that they would be quite happy to repeat the experience. In its own way I think that this short cruise of *Canberra*'s was a largely unrecognised milestone on the road towards gay liberation.'

Further research

We hope that people will follow up this work with more research. It would be useful if others were to augment the oral history accounts that do exist, particularly in Liverpool and Southampton, by tape-recording seafarers' memories. It would be a particularly good idea to study gay seamen's repartee when in confrontation with the law – it has been suggested that there were different regional cultural patterns of responding to the police (for example, London versus Liverpool). Shipping line records (most of which are kept at the National Maritime Museum, Greenwich) may offer accounts of management discussions about policies on gay crew. And there could be local studies of court records and newspapers from the 1940s to late 1960s showing prosecutions of gay seafarers for cottaging. We would like this book to trigger many explorations into this extraordinary period in seafaring and gay history.

Numerous questions still remain. To what extent was the extensive gay activity in the Merchant Navy in the 1950s and 1960s simply an inevitable product of women's exclusion? If so, what enabled people to suspend the usual homophobic attitudes found on land? And how can that atmosphere be created again and permanently, so that everyone is free to express a range of sexual identities from gay to straight without fear? Is any form of rampant sexuality a predictable outcome of social isolation and physical need? If so, why has homosexuality been illegal or outlawed for so long, rather than being seen as an inevitable situational expression?

To what extent was the camp atmosphere in the Merchant Navy in the 1950s and 1960s simply an extension of a particularly *British* sensibility? While mainstream societal attitudes to homosexuality in the UK were comparatively intolerant in this period, there also existed a long tradition of camp humour, stretching back to the music halls and manifesting itself in bawdy seaside postcards, sexual innuendo and the *Carry On* films of this period. The British have traditionally defused sexual tension by making a joke of it. Did Merchant Navy fleets from other countries that were characterised by negative attitudes towards homosexuality end up as similar havens for gay men who could use them as sites of performance and humour? And in what ways do other homophobic cultures implicitly or 'co-incidentally' facilitate the existence of 'gay-friendly' spaces?

We might also ask about the hidden gay history of the postwar Royal Navy, where there was less outrageous campery and more butch pursuit of camp men, as the stories about white-capped Stage Door Johnnies in Portsmouth suggest. In a way there is another *Hello Sailor!* to be written, one which examines the iconic butch bell-bottomed seaman who was *desired* but different from most of our informants. What are the relationships of the different types of masculinity that were performed in each navy and was camp a reaction to enforced male masculinity? Were sea queens of the John Wayne era actually arguing that machismo was just a bridge too far, and that they didn't want the daily strain of doing manliness? Or was it the case that being camp in a butch environment was yet more of a strain, but somehow worth the effort?

Finally, to what extent does the tolerance of gay culture in the Merchant Navy merely reflect the fact that the UK was on the cusp of Gay Liberation and the decriminalisation of homosexuality anyway? Were Merchant Navy men simply ahead of their time, making use of a peculiar window in social history? Perhaps gay men had developed their own subculture, but were yet to be accepted on land. And was it a broad and appropriate enough subculture or to some extent a cul-de-sac inhibited by heterosexual models and compulsory styles of femininity and masculinity?

The men we interviewed had experienced some of the most marked changes in the ways that they had viewed their own sexual identities, and the ways that society viewed them. Some had grown up in an atmosphere of ignorance, shame or guilt about homosexuality, feeling themselves to be the only people in the world in their situation. For many young men who had not been able to be open about their sexuality while ashore, the gay-friendly ships were a useful opportunity to explore their identities in a relatively safe situation, giving them an intensive socialisation into gay society. Life on the ships was often permissive and non-normative. People with stigmatised identities were accommodated there and validated, becoming unexceptional in a way that was not possible on land.

The Merchant Navy unwittingly did a favour to many gay men growing up in the mid to late twentieth century, providing a glamorous backdrop to hundreds of drag performances, exclusive parties and gay romances. For many of them, it was the time of their life.

Notes

1. There is a legend in the gay community that Qantas lost customers on a massive scale because it sacked all its gay cabin crew, as a new manager's wife didn't like them. It is said that passengers only returned when the super-efficient and competent gay flight attendants were reinstated.
2. Shilts, R. (1994) *Conduct Unbecoming: Gays and Lesbians in the US Military: Vietnam to the Persian Gulf*, St Martin's Press, New York, cited in http://hotwired.lycos.com/i-agent/95/28/index1a.html.
3. See http://.alternet.org/print.html?StoryID=9403.
4 Entry to Earthlink Network home page. Email: mlbakke!@bakkster.com. A useful summary (2000) of the US Servicemembers Legal Defence Network and the Don't Ask, Don't Tell policy can be found at http://.alternet.org/print.html ?StoryID=9403.
5. See http:www-tech.mit.edu/V112/N257/sailor.57w.html. See also Daryl Lindsay's *The Sting* article about US Navy drug investigators being accused of targeting gay sailors, which refers to health advocates fearing gay use of ecstasy increases the risk of unsafe sex and HIV infection: http://www.salon.com/news/feature/2000/07/18/sldn/index.html.
6. See http://onenews.nzoom.com/news_detail/0,1227,55950—7,00.html.
7. For a summary of gay cruising possibilities, see: http://www.cruisemates.com/articles/cruiseguide/gaylesbian/etiquette.cfm.
8. See Swashbucklers at http:// www.tototours.com/o2sail1.htm.
9. Bob Allen is quoted in a guide to gay etiquette at sea. See: http://www.cruisemates.com/articles/cruiseguide/gaylesbian/etiquette.cfm.

Appendix 1

Interviewees

The main seafarers who were interviewed for this book are described below. In some cases we have changed their names at their request. In others they did not want to give a great deal of biographical information, as they wished to remain unrecognisable for their own security today.

Martin
Steward. Camp name: Bessie. At sea from 1959 to c.1998.

Bill
Born 1954. Junior and fourth engineer with Denholm's Ship Management, Glasgow. At sea 1974–80. Ships sailed on include *Burmah Zircon, Norwegian Team, Seuca Team, Britannia Team, Troll Park, Chemical Adventurer, Chemical Explorer, Vancouver Trader*. Bill left the sea to go into the North Sea oil industry in Aberdeen. He's also worked as a social worker, and a Justice of the Peace. He's always been interested in politics and was a city councillor in Aberdeen.

Chris
Born 1938. Ships' writer. Storekeeper. Baggage steward. Laundry steward on *Carthage, Canberra, Perim, Chitral*. At sea 1958–64. Trained as a Registered General Nurse in 1975 and worked in Islington and Haringey as a nurse specialist in HIV/AIDS. Now retired, but still loves to travel and gives health talks to groups in Thailand.

Dave
Born 1931. Waiter, wine waiter and head waiter. At sea 1956–63. Ships sailed on included *Himalaya, Corfu, Iberia, Arcadia* and *Stratheden*. Presently enjoying retirement and has continued travelling, having made 30 visits aboard since 1992.

Robert
Ex-boarding school. Purser with British India Steam Company Ltd., at sea

1957–68. Ships sailed on included *SS Kenya* (London–East Africa), *Uganda*, *Nevasa* (Southampton–Malta), *Chantala*, *Chinkoa*, *Nardana*.

Frank
Born 1933. Cabin boy, messroom, restaurant, lounge, and bedroom steward, also public room attendent. At sea 1950–72.

Geoff
Writer, baggage steward, laundry steward with P&O. Later became a purser. At sea 1950–82.

Alan
Born 1939. Radio officer. At sea 1955–64. First four years working for Marconi, then with BP Tanker Company. Served on 16 different ships. Since leaving the sea has lectured in communications and electronics in nautical colleges and as a civilian in the armed forces.

Ian
Born 1960. After working in various hotels he became a waiter with P&O from 1981 to 1987. He worked for a short time on the old *Oriana* up to when it was scrapped, and was then a waiter on the *Canberra* until after the Falklands War. After that he was a public room steward and assistant barman on the *Sea Princess*. After leaving the sea, he worked in hotel management for a while, before buying a Post Office, where he is still a sub-postmaster. Ian also points out that one of his duties was to assist passengers on and off ships during launches. As he didn't learn to swim until 1998 – a fact he had managed to hide during his years at sea – it was fortunate that nobody fell in while he was there.

Appendix 2

Glossary of Maritime Terms

Note: Many terms have changed over time, particularly with the 1969 introduction of new job titles, for example 'Ordinary Seamen' are now 'SG2s'. And different words were used in different shipping companies. These explanations are as correct as possible for the period that this book covers.

Able Seaman, AB. A qualified seaman, over 21 years old, above an **Ordinary Seaman** but below a **Petty Officer**. Able Bodied Seamen did the more skilled manual work on the ship. Usually the career progression was that someone becomes an Ordinary Seaman, then at 18 an Efficient Deck Hand, and at about 21, or after a certain period of sea time, would be promoted to AB. Often ABs, EDHs and OSs are masculine men, sometimes butch. When gay men refer to 'sailors' they often mean these three classes of seafarer, or **Royal Naval** seafarers.

Before the mast. The term commonly used to describe **ratings** in distinction to **officers**: people who sailed before the mast were those with less privileges aboard. The phrase refers to the days when seafarers had their living quarters in the forecastle, at the front of the ship, with the masts behind them.

Bellboy. A young trainee on the hotel side of the ship, the equivalent to deck boys. They took the job after leaving school (aged 14, later 15 and usually after three months at college in Gravesend). They upgraded to **steward** at a particular age, usually 18. Bellboys worked in the catering/stewards department, responding to bells pushed by passengers. They took messages, operated the lifts, assisted in the dining room and at children's meals. The youngest members of a ship's 'family', they were often protected and sometimes petted by older crew who missed their own children at home. However, they could also be quite sophisticated, entrepreneurial and sexually active.

Bridge. The position where command of the ship as vehicle (not hotel) is usually exercised, from which the ship is navigated and controlled. It is the site of symbolic power on ship, equivalent to a plane's cockpit. Situated high up in the ship's superstructure, usually on the top deck to give the best visibility, it stretches across the width of the ship.

Cargo ship (Freighters in the USA). Any ship that primarily carries goods, and under 100 passengers. The term is not used much these days, because these ships are now described according to the cargo they carry, for example, 'container ship', 'bulk carrier' and 'tanker'. Some crew and passengers preferred cargo ships to passenger ships because they felt more like boarding houses than fancy hotels.

Crew. Sometimes used to refer to the entire complement of shipboard workers, sometimes used to refer to the lower levels of seafarers, non-**officers** or even simply manual workers.

Cruise ship. Vessel that takes passengers on long holiday voyages (cruises) between a number of ports, as opposed to ferries or to liners that go on regular scheduled voyages, normally between two ports. Formerly, some cruise ships, such as P&O's *Canberra*, were actually passenger ships which in holiday times diverted from their usual schedule as liners (ships that travel on scheduled routes or lines). They tend to have a light-hearted atmosphere.

Deck hand. One of the lowest grade of manual worker on the deck of a ship (not the engine-room or kitchen), doing manual, general maintenance tasks such as painting and cleaning. Also involved in handling ropes, springs and deck machinery that moor the ship to quays or buoys when it docks.

Forecastle (pronounced fo'c'sle). The compartments furthest forward, usually out of view of the **bridge** and so a place where shenanigans can be risked. Traditionally the living space for **ratings** was below this fo'c'sle deck. The name derives from the 'castle' built over the bows of old fighting ships, where archers stood to shoot at anyone entering the 'waist' of the ship (that area back towards the quarterdeck and on sailing ships the part of the upper deck between the fore- and main-masts).

Glory hole. A small compartment for storing unwanted items but traditionally the nineteenth- and early twentieth-century name for the small place where stewards have their accommodation. It was at the very front end of the ship (for'ard, **before the mast**). Historically, and significantly, the name for a tiny cell where prisoners were kept at court on the day of their trial. It also referred to a circular hole cut in an internal bulkhead (wall) through which gay men had sex.

Merchant Navy. Our P&O informants said that the joke at the time of their seagoing was that Britain had three navies: the Royal Navy, P&O (which was such a pukka shipping company, with a history of personnel wearing the company's special livery that it was seen as second to the

RN) and the Merchant Navy. The Merchant Navy is the collective term for the commercial shipping companies that own and operate ships of all types, which take passengers and goods, including mail, across the seas for profit. In contrast, the Royal Navy consists only of warships. The Merchant Navy is often seen as the poor sister of the Royal Navy and a more informal occupation. However, Merchant Naval ships played a major part in wartime by supporting Royal Naval ships and carrying civilian passengers and goods. Merchant seafarers are employed in it on (often short-term) contracts from particular companies, as in a hotel. They move from ship to ship, company to company, as opposed to **Royal Naval** personnel who have just one employer: the state. Lower-grade staff in the Merchant Navy are not usually in it for life, although officers are. It is not part of the armed forces and is less formal in atmosphere.

Mess. A canteen or café/dining room: the place where seafaring workers eat and relax. On the ships in the period we describe here there were separate messes for different grades and types of worker, for example, deck officers, engineering officers, petty officers, ratings, so it was one of the key daily ways that your status was made clear. One of its meanings for gay men was that at meal times they would not, particularly on a big, multi-divided ship, be able to cruise people of a different rank or department.

Officer. There are officers of various ranks in the three departments of the ship: deck, engine and catering. Deck officers (involved with the navigating and cargo stowage side of the ship's work) sometimes see themselves as 'gentlemen', and akin to their **Royal Navy** counterparts. They socialise with passengers.

Ordinary Seaman (OS). The lowest grade of seafarer in the deck department. Almost always a male occupation, OSs were involved with the general work of running the ship as a vehicle, for example, swabbing decks, painting railings.

Passenger ship. A ship that is designed to carry mainly passengers, and sometimes cargo and mail. Passenger ships could become cruise ships during holiday periods, but were usually liners that travelled scheduled routes at scheduled times. The traditional ports of departure were Liverpool, Southampton, Tilbury and London. Passengers could include migrants and business travellers as well as holiday-makers. The point was not so much just being on a ship, but getting to a destination – by ship. That is, passenger ships were not necessarily floating resorts like cruise ships; they were a means of overseas travel if commercial flying wasn't a viable option.

Petty Officer (PO). A senior rating, not an officer, usually someone who has worked his way up. They were the naval equivalent of a non-commissioned officer in the armed forces, or a foreman. Derived from the French word for small: *petit*. A Chief Petty Officer was called a 'Senior Leading Hand' and a Petty Officer was a 'Junior Leading Hand'.

Pig and Whistle. The traditional name for the crew bar on most merchant ships, situated down in the crew's quarters. Many ships did not have bars until the 1960s and initially they were just a serving hatch rather than a 'pub'. Crew bars were part of management's very strict (but frequently transgressed) way of controlling alcohol consumption aboard. Until at least the mid-1960s all that was on sale were soft drinks and Allsopps beer, not spirits. Higher staff were allowed to buy spirits and run up a bar bill. The 'Pig' was the main place for crew to socialise after 9 pm and a key site for gay cruising.

Purser. One who deals with the ship's *purse*. Pursers are the people who deal with the hotel management side of the ship, including passenger relations and accountancy. There is a hierarchy of pursers, at the top of which is the Chief Purser. Organisationally, they usually belong to the catering/stewards department. The Head Purser is strongly linked to the other 'senior managers' of the ship, such as the Captain, Chief Steward and Chief Engineer. They are not formally officers; different companies have different rules about this, but they are usually treated as officers. In the USA today, the Purser is called the 'Passenger Services Director'; in the Royal Navy the 'Pusser' dealt with crew pay.

Radio Officer. The officer responsible for ship-to-shore communication. This could include crucial operational matters like weather forecasts, and relaying of personal messages to families ashore. On many passenger ships they took down the news in Morse code overnight and got it typed up for the ship's daily newspaper the following day. Until the later twentieth century, these officers were usually the employees of the Marconi Company, not the shipping company, except in P&O's case. They therefore had a separate status which added to the loneliness arising from sitting alone in a small cabin all day. This was necessitated by them having to maintain scheduled radio 'watches' (shifts). With the advent of electronics, and the GMDSS (Global Maritime Distress and Safety System) satellite and telephone communication systems the job descriptions were re-rearranged, so since 2000 deck officers carry out what were the radio officer's duties.

Rating. Seafarers who were not officers. The word refers to the rate, rank or status of someone. Stewards, hairdressers and engine room greasers, for example, were ratings or 'leading hands'.

Royal Navy. This is one of the armed forces of the crown, dedicated to the protection of the realm. Its ships are warships of various types, not vessels that carry cargo or passengers for commercial profit. Often referred to as the Senior Service or the 'Grey Navy' (because of its ships' grey livery, unlike the white and colours of merchant vessels). The personnel in it are employed by the state, not private companies. In this period we describe they tended to be more formal and disciplined than those of the **Merchant Navy** (for example, they wore uniforms at all times) and sometimes saw themselves as superior to it. Royal Navy stewards and catering staff working in the RN often had a more relaxed attitude than those in combat roles. The phrase 'Hello **Sailor**' was originally applied to Royal Naval seamen.

Sailor. The word has two uses in popular culture. It is more usually applied to **Royal Naval** than **Merchant Naval** seafarers, and it is used colloquially to refer to manual, usually deck, workers in the Merchant Navy.

Stewards. People of various grades, mainly **ratings**, who work in the hotel side of the ship, the catering/stewards department, providing services *directly* to passengers. They include bedroom stewards and bar stewards. In some companies, waiters come under the umbrella term 'steward'.

Writer. A person who provided secretarial support services to departments and officers on ship, particularly in the purser's department at the equivalent of a hotel reception area. They usually had typing and language skills, and their duties included helping Junior Assistant **Pursers**, selling stamps in the Ship's Bureau, and recording crew overtime. The name probably derives from the days when captains, like senior church officials or members of Court, dictated letters and orders to gentleman clerks who produced finished documents in copperplate handwriting.

Further Reading

Baker, Paul (2002) Fantabulosa: *A Dictionary of Polari and Gay Slang*, Continuum, New York.

Baker, Paul (2002) *Polari: The Lost Language of Gay Men*, Routledge, London.

Bentley, Kevin (2000) *Sailor: Vintage Photos of a Masculine Icon*, Council Oak Books, San Francisco, CA and Tulsa, OK.

Bérubé, Alan (1991) *Coming Out Under Fire: The History of Gay Men and Women in World War Two*, Penguin, London.

Brighton Ourstory Project (1992) *Daring Hearts: Lesbian and Gay Lives of the 50s and 60s*, QueenSpark Books, Brighton.

Burg, Barry Richard (1983) *Sodomy and the Perception of Evil: English Sea Rovers in the Seventeenth Century Caribbean*, New York University Press, New York.

David, Hugh (1997) *On Queer Street*, London, Harper Collins.

Hunter-Cox, Jane (1989) *Ocean Pictures: The Golden Age of Transatlantic Travel 1936–59*, Webb & Bowyer, with Michael Joseph, London.

Jivani, Alkarim (1997) *It's Not Unusual: A History of Lesbian and Gay Britain in the Twentieth Century*, Michael O'Mara Books, London.

Kirk, Kris and Heath, Ed (1984) *Men in Frocks*, Gay Men's Press, London.

Power, Lisa (1995) *No Bath but Plenty of Bubbles: An Oral History of the Gay Liberation Front 1970–73*, Cassell, London.

Shilts, Randy (1993) *Conduct Unbecoming: Gays and Lesbians in the US Military*, Penguin, London.

Stanley, Jo (1996) *Bold in her Breeches: Women Pirates across the Ages*, Pandora/Rivers Oram, London.

Turley, Hans (1999) *Rum, Sodomy and the Lash: Piracy, Sexuality and Masculine Identity*, New York University Press, New York and London.

Warren, Carol A.B. (1974) *Identity and Community in the Gay World*, John Wiley and Sons, New York.

Weeks, Jeffrey (1977) *Coming Out*, Quartet London.

Zeeland, Steven (1995) *Sailors and Sexual Identity*, Haworth Press, New York.

Websites

There are many websites, although as they change so often, we have not included them here. Good search terms we have found are 'gay', 'homosexual', 'sailor', 'seafarer', 'seaman' and 'navy'.

Index

Bold type denotes main pages on the topic. Ship's names are in italic. Clubs, magazines, movies, pubs and shows are in bold. Gay nicknames are in quotes.

Massage 6
Matthau, Walter 56
Mauretania 54
Meatrack 99
Medhurst, Andy 118, 119, 144
Melly, George 9, 24, 46, 212, 222
Melville, Herman, 1, 24, 191
Men in Frocks 31
Mercury 36
Merman, Ethel 124
Mess (crew) 67, 99, 127, **238**
Meyer, Moe 118, 144
Migration 39, 50, 72
Military, the 13, 28, 29, 32, 39,
    65, 114, 119, 151, 162, 175,
    191, 207, 228
Mime 123–4
Minge, Stella 149
Minstrellisation 87
Misleading Ladies 122
'Miss L' 142
Mizer, Bob 8, 166, 168
Moby Dick 1, 9, 22, 24, 191
Mollies 76–7, 86, 88, 89
Mombassa 104, 157, 161
Money 191 (*see also* paid sex)
Monogamy 105
Monroe, Marilyn 59
Mort, Frank 186, 207
Morton, H.V. 56, 74
'Mother' 84, 86
Music x, 71, 123, 124, 126, 128,
    129, 163, 183
Music Halls ix, 31, 78, 121
Mullins, Laurie J. 205, 208

Naples 159
Nardana 235
National Maritime Museum, UK
    xiv, 231
National Union of Seamen (NUS)
    xiii, xiv, 4, 5, 27, 32–3, 41,

47, 48, 104, 116, 144, 178,
183, 205, 206, 207, 214, 215,
222, 225
Navies (of other countries) 8,
228–9, 232 (*see also* US
military)
Neptune ceremony 37, 120
Networks 67, 147, 150, 222 (*see
also* community)
Nevasa 235
New York xi, 1, 23, 39, 42, 51,
148, 154, 158, 162, 163, 164,
165, 170, 225
Newcastle 36
Newport, Rhode Island scandal
37
Newton, Esther 64, 74, 115, 135,
139, 145
Nicknames 59, **84–6**
Norwegian Team 234
Norwood, Rick xiii, 181, 186,
192, 193, 194, 198
Now Voyager 53, 57
Nurses (ship's) 105, 111 (*see also*
women crew)

Ocean Monarch 67
Officers 36, 37, 61, 62, 64, 65,
68, 92–3, 100, 102, 107, 109,
113, 121, 129, 147, 177,
188–9, 191, 192, 194, 210,
212, 216, 221, 225, 236, **238**,
239
As opponents of homosexuality
29, 123
Gay 6, 15, 20, 44, 61, 62, 63,
101, 156, 176, 178, 181, 184,
212, 226
Old Spice 154
'Olga' 85
Omner, Rosemary and Panting,
Gerald 48